ISRAEL AND CHINA:

FROM THE TANG DYNASTY TO SILICON WADI

By Mark O'Neill

Foreword ———————————— ①

"*Israel and China – from the Tang Dynasty to Silicon Wadi* adds new dimensions to the complexity of Shanghai and China's past and present as well as Jewish and British history. One of the minorities of empires has found a new voice in this fascinating narrative."

– Hugh Peyman, Founder of Research-Works and
author of *China's Change: The Greatest Show on Earth*

Foreword ———————————————— ②

Books offering an opportunity to better understand the world's most populous country, especially its history, are needed and welcome. China now is a world power, yet much of its history in earlier times and, especially, the history relating to its more recent industrialization, remains to be studied by many in the West. The book *Israel and China – from the Tang Dynasty to Silicon Wadi* examines China from a truly unique perspective – that of Israel and the Jewish people and the roles they played in China's history. They played roles from both inside China and, sometimes equally or even more important, from outside that country.

The book describes how many Jews maintained their Jewish culture and heritage or, perhaps, made compromises which were expedient or even necessary for survival. There's lots of good research here, research which documents facts and also allows for the recounting of many illuminating, uplifting, and sometimes tragic, stories. The destinies of many Jewish people were intertwined with those of the Chinese and, often, also with the destinies of other nations and ethnic groups as they, too, operated inside or outside of China. These destinies were played out as Jews migrated into or out of the country, established businesses and many other institutions, made political connections, married and had families, and lived their lives.

Anyone, whether history buff or scholar, interested in digging deeper into Chinese and/or Jewish history, will find that this book makes for a very good read.

– Lenore Lamont Zissermann, author of
Mitya's Harbin: Majesty and Menace

Contents

Introduction

"I believe in God and the hand of providence. Sometimes, if we are lucky, we can see God's guiding hand, and the story of the Jews in China is one of those lucky times. We see God's guiding hand, we have seen providence."

– Rabbi Asher Oser of Ohel Leah synagogue, Hong Kong

At a theological school in Jerusalem, five Chinese women in their 20s are intensively studying the Hebrew language and Judaism in preparation for formal conversion. In February 2016, they arrived in Israel from Kaifeng (開封), in the central province of Henan (河南). A total of 19 Chinese from the city have made *Aliyah* – the return of Jews from foreign countries to their ancestral homeland. The five young women are Han Chinese, similar in appearance to the other 1.3 billion people in China. But, during their childhood, their parents told them they were different to their neighbours – they were descended from Jews who had settled in Kaifeng over 1,000 years ago. After more than three years of intensive lobbying, the Israeli government was persuaded to allow them to enter the country. Their citizenship is conditional on completing the formal conversion through the country's Chief Rabbinate. Only then can they be officially accepted as Jews and Israelis.

These 19 are the most dramatic and visible link between the Israel of today, the Jews and China. Their ancestors came to the Middle Kingdom during the Tang dynasty (唐朝, 618-907 AD), in search of business opportunities, when it was the world's richest and most advanced country.

Those early Jews were within a few generations assimilated by a culture that, unlike the Christian nations of Europe, did not treat them as different or alien - and certainly not guilty of deicide. They enjoyed the same rights as other Chinese citizens; some passed the imperial exam and became officials. Others became wealthy businessmen, farmers or skilled craftsmen; a few became doctors. They assimilated and joined the middle and upper class of society.

This very success, and intermarriage with Chinese women, undermined their identity as Jews. They were cut off from their brothers and sisters in Europe and the Middle East; their knowledge of Hebrew and Jewish culture and history and observance of religious laws declined. By the early 19th century, the last rabbi in Kaifeng had died and was not replaced; the city's synagogue had fallen into disuse.

From the 1840s, a new group of Jews arrived. They came with the colonial powers, especially Britain, which forced the Qing government to cede Hong Kong and open ports on the east coast to foreign trade. Like their predecessors in the Tang dynasty, they came in search of business opportunities made possible by this new foreign presence; they became rich from the import of opium and textiles and the export of tea, silk and vegetable oil and later from property, manufacturing and transport.

The new arrivals, in Hong Kong, Shanghai, Tianjin and other ports, set up communities similar to those in Europe: they built their own synagogues, schools, cemeteries and social institutions. They invited rabbis to lead religious life and married within the community; their social interaction with Chinese was limited. Mostly Sephardic, they came originally from Baghdad and had moved to cities in British India. Sephardic Jews emerged as a community in the Iberian peninsula around a thousand years ago.

From the late 19th century, another group of Jews – Ashkenazis from Russia – arrived in China, this time in the northeast region of Manchuria. Ashkenazis are descendants of Jews who settled in Europe. They helped to create an international metropolis in Harbin; the community peaked at 25,000 in the 1920s. Like their brothers in Shanghai and Hong Kong, they built synagogues, schools and other social institutions and invited rabbis to guide them. They maintained the religious life and laws which they had brought from Russia and Eastern Europe.

The third group of Jews to arrive in China during the modern era were refugees from Nazi Europe. They started to arrive in the mid-1930s and reached 30,000, before the German invasion of the Soviet Union in June 1941 cut off the last escape route. They found refuge in Shanghai at a time when most countries in the world had closed their doors to the Jews. This is the most remarkable – and heroic – chapter in this book. Many came through visas provided by diplomats from China, Japan – and possibly Manchukuo – against the orders of their superiors.

The refugees were given entry into the international concession of Shanghai because the foreign officials who ran it kept the door open. The governments of the Republic of China and Imperial Japan, the invader, both welcomed the Jews; each proposed a designated area for them to settle and develop.

Because of the intensity of the war raging across China, neither "homeland" came to pass; but the proposals alone showed the esteem in which the Jews were held by the two governments – at the very moment when the Nazis and their allies in Europe were implementing "the final solution".

In Shanghai, the refugees lived in crowded and difficult conditions, cheek by jowl with thousands of Chinese, many also refugees and living on the edge of survival. Despite their own troubles, the Chinese treated these strangers who had suddenly arrived in their midst with kindness and courtesy.

The Japanese who controlled Shanghai from December 1941 refused to implement the demand of their Nazi allies for the mass extermination of Jews. This is the most astonishing – perhaps we can say miraculous – chapter of this story. A Jew living in most countries of continental Europe faced the daily threat of arrest and deportation to a death camp – but not in China and Japan.

During its occupation of the international concession from December 1941 to August 1945, Japan interned Jews because they held passports of "enemy" Allied countries, not because they were Jewish.

In the Pacific War from 1937 to 1945, millions were killed and injured – but the Jews were not targets and largely were spared. For them, Shanghai, Tianjin and Kobe were safer than Paris, Amsterdam and Vienna.

In the 10 years after the end of World War Two, nearly all the Jews left China – both the refugees and the long-term residents. They were driven out by the civil war between Nationalists and Communists, hyper-inflation and the policies of the new government after 1949 that nationalised private business and treated foreigners with suspicion. They left for the United States, Australia, Canada, South Africa and Israel, the new state established for them in May 1948. Only a small number returned to Russia or the countries in Europe from whence they had come.

A handful remained in China and devoted their lives to the services of the People's Republic. The only exception was the British colony of Hong Kong that was excluded from the Communist revolution; the community there was able to continue its business, religious and social life as it had done since the colony was founded in 1842.

The door to the mainland opened again after the death of Mao Zedong and the reform policies of Deng Xiaoping from 1978. The government welcomed foreigners as investors, experts, teachers, industrialists and businessmen. Jewish communities formed again, first in Beijing and Shanghai and, as the economy developed, in other cities. Once they reached a certain size, they also invited rabbis and recreated the religious and social life they had enjoyed in their home countries.

Today there are an estimated 10,000 Jews living in the mainland, with an additional 5,000-6,000 in Hong Kong. Tens of thousands more come each year as tourists, business people and students. The People's Republic of China (PRC) does not recognise Judaism as an "official religion" and has not given back to the community the synagogues they used before 1949. But it allows them their own religious and social life; it keeps a watchful eye on what they do and is happy that, unlike Christianity and Islam, they do not proselytise Chinese.

There is no anti-Semitism, neither official nor among the public. So Jews feel safer and more comfortable in Beijing, Shanghai and Guangzhou than in Paris, Marseilles and many cities in Europe; they can wear a kippah without fear of being attacked or abused. China's booming economy has created business opportunities they cannot find at home.

From its creation, the new state of Israel was eager to have diplomatic relations with China, one of five permanent members of the U.N. Security Council. But it took 42 years, until January 1992, before the two governments established such relations. This was because Mao chose to ally with "revolutionary" and Arab Muslim countries. Beijing called Israel a "Zionist entity" and a "tool of imperialist aggression".

The change came after its defeat by Vietnam during the invasion of spring 1979; Beijing sought the help of Israel to re-equip the outdated People's Liberation Army. This opened the door to trade between the two countries but exchanges had to be conducted in secret because they contradicted Beijing's public support for the Arab cause. Diplomatic relations also had to wait until the collapse of the Soviet Union, the biggest supporter of the Arab world.

Since 1992, relations have developed in a way no-one expected. In 2016, China was one of the biggest foreign investor in Israel, ahead of the United States. It is one of the principal sources of the venture capital which Israel's thousands of high-technology start-ups require. China has become Israel's third biggest trading partner and largest in Asia. Chinese companies are building large infrastructure projects in Israel and have acquired major Israeli firms. The government welcomes this investment, as a balance to capital from Europe and the U.S. and a way to win goodwill with a global superpower. But the welcome is not universal – critics say that China's market remains inaccessible to most Israeli firms and are suspicious of the motives of Chinese firms answerable to the state. Is the country selling to a potential enemy high technology, its most precious asset?

Beijing has close military and commercial ties with countries that hate Israel, such as Iran, Syria and Yemen. In addition, the 25 years of diplomatic relations have not produced a peace dividend for Israel – Beijing does not play an active role to solve the Middle East conflict, nor use its considerable influence with Iran and the Arab countries to broker a settlement.

In the historical context, the story of China is a happy one. Jewish history is long, complex and full of sadness. Primo Levi, a Holocaust survivor, wrote a statement that is etched on the walls of the Ort der Information (Place of Information) under the Memorial to the Murdered Jews of Europe in Berlin: "It happened, therefore it can happen again ..." A Jewish chemist and author, he wrote a book about his year as a prisoner in Auschwitz. He died in Turin in 1987, at the age of 67, after falling from a third-storey apartment landing; the coroner ruled his death a suicide. He was suffering from depression, in part because of the trauma of being a prisoner. Nobel laureate and Holocaust survivor Elie Wiesel said at the time: "Primo Levi died at Auschwitz forty years later".

Against this sombre background, the history of the Jews in China is full of light. They never suffered from anti-Semitism at the hands of Chinese, neither during the Imperial era nor the Republican and Communist periods. The attacks they suffered in Harbin in the 1930s were at the hands of Russian fascists, who brought their prejudice with them, and their Japanese collaborators.

During the Tang and succeeding dynasties, the Jews enjoyed the same rights as Chinese citizens and could practice their religion freely. In the century from the arrival of the British in the 1840s and since the open-door policy of 1978, the Jews in China have prospered in business and other fields and built their communities as they wished. Like Chinese, they suffered under the Japanese occupation in World War Two; and, like other foreigners, they decided to leave China during the Civil War and after the establishment of the PRC. But in neither case were they singled out.

"Chinese and Jewish cultures are the two oldest civilisations in the world and share a lot in common," said Pan Guang, the most eminent Chinese specialist on the history of the Jews. "Both highly emphasise the value of family ties and education. Although both have absorbed various exotic cultures, their central core has never changed since the beginning." (Note: "Jews and China – Legends, History and New Perspectives", by Pan Guang, on website of Centre of Jewish Studies, Shanghai).

Asher Oser, Rabbi of the Ohel Leah synagogue in Hong Kong, put it more poetically: "I believe in God and the hand of providence. Sometimes, if we are lucky, we can see God's guiding hand, and the story of the Jews in China is one of those lucky times. We see God's guiding hand, we have seen providence."

He also quoted the words of Salo Wittmayer Baron, one of the most distinguished Jewish historians of the 20th century. Baron was born in 1895 in Tarnow, Galicia, then part of the Austro-Hungarian empire and now Poland. Before the war, the town had 16,000 Jews but only 20 remained after the Holocaust. Baron survived because he moved to New York in the 1920s to become a professor. He lost his parents and sister during the war. In an interview in 1975, he said: "Suffering is part of the destiny [of the Jews], but so is repeated joy as well as ultimate redemption."

Jews arrive in China during the Tang Dynasty

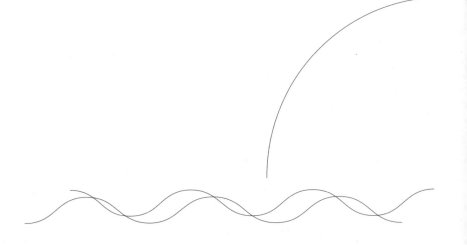

From

TANG

The Jews first came to China in large numbers in the
eighth century A.D., during the Tang dynasty (618-907),
when it was the world's biggest and most advanced
country. They came by land across Central Asia and
by ship to the ports on the southeast coast, mainly
Guangzhou. They lived in many cities, including Xian,
Luoyang, Kaifeng, Guangzhou, Hangzhou, Ningbo,
Quanzhou, Beijing and Nanjing.

They moved to China for the same reason as other
foreign merchants did and do today, for business and
commercial opportunities. Scholars report arrival of Jews
much earlier, even during the Zhou dynasty (1,045-
256 BC), but lack archaeological or written evidence for
their presence.

During the Tang dynasty, China was the world's biggest
economy and trading power. Its output accounted for
about half of global GDP. It produced large quantities
of goods for export, including tea, silk, lacquer ware,
porcelain and silver.

The main trading port was Guangzhou, capital of
Guangdong province. Living there to conduct this trade
were tens of thousands of foreigners, including Jews;
these groups had their own restaurants, community
associations and places of worship.

The national capital was Changan (長安 西安), then the largest city in the world with a population of one million, including Jews. It had a diverse population who practised many religions, including Buddhism, Zoroastrianism, Nestorian Christianity and Islam as well as Judaism.

Settle in Kaifeng (開封)

The first large settled community of Jews was in what is now Kaifeng, then called Dongjing (東京, Eastern Capital)in Henan province during the Northern Song dynasty (960-1127 AD). The Emperor had his palace in Dongjing, which had a population of over 400,000. Among the residents, as in Changan and Guangzhou, were many foreigners, including Arabs, Turkic people and Persians as well as the Jews.

Most scholars believe that these Jews migrated from what are now the modern states of Iran and Iraq. During this dynasty, China was still an economic powerhouse that led the world in trade. It was a major manufacturer of iron products, used for military and civilian purposes. It printed the world's first government-issue paper money. Merchant ships carried Chinese iron, swords, silk, velvet, porcelain and textiles as far afield as Southeast Asia, India, the Middle East and East Africa. This created an excellent commercial environment for the Jews and the other foreigners.

"After the Jews arrived in Kaifeng, they were well treated by the Song dynasty and allowed to become Chinese citizens," according to Professors Pan Guang and Wang Jian. (Note 1) "They could preserve their native customs and religious beliefs and settle in Kaifeng. In education, work, buying and selling of land, marriage and the right to move, they enjoyed the same rights and treatment as Han Chinese. They never faced discrimination."

In this climate, they prospered and became a wealthy class and their religious activities flourished. In 1163, they built the Israel synagogue. In 1279, with the support of the government, they rebuilt and enlarged the structure to a size of 10,000 square metres.

"The Ming dynasty (1368-1644) was the golden era of the Jewish community in Kaifeng. It had more than 500 families, with about 4,400 to 5,000 people. They included those who had passed the imperial exam and entered the court or became county officials. Others became very rich through business. There were highly skilled craftsmen and wealthy farmers. A small number became doctors and professionals. They were in the middle and upper class of Chinese society." (Note 2)

The Ming dynasty coincided with some of the most intense persecution of the Jews in Europe. They were expelled from Spain in 1492 and from Portugal in 1497; tens of thousands were also expelled from Austria and Germany during this period. Children in Christian countries were taught that the Jews were responsible for the death of Jesus.

Since there were almost no Christians in China, the Jews living there did not encounter this hatred. They enjoyed rights and freedoms denied to their brothers and sisters in many countries of Europe.

In the Kaifeng Museum, there are rooms with pieces that show the Jewish presence in the city during the Ming period. These include a restored tablet from the synagogue and two tombstones. "The writing on these is evidence of the religious activities on the Jews of Kaifeng and of their political status, social position and living conditions," said the *Overseas Chinese* magazine (僑園) in its issue of June 2016. (Note 3)

This very success of the community and integration into China's social and professional life threatened their identity as Jews. To integrate better, they took Chinese names and spoke Mandarin in their daily life; they used Hebrew only for religious purposes. Initially, they married within their community but, during the Ming period, they started to marry Han Chinese wives; they wore Chinese clothes and decorations. A majority of Jews who had come to China were men; there was a shortage of Jewish women to marry.

Decline and disaster

In 1642, the Ming dynasty faced a major peasant revolt. Surrounded by a rebel army, the Ming general commanding Kaifeng ordered the dykes of the Yellow River to be breached; this caused an enormous flood of the city. About half of its 4,000 Jews were drowned; the synagogue was covered in water and many holy books lost. Through great efforts, the community rebuilt the synagogue in 1663 and recovered some of the holy books. But the number of the community fell to 2,000. Over the next 200 years, it continued to diminish. One reason was the decline of Kaifeng itself. The national capital in the Song and a major commercial centre in the Yuan and Ming dynasties, it went into decline from the start of the Qing (1644-1911); its population fell to 200,000 and its economy shrank.

Many Jews left to seek better opportunities elsewhere. The city was flooded several times more; in 1841, a breach of the dykes of the Yellow River caused it to be flooded for eight months. From the late 17th century, the community had no money to repair the synagogue; by the middle of the 19th century, it had fallen into disuse.

Another reason for the decline was the closed-door policy of the Ming and Qing governments. This meant that the community could no longer maintain the contacts of previous generations with the Jewish world outside China. Its last rabbi died in the early 19th century and was not replaced; there was no-one qualified to carry out religious services.

As Jewish people entered more into mainstream Chinese society, so the process of assimilation deepened. "The Jews were scattered in different places and the community in Kaifeng died out," according to *Overseas Chinese*magazine (June 2016). "After the flood of 1842, the synagogue was flattened. There was no-one to rebuild it." (Note 4)

Professor Pan Guang said that the decline of the Jewish character of the community was mainly the result of two factors. One was that they had been cut off from the outside world for 200 years. The other was that the treatment they received was the opposite of that given to their brothers and sisters in Europe.

"They had equal rights and status with other residents of Kaifeng. The different dynasties treated them well and without discrimination. They could work in the government and prosper in business. In Europe, by comparison, they suffered discrimination in economy, politics and culture and were not treated equally. So, they were kept outside mainstream society. In China, their equal treatment naturally led them to assimilation." (Note 5)

Just as the community was dying out, so westerners interested in Judaism arrived in China. Due to treaties that followed the two Opium Wars of the mid-19th century, the European powers won the right of their citizens to live in China. Among them were Christian missionaries. Some discovered the Jewish history of Kaifeng for the first time; intrigued by it, they began to do research.

In February 1866, an American missionary named William Alexander Parsons (WAP) Martin visited Kaifeng. He found the synagogue in ruins and stones from it in a ditch; of the eight families said to be Jewish, six had married Han Chinese and two Muslim Hui. These missionaries concluded that the community in Kaifeng was unable to speak or read Hebrew, did not perform religious rituals and had lost its Jewish character through assimilation and intermarriage.

The missionaries hoped to revive the interest of these "Jews" in the Bible and introduce the New Testament to them; but they found they had no interest. Nonetheless they marvelled that sons and daughters of Israel had reached this city, so far and remote from the Holy Land. While they no longer practised the rites of their forefathers, they were aware that the ancestry made them different to the Chinese among whom they lived.

In 1900, the Jews of Shanghai sent a letter to their brothers in Kaifeng inviting them to visit. They arrived in March 1902. At a meeting on the evening of March 26, they were received for two hours by their Shanghai brethren.

"Questioned as to whether any of them knew anything of their religion, they said that, for a long period before the Taiping Rebellion, they were gradually declining and their faith was rapidly being forgotten." The Taiping Rebellion was a 15-year (1850-1864) uprising that cost 20 million lives.

The Jews of Kaifeng said they did not observe any of the ordinances of the Jewish religion nor "the idolatrous practices of the heathen." (Note 6)

There followed visits and contacts between the two sides, but the Shanghai Jews could not raise sufficient funds to rebuild the Kaifeng synagogue, mainly due to financial constraints.

In 1911, an uprising overthrew the Qing dynasty after more than 260 years; the Republic of China was born. The next year, the new government signed a land agreement with seven Jewish families in Kaifeng to build a synagogue. The next year the families sold the nearly 10 mu (0.7 hectares) of land to a Protestant church for 1,300 dollars (1,300元大洋). (Note 7)

During censuses conducted by the Nationalist government, the members of the Kaifeng community were unable to provide written family records; their only memory was oral.

Making *Aliyah*

The state of Israel was founded on May 14, 1948 as a homeland for Jews throughout the world. It became a base for Zionist groups who believe it their duty to "bring home" members of the Jewish race scattered overseas. This is called in Hebrew *Aliyah*, meaning "ascent to Jerusalem". The descendants of the community of Kaifeng could, therefore, apply to emigrate if they could prove their Jewish ancestry and convince the religious authorities in Israel that they were real Jews.

In 1949, a Communist government took power in China; it promoted atheism and recognised only five "official" religions; Judaism was not one of them. The entry of the People's Republic of China on the northern side in the Korean War (1950-53) resulted in a western trade embargo and the freezing of relations with the western world for three decades. These conditions made it impossible for the community in Kaifeng to make contact with the Jewish world outside China, invite a rabbi from abroad and resume their religious life.

It was a "revolutionary" era, during which practice of religion was difficult, sometimes impossible. It was extremely hard for Chinese to obtain permission to leave the country. During the Cultural Revolution (1966-76), fanatical Red Guards made sustained attacks on all forms of religious practice.

Contact with the outside world only became possible after the death of Mao Zedong (毛澤東) in 1976 and the open-door and reform policies of the early 1980s. Chinese were allowed to go abroad, to work, study or settle.

According to the 1987 census, there were 159 people of Jewish descent in Kaifeng, all with Chinese family names and all having married Han or Hui partners. (Note 8) The Number Four People's Hospital had been built on the site of the ancient synagogue.

"In the 1980s, the Henan provincial people's hospital and the Kaifeng Hygiene Bureau carried out DNA analysis of a dozen people of Jewish descent. They found that their blood type was similar to those of Han people and unlike that of Jews overseas. They concluded that the blood lineage came from a group of Jewish people from the two rivers of Iraq (Tigris and Euphrates), close to the Jews of Armenia and Arabia." (Note 9)

The view of the Chinese government is that, while Jews existed in Kaifeng in the past, they do not now. It says that they have long been assimilated into the Han nationality and classifies them as Han or Hui on their identity documents. It does not recognize them as a religious group, because Judaism is not one of the five official religions. A majority of Jews also believe that these descendants in Kaifeng are not Jewish; they say that, to prove his or her Jewish ancestry, a person must have written documents. In addition, the descendants had for many decades no religious practice or learning, no rabbi and no synagogue.

Since 1949, religion has been a sensitive issue in China, especially if the government perceives foreign institutions or individuals "interfering in domestic affairs". Foreigners are banned from proselytising. The Kaifeng city government has not allowed construction of a new synagogue that would be the best place for regular religious worship and to revive the community. It is even less likely to in the conservative social climate created by Xi Jinping (習近平) since he became general secretary of the Communist Party in November 2012.

The open-door policy has enabled people from outside to visit Kaifeng and look again at this unusual example of the Jewish diaspora. Initially, the city government welcomed this, hoping for an influx of investment from wealthy Jews. But those who came did not bring the desired factories or R & D centres but, instead, prayer books and religious items which they wished to share with their long-lost brothers and sisters.

The community in Kaifeng asked for recognition as Jews, but the government refused, saying that it would not revise its decision to recognise only five religions. Some visitors even invited these descendants to emigrate to Israel. One of the most prominent is Moses Zhang Xingwang (張興旺), born in 1947, who has served as a member of the city's People Political Consultative Conference (政協). He is a retired sports teacher; his apartment is filled with symbols of Judaism, including a menorah (seven-branched candlestick), a Star of David flag and copies of the Torah. On the wall are photographs of the Wall of Lamentations in Jerusalem and of himself with visiting Israeli VIPs. At weekends, with a prayer shawl around his shoulders, he tells children of the community stories about their Jewish heritage and the Lost Tribes of Israel. He is careful not to proselytise.

He wants his ashes to be interred in Israel when he is dead; he calls it "the land of my ancestors". He told the *Overseas Chinese* magazine: "after the reports appeared in the newspapers, overseas Jewish groups came here and asked us to 'return' to Israel to settle. I refused. Although I have Jewish blood inside me, I was born and grew up in China. I have a deep feeling for China." (Note 10)

In 2003, an American Messianic Jew named Tim Lerner opened a school in Kaifeng called *Yiceleye* (Israelite); it instructed the descendants of the community in Hebrew and organised Shabbat dinners and festival celebrations. Lerner arranged for young members of the community to earn scholarships to live and study in Israel. He was helped in this by Shavei Israel, an organisation dedicated to bringing back "lost Jews" to their homeland. It has worked to bring back Jews in India and Siberia and to educate "hidden Jews" in Poland and other countries in eastern Europe.

Messianic Jews are a minority among the world's Jews; many rabbinical authorities do not recognise them as Jews at all. Messianic Jews believe that Jesus is the Jewish Messiah and believe in both the Old and New Testaments; mainstream Jews regard only the Old Testament as authoritative scripture. In 2006, Lerner had his visa revoked by the Chinese government on suspicion of evangelising. He said he did not try to convert anyone but established the school to help the community in Kaifeng "learn the Jewish lifestyle". Some Jews are suspicious of Lerner's motives; they think his final aim was to convert the members of the community to Christianity.

Bringing back the "lost Jews"

Shavei Israel is an organisation based in Jerusalem that, as of late 2017, had helped 19 members of the Kaifeng community emigrate to Israel. Its website describes its mission: "we extend a helping hand to all members of our extended Jewish family and to all who seek to rediscover or renew their link with the people of Israel. Our endeavor is to strengthen the links wherever they may have been weakened by history, distance or social parameters.

"The Jewish people are currently facing a demographic and spiritual crisis of unprecedented proportions. Our numbers are shrinking, Jewish commitment is waning, and more and more young people are leaving the fold. And yet, simultaneously, an extraordinary awakening is taking place. From northeastern India to southern Spain, from the coast of Portugal to shores of Brazil, countless numbers of people are trying to make sense of their Jewish ancestry.

"Shavei Israel is the only Jewish organisation today that is actively reaching out to 'lost Jews' in an effort to facilitate their return…Shavei Israel does not proselytise nor does it support any form of missionary activity. It responds to personal expressions of desire to return to Judaism."

In April 2014, the community in Kaifeng held one of its first Seder meals in generations, according to the *Jerusalem Post*. (Note 11) It was organised by Shavei Israel, which sent Tzuri (Heng) Shi, a former Kaifeng resident who emigrated to Israel and officially converted, to conduct it. It gave him all the materials necessary to carry out a ceremony, including *Haggadot* – the text that sets out the reading of the Passover Seder – in Hebrew and Chinese.

"We are proud and excited to organise this historic event," Michael Freund, founder and chairman of Shavei, told the newspaper. "Kaifeng's Jewish descendants are a living link between China and the Jewish people, and it is very moving to see the remnants of this community returning to their Jewish roots as they prepare for Passover."

Singing the Israeli national anthem in Chinese

The most recent migrants at time of writing were five women in their 20s from Kaifeng who arrived at Ben Gurion Airport on February 29, 2016. They astonished waiting reporters by answering questions in fluent Hebrew – two had spent four years at a religious boarding school in Israel and the others had been learning the language in Kaifeng, some through online teachers in Israel. They also sang the Israeli national anthem in Chinese.

The five young ladies were taken by minibus to the Jeanie Schottenstein Center for Advanced Torah Studies for Women in Jerusalem to study Hebrew and Judaism for several years; this prepares them for formal conversion to Judaism through the Chief Rabbinate of Israel.

Shavei Israel is paying their living and study costs at the college. Only on completion of this conversion process and the approval of the rabbinical authorities can they receive Israeli citizenship.

In interviews published on the Shavei Israel website, the women explained that, as children, they had been told by their parents that they were Jewish. "My father told us that our ancestors came from Israel," said Li Jing (李靜), 28. "When my father first told me, I was filled with pride. But then I was bit puzzled. I mean, what does it mean to be a Jew? We kept the Sabbath, celebrated the New Year and all the holidays. I only eat food that is kosher."

She studied business English at a university in Xian (西安) and worked as a customer services manager in Kaifeng; she studied Hebrew and English online with a tutor provided by Shavei Israel. The organisation arranged for two of the five – Li Yuan (李圓), 27, and Yue Ting (岳婷), 26 – to study at the Yemin Orde religious boarding school near Haifa from 2006 to 2010. Li Yuan has a degree in education and worked as an administrator of a middle school in Kaifeng. Yue Ting graduated from Henan University (河南大學) and worked as a teacher in Kaifeng. "Israel is where our ancestors lived," said Yue. "My father has always wanted me to go back. He knows I belong there – even more so after I studied at Yemin Orde. I only understood about my Jewish roots on a very simple level before I went to Israel. Through years of study and practice as I grew old, I got to know more about Jewish law. I feel very proud to be a Jew." On its website, Shavei Israel has established "Campaign Kaifeng", asking readers to donate to help the five young Chinese women build their new

Five young women from Kaifeng who made *Aliyah* to Israel in February 2016 stand in front of the Western Wall in Jerusalem. (Credit: Shavei Israel)

lives in the Holy Land. (Note 12)

Becoming a Jew is no simple matter. Mainstream Judaism does not evangelise. The tradition passes through the mother's line; a person must study and learn Jewish culture and traditions. The Chinese descendants of the Jews of Kaifeng do not meet these criteria; nor do they have sufficient historical documents to prove their Jewish ancestry. So, they need sponsorship and organised help from groups like Shavei Israel to obtain the papers they need to go to Israel and undergo the necessary religious and language training there.

The Rabbinical courts who determine whether a person is Jewish or not are strict in their rulings; they are suspicious of impostors, including those who might have economic motives to emigrate to one of the world's most prosperous countries.

Beijing suspicious

Beijing has not wholly welcomed these contacts between its citizens and these groups from Israel. According to *The New York* Times, starting from 2015, the city government closed organisations that promoted the Jewish revival, removed Jewish monuments and signs from public places and banned the community from gathering for religious services on holidays. (Note 13)

"The community says that the government's crackdown is not one of anti-Semitism but rather stems from the government's fear of outside influence from all religions not officially recognised by the state," it said. As a result, those members who wish to be observant must do so in small groups at home, sometimes watched by police or security officials.

The crackdown is not against Jews alone but all religious groups who have contacts with the outside world. Beijing perceives foreign religious organisations, especially Protestant ones, as a threat and with a political agenda to turn its people against the Communist Party. The measures have been severe in the southeastern city of Wenzhou (溫州), known as the "Jerusalem of China", because an estimated 15 per cent of its population are Christian, the highest percentage in the country. It is in Zhejiang province.

From early 2014 until late 2017, workers with cranes and bulldozers, backed by armed police, have removed more than 1,500 crosses from church roofs and demolished churches in Zhejiang, even those belonging to the official Protestant organisation. In a major speech in April 2016 to a National Religion Work Meeting, Communist Party chief Xi Jinping said that the country "must develop a Socialist Chinese religious theory and drive out foreign infiltration. Communist Party members must believe in atheism and absolutely must not seek personal value or beliefs in religion." So, the measures in Kaifeng are not against Judaism per se but against foreign influence and "interference" in the religious life of Chinese.

Notes

1   *The Jews and China* (猶太人與中國) by Professors Pan Guang (潘光) and Wang Jian (王健), Shishi Publishing Company (時事出版社), 2010, page 9.

2   Pan and Wang, page 10.

3   "The Descendants of the Jews of Kaifeng"(開封猶太人後裔，身份之謎被揭開) in *Overseas Chinese* magazine (僑園), June 2016.

4   Article in *Overseas Chinese* magazine (僑園).

5   Pan and Wang, page 14.

6   *The Jews in Kaifeng, Reflections on Sino-Judaic History*, by Chan Sui-jeung (陳瑞璋), The Jewish Historical Society of Hong Kong, 1986, page 37.

7-10 *Overseas Chinese* magazine, pages 57-58.

11   *Jerusalem Post*, 10/4/2014.

12   Website of Shavei Israel.

13   *The New York Times*, 26/9/2016.

Harbin,
the Jewish capital of
Manchuria

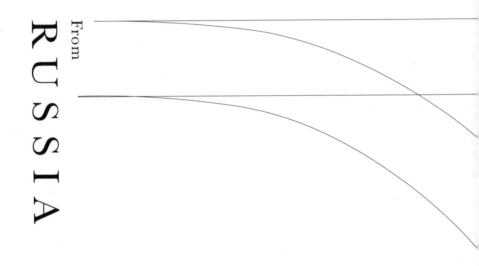

From

RUSSIA

The centre of Jewish migration in northeast China in the late 19th century was Harbin in the remote province of Heilongjiang, 1,340 kilometres south from the Russian border. The first Jew arrived there from Russia in 1898 as part of the China Eastern Railway (東清 鐵路) venture and the community peaked at about 25,000 in the 1920s. They established factories, banks, hotels, shops and international trading firms; they built synagogues, schools, hospitals, a music academy and a Jewish cemetery that had by 1958 nearly 3,200 graves.

The grandparents of Ehud Olmert, Israel's Prime Minister from 2006 to 2009, lived there; his parents grew up in Harbin before leaving in 1930 and emigrating to Israel in 1933. The last member of this community died in Harbin in 1985.

In the middle of the 19th century, no-one could have imagined such a history. The city of Harbin did not exist. Its name, according to a Chinese scholar, was derived from "Heaelabin", the name of a small cluster of Manchu villages of fishermen on the banks of Songhua river. Harbin was an ethnic village some 50 kilometres to the southeast of that cluster of villages. Its only factory produced rice liquor.

The Qing dynasty which took power in 1644 were

Manchus from the vast area of Manchuria in northeast China that later formed the three provinces of Liaoning (遼寧), Jilin (吉林) and Heilongjiang (黑龍江). A fraction of the majority Han population, the Manchus believed that, if they allowed free migration to the sacred region, millions of Hans would settle in their homeland and it would lose its Manchu character. So, the Qing emperor banned such migration. The ban was not strictly observed; toward the end of the dynasty, emperors allowed Han victims of floods and other disasters to move there and Manchu landlords needed peasants to farm their large estates.

But, overall, the region was sparsely populated compared to the rest of China. One reason was the harshness of the climate; in Harbin, winter temperatures fall as low as minus 40 degrees Celsius. In the 1850s, who could have imagined that this bleak and inhospitable region would become an important place of settlement for sophisticated urban Jews of the Russian Empire and elsewhere?

New railway creates international metropolis

Their migration was the result of two important historical events. One was a secret treaty signed in June 1896 between Tsarist Russia and the Qing empire. Under this, Beijing gave Russia permission to build a railway across Heilongjiang and Jilin to its warm-water port of Vladivostok (海參崴) on the Pacific Ocean; it also gave the Tsarist government the right to station troops to protect the railway and gave them and other Russians extraterritorial rights. The line, which began in Chita in Siberia, cut dramatically the time needed to reach Vladivostok from European Russia.

Beijing agreed to the line in exchange for help from the Russian military against a possible invasion by Japan; the new line would facilitate the movement of troops and the food and equipment they needed.

The terms of the treaty were not made public until 1922, after the fall of the two imperial dynasties who signed it. The agreement gave Russia and its citizens rights similar to those enjoyed by citizens of Britain, France and Germany and other foreign powers elsewhere in China. It was the trigger for the development of Harbin, which became the centre of the new line, the China Eastern Railway (CER) .

Construction began in July 1898; regular traffic between St Petersburg and Vladivostok began in July 1903. The Russians selected the location where Harbin would be established as headquarters of the CER and their military and administrative centre in Manchuria; they built a Russian city outside the borders of their empire.

It became in effect the capital of a Russian colony. In 1898, a Russian administration was established to run the city, a power it exercised until 1920, but de facto continued until the 1930s. By 1902, 12,000 Russians were living there, including managerial staff and technicians of the CER.

A census conducted by the CER in 1913 found a population of 69,000, of whom 34,000 were Russians, outnumbering the 24,000 Chinese, as well as 5,000 Jews. It found 53 nationalities speaking 45 different languages; Russian came first, followed by Chinese, Polish and Yiddish. Only 11.5 per cent of the residents had been born there. Of the 40 members of the city council in 1909, 12 were Jewish. Without import or export duties, it became an international city that attracted nationals from more than 30 countries, with 28 foreign consulates and hundreds of shops, factories and banks. Many Chinese entrepreneurs moved there to set up in business and take advantage of its growing economy.

Driven out by persecution

The creation of this new city was the pull that attracted the Jews. What pushed them were new opportunities and the pogroms to which they were subject in the two last decades of the 19th century. From the assassination of Tsar Alexander II in 1881 until the start of World War One in 1914, more than two million Jews left Russia; a majority went to North and South America, as well as to South Africa and western Europe. A smaller number went to Harbin.

Acting on the advice of his Finance Minister Count Sergei Witte, Tsar Nicholas II encouraged the relocation of a number of wealthy businessmen whom the minister described as "the strongest of the strong"; they would create the power to move goods from the region to Russia and Europe.

This migration offered freedom of religion, study and employment in Harbin. The first arrivals worked as managers, architects and technical staff of the CER. Others set up businesses related to it, supplying timber and other raw materials, parts and components, and selling daily necessities to its Russian and Chinese employees. Some Jews served in the

Russian military, others came from Poland, Lithuania, Estonia and Latvia. Jews were encouraged to go to Harbin because the laws and restrictions on Jews in Russia, such as exclusions from certain professions and quotas in universities, did not apply there. They could live, work and worship where they chose and freely decide the education of their children.

They encountered anti-Semitism but it was far less than in the Motherland; Russian-speakers, they felt at home in the Russian atmosphere of Harbin. By 1903, there were 500 members of the community there; they set up a Jewish association, built the first synagogue in 1909 and hired a rabbi to lead it. Jews went to other cities along the CER – Manzhouli (滿洲里), Hailar (海拉爾) Qiqihar (齊齊哈爾) – as well as Shenyang and Dalian.

Soybean, fur and timber

The new arrivals soon discovered the rich economic potential of Manchuria. While the climate is harsh and permits only one harvest a year, the unique black soil is fertile, especially for soybean, sugar beet, animal husbandry and dairy production. There were thousands of hares, squirrels, ermine, tigers, bears and other animals, which created a booming trade in furs.

In addition, as a city outside the jurisdiction of China, it was tax-free. In 1908, a Jewish entrepreneur built Manchuria's first sugar beet processing plant, covering an area of 10,000 square metres; he imported equipment from Poland. In 1909, another started a soybean export company; also using the most modern equipment from Europe, he set up a plant to process the beans and export them to the United States.

In 1904/5, Russia fought a 19-month war with Japan for control of northeast China. The battlefields were in southern Manchuria and the seas around Korea, Japan and the Yellow Sea. The Japanese won an overwhelming victory. It was an industrial conflict, presaging the Great War ten years later; together, the two sides lost about 140,000 men and more than 70,000 Russians were taken prisoner.

The war was good for the economy of Harbin, the main logistical centre for the Russian military; there was no fighting there and the city was not damaged. The defeat worsened unrest and social conflict within Russia.

Anti-Semitism intensified with the publication in Russia in 1903 of the notorious *Protocols of the Elders of Zion*, a forged text that purported to describe a Jewish plan to take over the world. After the war, many Russian Jewish soldiers and prisoners-of-war did not wish to return home. Some settled in Harbin and other cities in Manchuria; others joined Jewish communities in Shanghai and Tianjin.

By 1916, there were 6,000 Jews in Harbin. The Jewish and Russian populations increased again after the Bolshevik revolution of 1917. Thousands of White Russians, including nobles, intellectuals and business people, fled to the largest Russian city outside its borders.

"There were so many people that all the hotels in Harbin were full to overcrowding," said an article on "Moscow of the Orient" in one of

China's main historical magazines, *National Humanity History* (*NHH*, 國家人文歷史*, July 2016).

"With nowhere to stay, many slept on the streets. These were not refugees with nothing; they brought a large amount of assets, which they invested in large buildings. The major structures of Harbin were constructed during this period. The number of Russians overtook that of Chinese. The city became the largest centre for Russians in China. The Russians intended to stay there permanently." (Note 1)

Harbin did not look like other cities in the interior of China. Its buildings reflected the style and taste of the different nationalities that constructed them. By the mid-1920s, the Russian population of Harbin reached 120,000, its peak, with 30,000 others living in smaller towns on the railway; about 10 per cent of the Russians were Jews.

Trading with the world

The period between 1917 and the Japanese occupation of 1932 was the golden age of the Jews in Harbin. While it was a majority Russian city, it was different in governance and culture to the mother country. The young Republic of China, founded in 1911, was weak and distant, its capital in Beijing and, from 1927, in Nanjing; it exercised little authority over a city so remote. Nor did Zhang Zuolin (張作霖), the warlord of Manchuria; his headquarters was in Shenyang, more than 500 kilometres to the south. His policy toward Harbin was laissez-faire. It was only in 1926, 28 years after the establishment of Harbin, that Chinese took over the council and

Kataskya Street in downtown Harbin, 1920s.

Ossinovsky home in Harbin, 1922.

governance of the city.

The Jews found themselves in an international city that gave them freedoms they did not enjoy in many countries around the world. By 1928, the city had more than 4,700 trading firms, large and small, and transport links to 100 ports and cities around the world, including Tokyo, Moscow, Warsaw, Berlin, Paris, London and New York.

That year, it had 42 oil-processing plants, 23 flour mills and eight liquor factories; in addition, it had textile and machinery plants. There were more than 3,000 companies with foreign investment, including major Japanese firms such as Mitsui (三井), Mitsubishi (三菱) and Nisshin (日清). The main foreign investors were Russia, Japan, the U.K., the U.S., France and Germany.

Manchuria became one of the world's largest producers of soybean. The crop accounted for 85 per cent of the region's cultivated area; although the summer growing season was short, the beans matured very quickly. The fertile soil of the region also grew corn, wheat, hemp, tobacco and potatoes. Harbin's trade expanded rapidly, from 17.85 million silver taels in 1908 to 75.25 million in 1926 and 99.46 million in 1928; exports greatly exceeded imports. (Note 2)

Amid this rapid economic growth, Jewish companies and entrepreneurs found many opportunities. Chinese scholars have described this expansion into Manchuria as creating the colony of "Yellow Russia". The Sino-Russian Bank (華俄道勝銀行) in Harbin issued rubles; those buying tickets on the

A.M. & D Samsonovich Brothers Chamber of Commerce, 1912.

Advertisement for Jewish MARS
chocolate and sweet factory, 1925.

CER or doing business with it had to use this currency.

By 1914, 100 million rubles were in circulation in Manchuria, of which 40 million were in Harbin and 60 million in towns and cities along the CER. This figure was one-sixteenth of the total in circulation in the whole of the Russian empire. It was then the strongest currency in Manchuria; with no centralised government, the region had more than a dozen currencies, issued by different warlords and organisations.

Synagogue, schools and orchestra

It was only natural that the Chinese would learn something from the Russians. In this case, it was a belief in stereotypical notions that the Jews can influence international trade, business and money. A 1911 memorandum sent by the Chinese Chamber of Commerce of Harbin warned the Chinese Trade Minister in Beijing that involving Jews in the preparation of a new trade agreement with Russia will have great consequences on the deal because the Jews will use it for their own advantage.

In general, China had no tradition of anti-Semitism. It was quite the opposite. Just a year after the Balfour Declaration of the British government in 1917, China expressed support for a Jewish homeland. In December 1918, in a letter to Mr. E. S. Kadoorie, one of the leaders of the Jewish community in Shanghai, Chen Lu, Chinese Vice-Minister of Foreign Affairs (外交部次長陳籙), said that, like Britain, his government endorsed the establishment of a Jewish national home in Palestine.

In this hospitable environment, Jewish life and business flourished. The community opened its first synagogue in January 1909: and a second in 1921. Both had cantors who led the prayers and a children's choir who sang during Jewish holidays.

The first rabbi, from Russia, fell ill and died soon after his arrival. The second moved to the community in Tianjin and then the U.S. It was the third, Aharon Moshe Kiselev, who became renowned in Harbin, other communities in China and in Europe.

Born in 1866 in the Chernigov region of Russia, now Ukraine, he was a gifted Talmudic scholar who spoke Yiddish, Hebrew, Russian and German. He arrived in 1913 and served the community for 36 years until his passing in September 1949.

He lived through the 13-year Japanese occupation, the Chinese civil war and the departure of most of his congregation. "Rabbi Kiselev was the spiritual leader of the Jews in Harbin, China and all of the Far East," wrote Teddy Kaufman, who was born in Harbin in 1924, was a personal secretary to Kiselev for a time and was director of the Association of Former Residents of China in Israel for nearly 40 years.

"It is to him that we owe the flourishing of the religious life of the Jews in China that went on parallel to our traditional national education."

The community also employed a circumciser (*mohel*) and (*shochet*) a person trained to kill animals and birds according to religious law; they travelled to Jewish communities in Heilongjiang to perform these services. It also set up a cemetery where the dead were buried according to Jewish ritual; a manager lived on the premises with his family. It is the only Jewish cemetery in mainland China that has survived until today. (Note 3)

According to the *National Humanity History* (*NHH*), the Jews who went to Harbin after the 1917 Revolution brought assets with them and included business people, bankers, doctors, engineers, authors, musicians and poets.

"By 1920, their number exceeded 10,000, more than in Shanghai and making Harbin the largest Jewish centre in the Far East. At the peak, the number reached 25,000." (Note 4) Between 1918 and 1930, the community published over 20 newspapers and periodicals, all in Russian except one in Yiddish. Famous Jewish artists and musicians came to the city to perform.

The Jewish residents set up institutions to support their community, according to *The Jews and China*, by Professors Pan Guang and Wang Jian of the Shanghai Centre for Jewish Studies. These included synagogues, welfare organisations, an old people's home, a refugee relief committee, primary and secondary schools and academies of commerce and music.

"In 1918, the residents set up a school for children of Orthodox Jews, with teaching of Hebrew and religious texts. In 1921, the Mishmeret Cholim (Guardian of the Sick) Fund was set up to provide free medical treatment to poor Jews of Harbin and those who lived along the route of the CER. It began with two clinics and in November 1934 founded a Jewish hospital, with 25 beds, and hired the most famous medical specialists in Harbin. Its director was Dr Abraham Kaufman." (Note 5) Teddy Kaufman was his son.

Dr Kaufman was a leader of the community in Harbin for over 30 years. He was born in November 1885 into an Orthodox family in a small Jewish village in west Ukraine, part of the Russian empire. He studied medicine at the University of Bern in Switzerland. After graduation, he returned to Russia to work and he became an ardent Zionist.

In February 1912, he emigrated to Harbin with his new wife and started work as a doctor. For the next 30 years, he was one of the most important leaders of the Jewish community in the city, active in many spheres of life. From 1919 to 1931 and from 1933 to 1945, he was chairman of the Jewish community of Harbin; he was also a board member of the World Zionist Organisation and chairman of the Jewish Zionist organisation of China. He was active in charity toward Jewish refugees coming from Europe; from 1921 to 1943, he edited a weekly Russian-language newspaper *Jewish Life*.

The cultural life of the Jewish Association in Harbin was rich. In 1910, the community set up a theatre, which hosted dance and musical performances. In 1918, a famous Jewish musician and conductor came from Russia and took over the CER orchestra. Thanks to his hard work, it became the top-ranking orchestra in the Far East. (Note 6) Mainly composed of Russian players, it was the first classical musical orchestra in

A patient in the Jewish hospital in Harbin, 1927.

Advertisement for Logivich
Moscow Pharmacy in Harbin,
1916.

Licence to practice pharmacy given to
Michael Pektorovitz in Harbin.

China. In 1912, the community opened a library with more than 13,000 books.

Zionism in China

In November 1917, the British government issued the Balfour Declaration, saying that it viewed "with favour the establishment in Palestine of a national home for the Jewish people, and will use their best endeavours to facilitate the achievement of this object". It was a milestone in the history of Zionism.

The declaration had an echo on the other side of the world in distant Harbin. That year, a Zionist organisation was set up there and Dr Abraham Kaufman became its leader. Rabbi Kiselev was a supporter. "In March 1919, Harbin hosted the Far East Zionist representative conference, with delegates from cities all over China and the Russian Far East." (Note 7)

In the early 1920s, several groups of young Jews from Harbin emigrated to Palestine. As the young Soviet Union increasingly restricted Zionism, Harbin became its centre in the Far East. From 1920, the Jewish community published a newspaper in Russian, *Siberia-Palestine*; it was later called *Jewish Life* and circulated throughout Manchuria and north China. After 1929 a branch of Betar was set up in Harbin. Betar is a Zionist youth movement founded in 1923 in Riga, Latvia by Vladimir Jabotinsky. The Harbin branch provided sports and cultural activities and military training and attracted many young Jewish people who were looking for action instead of ideology.

One of the members of Betar in Harbin was Mordechai Olmert, father of Ehud, a future Prime Minister of Israel. Unlike most Jews, he chose to study not at a Russian-language school but a Chinese one and spoke Mandarin. He left Harbin for Palestine in 1930; Bella, his wife to be, left a few years later. In 1947, he returned to Harbin, as part of a fund-raising tour among Jewish communities in China. His father J.J. Olmert is buried in the community's cemetery in Harbin.

Banks and brothels

The first Jews in Harbin worked in jobs connected to the CER. But they soon moved into other sectors of the economy, including hotels, shops, cafes, bakeries, breweries, tobacco, coal mining, timber and flour milling.

"Jewish businessmen were very active in industry, commerce and international trade…One was a pioneer in the export of soybean from Manchuria. In 1909, with a British partner, he invested 170,000 pounds to set up the Sino-British Oriental Trading Company (華英東方貿易有限公司) it set up branches in major cities around Asia, to facilitate the trade. In 1914, he imported the most modern crushing equipment from Europe for a soybean oil factory, exporting the finished product to the United States." (Note 8)

In the early 1920s, members of the community set up the Jewish People's Bank (猶太國民銀行), initially to provide credit to Jewish businesses and later extending it to many kinds of customers. By 1935, it was serving 1,184 customers with a wide range of financial services. It closed in 1950, after a history of more than 30 years, the longest of any foreign-invested bank in Harbin.

Jewish entrepreneurs established other financial institutions. "Others set up dance halls, theatres, billiard halls, casinos and brothels in the city and outskirts." (Note 9)

The Great Depression of 1929 had a serious impact on the community in Harbin, especially those involved in international trade.

Like their brothers and sisters in Shanghai, the Jews of Harbin had limited contact with Chinese people. In their schools, the students learnt Russian, English, French and Japanese but rarely Mandarin. With their business partners and servants, they spoke Russian. The Chinese who wanted to have dealings with them had to learn Russian, just as the Chinese of Shanghai had to learn English or French.

"Few Jews (in Harbin) had interest in speaking Chinese or [in] Chinese culture," according to Wang Zhijun and Li Wei. (Note 10) "The Jews of Harbin lived in quite a closed world. They maintained close contacts with the latest developments in Jewish civilisation around the world. They enjoyed the same rights as other foreigners and lived in the way they wanted. They did not need to change their language or style of life."

With the other Europeans, they lived in an area of Harbin called "Russian

Members of the Betar movement in Harbin, 1930s.

Jewish People's Bank in Harbin, 1923.

Harbin Jewish Home of the Aged
and Soup Kitchen, 1920.

city" (俄國城); the Chinese lived in what was called "China city" (中國城) Intermarriage between Jews and Chinese was very rare.

In this respect, the Jews were like other foreign residents of China of that era who retained their own style of life, language and cuisine. They did not expect to remain in China over the long term and wanted to keep family and professional ties to their mother country. Many considered China a weak and backward country that had missed the chance to modernise.

Without a country of their own, the Jews had even more reason to strengthen their own community, religion and way of living. They had escaped from Russia and Eastern Europe in order to practise the Jewish life denied to them in those countries; so, they had even more reason to maintain and cherish it in Harbin.

International city becomes Japanese outpost

In 1931 came a blow more serious than the Great Depression -- the Japanese takeover of Manchuria. The occupation of Harbin in 1932 ended the remarkable freedom which Harbin had enjoyed as an international city for the previous 30 years.

Japan had several motives for the takeover. The most important was to expand its "sphere of influence" in the region. Another was to prepare for a possible war with or invasion of the Soviet Union. A third was to control the soybeans, corn, wheat, timber, coal, iron ore and other resources Manchuria had in abundance – many of the sectors in which

Jewish businesses were active. A fourth was the personal enrichment of the civil and military officials involved; wealthy and prominent, owners of major Jewish companies were obvious targets for extortion and kidnapping.

As a result of the invasion, Harbin lost much of its international character; Japanese companies moved to monopolise the most profitable sectors of business. The city's large trade surplus turned into a deficit.

In 1935, the Soviet Union sold the CER for 170 million Japanese yen to the puppet government of Manchukuo; so, the railway passed under Japanese control, greatly damaging the interests of Jewish individuals and companies which worked for and did business with it.

The new rulers were anti-Communist and anti-Soviet. They worked with the fiercely anti-Soviet White Russians, such as the Russian Fascist Party, who had brought their anti-Semitism with them. With the connivance of the Japanese police, there were outbreaks of anti-Semitic violence of the kind that the community had fled to Harbin to escape. There were attacks on Jewish individuals and property.

"From 1932 to the first half of 1936, 31 Jewish shops in Harbin closed, involving capital of 1.961 million yuan. The Jewish population in the city fell to about 8,000 in 1935 and about 5,000 in 1939. The golden age of the community in Harbin would never come again." (Note 11)

Some moved to other cities in China with an important Jewish community, such as Shanghai, Tianjin and Qingdao, and were outside the control of the

Japanese military – though only for a time. Others who could obtain visas emigrated to the U.S., Australia, Brazil and other countries.

Triumph and Tragedy

One of the most prominent buildings in Harbin was and is the Hotel Moderne, which opened in 1913. It was built by a Russian Jew named Iosif Kaspe. He served in the Russian Army in the war with Japan of 1904-05; after it ended, he decided not to go home but to settle in Harbin.

Kaspe started selling used clothes on the streets of the young city, then opened a small shop repairing watches. He was a sociable man with excellent technical skills and the business prospered. With his profits, he opened a second shop selling silver ornaments and jewellery; it also did well. As the railway hub of Manchuria, the city was booming and lacked a top-class hotel.

"Seeing the rapid growth of the city, he hired a famous Russian architect and imported high-quality materials from Europe and the U.S. In 1913, he opened the Moderne as the first foreign-invested hotel in the city. Built in the European style with three floors, it had 160 rooms, restaurants, meeting halls, dance floor, cinema and a theatre.

"It attracted important guests, including Song Qing-ling (宋慶齡) [Sun Yat-sen's widow] and [Republic of China statesman] Wellington Koo (顧維鈞), and was, before 1949, the most high-class hotel in northeast

China." (Note 12)

Kaspe hired famous chefs, magicians, dancers and performers; the hotel became a centre of social life for the rich and powerful of Harbin, as well as a political hub for foreign persona and Chinese leaders. He invested in cinemas and theatres; he was also a philanthropist, providing funds to the victims of natural disasters that befell Harbin.

But, like other foreigners, he knew China would be unstable under the Japanese and that he had to prepare an alternative future for himself and his family. According to the *Global People* (*GP*) magazine, (Note 13) Kaspe had transferred all his assets to his two sons whom he had sent to study in France and who had French nationality. He flew the French flag over the front of his hotel as a form of protection.

Things changed after September 18, 1931, when the Japanese military took over the region and, the next year, created a new "country" under the name Manchukuo (滿洲國), headed by former Qing Emperor Pu Yi (溥儀). Some residents of Harbin welcomed the new rulers; among them were many White Russians who had supported the Tsar and escaped to Harbin after the Bolshevik Revolution.

Fervently anti-Soviet, they hoped that the Japanese army, also anti-Communist, would invade their homeland, overthrow the Soviet regime and enable them to go home. These White Russians were anti-Semitic; they resented the wealth and success of the Jewish community of Harbin.

Kaspe's fortune also attracted the attention of Japanese officers who used their new power to enrich themselves. "Many shops had to pay all kinds of fees. The Moderne Hotel with its large profits especially attracted the attention of the Japanese, who also recognized the place for its social and political importance and symbolism. They offered to buy it for one million yuan but Kaspe would not agree." (Note 14)

The animosity between him and the new rulers intensified in 1932. The League of Nations sent a five-member Lytton Commission, headed by a British nobleman Lord Lytton, to investigate whether Manchukuo was a country based on the wishes of its inhabitants or a Japanese puppet regime.

"On September 9 (1932), the Lytton Commission arrived at the Moderne Hotel, with a total of more than 100 people, including 26 officials of the Japanese and Manchukuo governments. Government agents occupied the rooms next to those of the commission, posing as tourists, and flooded the hotel to prevent anyone meeting its members. The Commission spent 12 days in Harbin and received 1,500 letters and petitions." (Note 15)

Its report in October supported the Chinese case and concluded that the new state was not the result of a genuine independence movement. When the League of Nations approved the report, Japan walked out and withdrew from the institution.

"The Japanese and Manchurian governments were enraged. Their suspicions turned toward Kaspe, whose movements within the hotel they had been unable to limit. Michitaro Komatsubara (小松原道太郎), head of the Japanese secret police, ordered the kidnapping of Kaspe. But this was not easy, since he employed many Russian security men in his hotel day and night and was surrounded by bodyguards whenever he went outside." His house was surrounded by a barbed wire fence and several fierce dogs patrolled the entrance and yard.

Instead, they decided to kidnap his son Semion, 24, a talented musician who had just graduated from a music academy in Paris and had become a professional pianist. He came to Harbin on the invitation of his father who arranged a performance tour throughout the region for his son. Semion was spending the summer of 1933 in Harbin with his girlfriend. The Japanese side provided the weapons and the money for the kidnap and a White Russian officer of the city's police force the manpower.

On the night of August 24, when a chauffeur was driving Semion and his girlfriend home from a party, he found his car blocked by another car. Armed men stepped out, held a gun to his head and bundled him into their car; they gave his girlfriend a letter to deliver to Iosif, demanding a ransom of 300,000 yuan and saying that, if he told the police or the French consulate, they would kill his son.

Unperturbed, Iosif informed the police and the consulate and asked them to use diplomatic leverage; he informed the media that he would not pay a cent in ransom and said that no-one would dare to harm Semion.

While an official investigation was launched, he negotiated with the kidnappers and brought the price down to 30,000 yuan. Days passed with no news. Angry and frustrated, Iosif hired an Italian private detective with good contacts in the intelligence community. After his investigation, the detective reported that the kidnapping was an operation of the Japanese military police who used the White Russian Fascists.

Fearful that Kaspe was not going to pay, the kidnappers sent him an envelope with Semion two earlobes covered in blood and a letter from Semion asking for a payment of 150,000 yuan; Iosif offered 35,000.

Kaspe decided to pressure the Japanese government. At his request, the French consul told the media that the Japanese military police were involved in the kidnapping; the story was carried in media around the world, causing grave embarrassment to the Tokyo government.

The Japanese police started to pursue the case; on November 28, at Harbin railway station, they arrested two of the gang members who revealed where the young man had been held. When the military police chief heard that one of the other gang members was trying to make a private deal with Kaspe, he summoned the man to a meeting, at the cargo yard of the same railway station, and shot him dead.

He also ordered the death of Semion, in an attempt to prevent the details of the kidnapping coming out; he was killed on December 3. The body was finally found that day, after over 100 days of captivity, and the remaining kidnappers arrested. "All that was left of this outstanding young man was a skeleton, an unbearable tragedy," said *Global People*. The death caused an outcry, at home and abroad. Thousands, including

Jews, Chinese and other nationalities, attended his funeral in Harbin.

In March 1936, three Chinese judges sentenced the kidnappers to death. But this verdict was overturned in January the next year, under Japanese pressure. The kidnappers walked free from prison, after it was ruled that they acted for patriotic reasons. Broken-hearted, Kaspe left Harbin to join his wife and other son in Paris. He died in France in October 1938.

His wife Maria and younger son Vladimir were stripped of their French citizenship in 1941 and forced to leave the country. They sailed to Casablanca and, from there, Vladimir went to Mexico; he became a well-known architect and professor in Mexico City where he died in 1996. The whereabouts of Maria are not known.

After Kaspe's departure to France, the hotel was managed by his cousin Moses Zimin and later by another member of the community. The Japanese never took over his hotel. This tragedy had a serious impact on the city's Jewish community and their confidence in the new government to protect them. The hotel Kaspe founded was taken over by the new Chinese government after 1949. The hotel lives on and celebrated its 100th anniversary a few years ago. Visitors can still hear piano music on the terrace where Semion played.

The Fugu Plan – a Jewish homeland in Manchuria

Japan regarded Manchuria in the same way as European powers saw their colonies and the young United States saw the Mid- and Far West – empty

Hotel Moderne, opened in 1913 by Iosif Kaspe and flying the French flag.

Jewish community leaders at Soskin silver wedding celebration in Hotel Moderne, 1930

land where they could settle surplus population, develop agriculture and industry and carry out projects impossible at home.

Japan consisted of overcrowded islands with few natural resources. Colonization required substantial investment to build the housing, roads, railways, power lines, schools and hospitals needed to attract mass migration.

In the summer of 1937, Japan foolishly launched an unwinnable war with China that cost hundreds of millions of yen a year; it did not have the surplus capital it needed to develop Manchuria. Initially, it hoped to attract this from European and American investors. But, after the Lytton Commission report and Japan's withdrawal from the League of Nations, Europeans and Americans would not invest there.

Even worse, the migration of thousands of Japanese farmers to the "paradise" of Manchuria was going slower than planned; the climate was harsh, local people were hostile and the necessary infrastructure did not exist. Many settlers returned, disillusioned and disappointed, to Japan.

And so was born the "Fugu Plan" (河豚計劃) devised by several Japanese specialists on the Jewish question and first made public in 1934. "Fugu" is the Japanese word for pufferfish, a prized delicacy in the country's cuisine. But, because the fish contains a poison, preparation of it is strictly controlled by law in Japan; only chefs with three years of rigorous training are allowed to prepare the fish.

The specialists, civil and military officials, believed that Japan should take advantage of the emigration of Jews from Europe to settle them in Manchuria, in a special autonomous zone such as the one Stalin established in Birobijan; the new migrants would bring capital, skills and technology to develop this virgin land. They would be given freedom of work, religion, culture and education denied to them in Europe; official documents spoke of settling tens of thousands.

Those who devised the "Fugu" plan wanted at the same time to win the goodwill of the wealthy and powerful Jewish community in the U.S. who would, as a result, fund the new settlements and look favourably on Japan. They also wanted to earn the goodwill of the U.S. government, so that it would end its opposition to Japan's invasion of China.

Those backing the plan came from both business and the military. In an article in 1934, Yoshisuke Aikawa (鮎川義介), founder of the Nissan (日產) conglomerate that included the motor company, proposed that 50,000 Jews from Germany be resettled in Manchukuo, using capital from American Jews, to develop the region and form a defensive wall against the Soviet Union. In 1937, he moved the headquarters of his company to Manchukuo, where he established the Manchurian Industrial Development Company (滿洲重工業開發株式會社).

Within the military, a main architect of the plan was Norihiro Yasue (安江仙弘), a graduate of the Army Officers' College and a Colonel in the Army Intelligence Bureau. He had served in the Japanese army that invaded Siberia in 1918, in an attempt to defeat the Bolshevik Red Army. He spoke Russian and knew well the plight of Jewish people in Europe and Russia.

In 1926, the Ministry of Foreign Affairs sent him to Palestine to research the Jews. He met many people, including David Ben-Gurion, Chaim Weizmann, businessmen, farmers and rabbis. He visited kibbutzim established by the new settlers and was greatly impressed by their energy, organisation and patriotism to rebuild their ancient country. Yasue believed such people would be a great asset to the Japanese empire. He and his colleagues outlined a plan for large-scale settlement of Jews in Manchukuo; it was supported by the Guandong Army (關東軍 – east of the pass – *shanhai guan*), the Japanese army that controlled the "country" and saw that the migration of their own people was not going smoothly.

Official documents called for settlement of tens of thousands of Jews in Manchukuo and the suburbs of Shanghai; they would have complete freedom of religion and education but would need to be under surveillance to ensure that they did not enter the mainstream of Japanese politics and economy.

The plan called for substantial funding from the wealthy Jewish community in the United States. To this end, Japan would send delegations to the U.S. to explain the project and invite Jewish rabbis to Japan to introduce their religion to the public. Architects of the plan also planned to attract U.S. media and film-makers from Hollywood to publicise it.

But the Japanese "stick and carrot policy" toward the Jewish community, the frequent arrest of Jewish persons, the murder of Semion Kaspe and the immunity given to his killers had enraged the Jewish community of Harbin; many had left for Shanghai and Tianjin, cities where they felt safer.

White Russians had committed attacks on Jewish individuals and property in Harbin, with the blessing and surrogates of the Japanese police and intelligence units.

The first thing the government needed to do was try to win back the support and confidence of the Jewish community. It gave this mission to Norihiro Yasue. He was well-equipped for it; he was sympathetic to and knowledgeable about them. He spoke Russian, the main language of the Jews of Harbin.

Like other senior officers in the Japanese military, he remembered a loan of US$200 million given to Japan by Jacob Henry Schiff, an American Jewish banker, in 1904-05, which was critical in winning its war against Russia by funding the large-scale purchase of munitions. Schiff made the loan after British bankers in London refused, for fear of upsetting Russia, a great power.

Being a Jew, Schiff held its regime responsible for terrible pogroms that had left hundreds of Jews dead. In 1905 and 1907, Schiff received honours from Japan; he was the first foreigner to receive an honour in person from Emperor Meiji (日皇明治) in the Imperial Palace. For Japanese, this loan was evidence of the power of Jewish capital and the fact that Jews accepted Japan as an important partner in the world.

Like China, Japan was one of the earliest countries to support the idea of a Jewish state in Palestine. In December 1918, the Japanese government sent a message to the Shanghai Zionist Association stating its "pleasure of having learned of the advent desire of the Zionists to establish in Palestine a National Jewish Homeland...Japan will accord its sympathy to the realisation of your [Zionist] aspirations."

Courting the Jews

In Harbin, Yasue befriended Dr Abraham Kaufman, the leader of the city's Jewish community. He often visited his house, where they held long discussions in Russian on the future of the Jewish people and Palestine. Kaufman protested to him about the anti-Semitic violence and hatred in the newspapers of the White Russian community in Harbin.

In 1934, Yasue helped him form the Far Eastern Jewish Council (FEJC), an official body to represent the views of the Jews in Manchuria. Yasue and his colleagues took steps to curb the anti-Semitic activities of the White Russians and closed its most virulent anti-Jewish newspaper *Our Road* (我們的道路).

The FEJC held its first conference in December 1937, in Harbin. It was attended by more than 700 Jews, from Harbin, Qiqihar, Shenyang, Tianjin and Shanghai as well as Kobe (神戶) and Yokohama (橫濱) in Japan. Also in attendance were senior Japanese military officials, including Yasue, and two White Russian Generals. Hanging on the wall were the flags of Japan, Manchukuo and Zionism; a Russian band played the national anthems of the three.

In his speech, Yasue said that, while the Jews had had conflicts in other countries, this had never happened in Japan. "We will treat the Jewish question from the standpoint of justice. The Jewish people have a rich spirit of intensive study, are hard-working, gifted in economic and social affairs and have made contributions to science...If the Jews can recover their country, then the Jewish question will be solved."

The conference closed after three days, with resolutions that the Jews would help Japan and Manchukuo build a new order in Asia and a protest against the anti-Semitism of Nazi Germany. It also set up a Far Eastern Jewish Self-governing Committee. The Jewish leaders thanked Japan for treating Jews equally, while other countries were persecuting them.

The event and news coverage of it served the interests of both Tokyo and the Jews. For Tokyo, it sent a message to the large Jewish communities in Europe and North America that their brothers and sisters in areas under Japanese control were being well treated and co-operating with the new ruler. For the Jews of Manchuria, it showed their legal status and position and the support of Tokyo for a Zionist state. That year the Manchukuo government gave Dr Kaufman a medal in recognition of his public service.

A second and third conference were held in 1938 and 1939. The second opened on December 26, 1938, also with about 700 delegates. It was opened by Dr Kaufman, followed by a blessing from Aharon Kiselev, Chief Rabbi of the Harbin community. In his speech, Dr Kaufman spoke of his distress and sympathy for the Jews under attack in central and eastern Europe. He criticised the British government for not implementing the Balfour Declaration and for restricting Jewish immigration to the Holy Land.

Among the speakers was Setsuzo Kotsuji (小辻節三), a professor and the only Japanese at that time who could read and speak Hebrew. He addressed the conference in Hebrew: "From a young age, I have had a deep interest in the study of the Hebrew language and the Jewish race and history," he said. "So, I have more concern and sympathy for them than other people. I hope for the foundation of Israel in Palestine at an early date." His fluent Hebrew deeply moved the audience. He was adviser on Jewish affairs to the South Manchurian Railway Company (南滿洲鐵道株式會社), one of the largest Japanese conglomerates in Manchuria. In chapter five, we explain in detail about Kotsuji-san and his service to the Jewish people.

In March 1938, thousands of Jews fleeing Nazi persecution arrived on the Trans-Siberian railway at Otpol station on the Soviet side of the Manchurian border. The Manchukuo government refused them entry. Dr Kaufman went to see Kiichiro Higuchi (樋口季一郎), a major-general in the Imperial Army and head of its department for special missions in Harbin; he asked him to allow the Jews to enter.

Higuchi had a profile similar to that of Yasue. A fluent Russian speaker, he had served as military attaché in Poland, travelled in Germany and knew well the situation in Europe. He overruled the government and sent

13 trains, each of 12 cars, to transport the Jews over the border. He sent subordinates to arrange for them to settle in Harbin, Shanghai or overseas. In December 2009, 39 years after Higuchi's death, an olive sapling given by Israel's ambassador to Japan was planted in a park in front of the city hall of Gifu (岐阜), his home place, in recognition of what he had done. (Note 16)

Harbin Jewish leader receives Japanese Imperial award

In May 1939, Yasue arranged an official month-long visit by Dr Kaufman to Japan, where he met senior officials, including the Finance Minister; he became one of the few foreigners to be given an imperial award. Dr Kaufman used the meetings to express the needs and views of the Jews in Manchukuo; the officials assured him that the Japanese government would treat them without discrimination. He formally thanked Prime Minister Nobuyuki Abe (阿部信行) for the protection Japan had given to the Jews in East Asia.

Dr Kaufman's personal dealings with the Japanese were a matter of grave concern to the leading Jewish organisations in the U.S., who were alarmed by the information he was passing to them. The Jewish Congress in America issued a secret directive putting an immediate stop to any exchange of information between the organisations and Kaufman.

We may imagine the sentiments of Dr Kaufman and his colleagues in Harbin. The three conferences were held in the years when European Jews were desperate to leave but could find no place to accept them – even countries in the west with large Jewish communities.

They included the United States, the country with the world's largest and most powerful Jewish population. In June 1939, the St Louis, a vessel which had left from Hamburg with more than 900 Jews, was not allowed to land in Miami and was ordered to return to Europe; about 250 of the passengers would die in the Holocaust.

That same year the U.S. Congress rejected a bill to accept 20,000 German Jewish refugee children, over and above existing visa quotas for Germans, despite the fact that 1,400 Americans had written to Congress saying they would accept a refugee child.

By contrast, senior officials of Asia's biggest industrial and colonial power were courting the Jews and inviting them to settle and invest. Yasue and his colleagues held many meetings to discuss how to encourage and establish Jewish settlements in and around Harbin. In 1939, Yasue and two others proposed a second autonomous region for the Jews close to Shanghai.

In December that year, Yasue and his colleagues held the Third Conference of Jewish Communities in the Far East in Harbin. But there was no fourth one in 1940. As Japan began preparations for war with the United States, such an event was no longer useful.

However, the three conferences did have great significance for the Jews in China. They gave them a legal status and support and protection from the new ruling power. This was particularly useful for the many Jews who held no passport and were stateless. It strengthened their position against the anti-Semitic members of the White Russian population in Manchuria. And it enabled them to influence Japanese policy in their favour; helping to keep the door open to admit thousands of Jewish refugees from Europe into areas of China controlled by Japan. (Note 17) But this influence was limited: the later enclosure of Jewish refugees in a segregated area of Shanghai and the execution of Polish Jews there showed the cruelty of the Japanese.

Accepting the Jews

This Jewish sentiment was shared at the highest level of the Japanese government. On December 6, 1938, in Tokyo, the Prime Minister, Foreign Minister and ministers of the Army, Navy and Treasury held the "Five Ministers' Conference" (五相會議) to decide the government's position on the Jewish question.

The Army and Treasury ministers argued that Jews would be a great asset for Japan, bringing capital and influencing world opinion in their favour. Opinions were divided, the meeting was intense and lasted well into the night; the ministers wanted to preserve good relations both with their allies Germany and Italy and also with the global Jewish community.

Finally, the pro-Jewish lobby won the day; the cabinet adopted three principles that would be followed by Japan for the next four years. One was that the Jews living in Japan, China and Manchuria would be treated fairly and in the same way as other foreign nationals; they would not be expelled. Second, Jews entering the three would be dealt with on the basis of existing immigration policies. Thirdly, no special effort would be made to attract Jews, except businessmen and those with technical skills useful for Japan.

As an immediate result of the meeting, about 15,000 Eastern European Jews in the Japanese district of Shanghai were given residence in what later became the "Jewish ghetto" there.

This is a record of the meeting from the website of the Japanese Foreign Ministry: "The meeting of the most high-ranking body of national policy on December 6 set the guidelines for the policy of Jews in Japan before the war. At that time, its ally Germany was persecuting the Jews. Despite this, the guidelines stated clearly that the Jews should be given the same treatment as other foreigners. On December 7, the Foreign Minister sent the guidelines to major embassies." (Note 18)

These principles would prove invaluable for the next four years to the thousands of Jews resident in Japan and in the large parts of China controlled by the Japanese military, as the Japanese government resisted pressure from its Nazi ally to follow its example in the "Final Solution".

"Fugu Plan"not implemented

The "Fugu Plan" ran to 90 pages and called for the settlement of 30,000 Jews in an area of China controlled by Japan, an area that would be expanded. Jews in the United States would pay for the construction, with an initial payment of US$100 million. It called for experts to be sent to the western countries, especially the U.S., to explain the plan and for eminent Jewish figures to be invited to see the new area. (Note 19)

But the plan was not implemented. It never won the approval of the U.S. Jewish community nor brought the capital needed. One of its strongest opponents was Stephen Samuel Wise, an American rabbi and close friend and adviser to President Franklin Roosevelt; he was president of the World Jewish Congress from 1936 until his death in 1949. He argued that co-operation between Japan and the Jews was "unpatriotic" and would contravene the spirit of the economic boycott that Washington was enforcing against Japan.

In September 1939, Germany and the Soviet Union invaded Poland. In July and August 1940, the Soviet Union annexed the three Baltic States. On September 27 1940, Japan signed in Berlin with Italy and Germany the Tripartite Pact, which brought it closer to the Nazis. The next day, Yasue was dismissed from his post as head of army special operations in Dalian and became a reserve officer; the fourth conference of Jewish Communities in the Far East planned for December that year was cancelled.

In June 1941, Germany invaded the Soviet Union, closing the main escape route for European Jews to Japan and China. After the attack on Pearl Harbour in December 1941, any support from the Jews of the U.S. was out of the question. In early 1942, the Japanese cabinet formally revoked its decision of December 7, 1938 and the Fugu plan at the same time.

But Yasue and his pro-Jewish colleagues in the government remained active and worked against implementation of Nazi policies toward the Jews. They and Dr Kaufman played an important role in 1942. In July that year Josef Meisinger, a Colonel in the Gestapo and its liaison officer at the German embassy in Tokyo from 1941 to 1945, visited the Jewish district of Shanghai and proposed the "final solution" for those living there. The lobbying of Kaufman, Yasue and his colleagues within the government was one factor in preventing the implementation of this horrific proposal. We will describe this episode in more detail in chapter four.

Heavy price

Dr Kaufman paid a heavy price for his co-operation with the Japanese during the war. On August 9, 1945, the Soviet Army with 1.5 million men invaded Manchuria. The Japanese forces opposing them had been greatly weakened by withdrawal of their best units and most of the heavy artillery to fight the Americans in the Pacific and the Nationalist army in south China.

The Soviet invasion was a great success; its forces quickly occupied Harbin. Emperor Hirohito announced Japan's surrender on August 15. On August 21, the Soviets held a large reception in Harbin to celebrate the end of the war; they invited the leaders of different communities in the city, including Dr Kaufman and two of his colleagues. The three were arrested by the Soviets and accused of "collaboration with foreign forces". They were held in the Harbin prison for over three months and then taken to the Soviet Union, where they were imprisoned in a gulag-labour camp.

They were not alone; thousands of other innocent emigres in Harbin were arrested by Soviet agents; their "crime" was to have represented their communities to the Japanese government. Most of them died in the camps. The new state of Israel issued a passport for Dr Kaufman to move there; but the Soviets refused to let him go.

After his release in 1956, Kaufman moved to Karaganda in Kazakhstan. On March 25, 1961, the man who had become a Zionist 50 years earlier finally reached the Holy Land; he spent the last 10 years of his life as a pediatrician there. He died in Tel Aviv in 1971.

During his lifetime, he had made an enormous contribution towards helping and protecting the Jews of China, and of Harbin in particular. This would have been impossible without his 10 years of close collaboration with the Japanese; it gave him a privileged access enjoyed by few foreigners in China.

"This close co-operation with the Japanese invader harmed the feelings of the Chinese people," said historians Wang Zhijun and Li Wei. "This is undeniable." (Note 20). Yes, but how else could Dr Kaufman have saved his people? During the 20th century, many Jews had extraordinary odysseys, as they fled persecution in search of a better life, in the Promised Land or elsewhere. Dr Kaufman ranks among them – his odyssey took him from Ukraine to Switzerland, Harbin, Tokyo, a Soviet labour camp, Kazakhstan and finally, at the age of 76, to Israel.

Notes

1   "Moscow of the Orient" (東方莫斯科) by *National Humanity History* (*NHH*) magazine (國家人文歷史), July 2016.

2   *Harbin Jews in Early 1900s: Their Political and Religious Lives* (20 世紀上半期 哈爾濱猶太人的宗教生活與政治生活), by Wang Zhijun (王志軍) and Li Wei (李薇), People's Publishing House (人民出版社), April 2013, pages 2-12.

3   Rabbi A.M. Kiselev and the Religious Life of the Jews in Harbin, by Teddy Kaufman, a report delivered at the International Seminar in Harbin.

4   *NHH* magazine

5-9 *The Jews and China* (猶太人與中國) by Professors Pan Guang (潘光) and Wang Jian (王健), Shishi Publishing Company (時事出版社), 2009, pages 158-165.

10 Wang Zhijun and Li Wei, pages 307-308.

11 Pan and Wang, page 167.

12 *NHH* magazine

13-15 Material on the Kaspe kidnapping comes from articles in three Chinese magazines – "Moscow of the Orient" (東方莫斯科) by *National Humanity History* (*NHH*) magazine (國家人文歷史), July 2016; "The Tragic Destiny of the founder of the Modern Hotel" (馬迭爾創始人的悲劇命運), *Global People* magazine (環球人物), 2011, Number 27; and "The Harbin Kidnapping of 1933 that shook the world"(1933 年震驚中外的哈爾濱綁架案) in *Eye on History* (看歷史), January 2017.

16 *Asahi Shimbun* (朝日新聞), 4/5/2010.

17 Wang Zhijun and Li Wei, pages 269-279.

18 Japanese Foreign Ministry website (http://www.mofa.go.jp/mofaj/), diplomatic records of early period of Showa war.

19 Pan and Wang, page 51-52.

20 Wang Zhijun and Li Wei, page 241.

Chapter Three

The making of Shanghai – 1840-1941

From **OUTSIDERS**

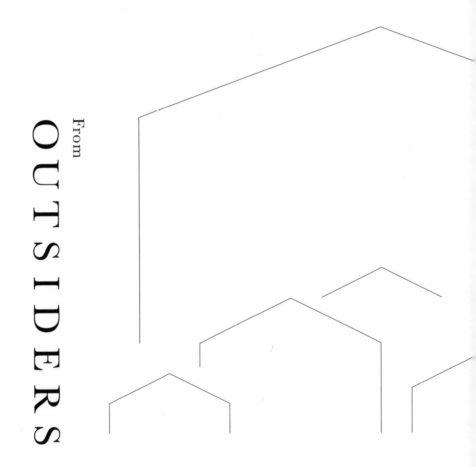

The Jews made an enormous contribution to the new international city of Shanghai that was born out of the First Opium War of 1839-1842. They built factories, hotels, schools, hospitals and apartment blocks for the rich and the poor; they managed buses, trams and other public utilities.

Most foreigners only stayed long enough to finish their posting or earn the money they came for. But the Jews settled in the new city and made it their home; they re-invested the money they had earned. This gave them knowledge, experience, contacts and connections others did not have and that enabled them to take full opportunity of one of the fastest growing cities in the Far East.

As long-term residents, they were more willing to invest in property. Some became fabulously wealthy. They were one of the most important foreign business communities in Shanghai.

Many of the buildings they constructed remain today. While the new district of Pudong (浦東), on the east side of the Huangpu River (黃浦江), is a creation of the post-1978 reforms, the downtown area of Puxi (浦西), on the west side, retains a broad footprint of Jewish property firms.

To CITIZENS

The city they helped to build was unique. The foreign concessions of Shanghai were in China but not under Chinese rule. They were controlled by foreign imperial powers, especially Britain, France and the United States, of whom the British were the most important. In 1846, the British concession covered 1,080 mu (72 hectares) in size, with 120 British residents. Within the concession, foreigners – but not Chinese – could lease land in perpetuity.

The American concession was established in 1848 and the French one the following year. In 1854, the three countries created the Shanghai Municipal Council (工部局) to govern this new area. In 1863, the British and Americans merged their areas to form the International Concession (上海公共租界); the French continued to run their own concession to the south.

On this small piece of Chinese soil, the foreigners built a modern European city with paved roads, electricity, running water, trams and buses; it had its own laws and regulations, including the right to buy and sell land. By 1915, the foreign concessions had increased to 70,000 mu (4,670 hectares), 12 times their size in 1848.

Like other migrants, the Jews who moved there were taking a big gamble – that the economy of the new city would develop in a healthy and stable way and provide them with better business opportunities than in Baghdad, Batavia (modern-day Jakarta) or Bombay.

This was not a given. There was always the risk that, angry at being forced to give up this land and legalise the sale of opium, the Chinese government would take it back. It could mount a military attack or foment strikes and unrest among its nationals living in the concessions; the Chinese always greatly outnumbered the foreigners.

In addition, foreign businesses relied heavily on import and export trade. Would the shipping routes between Shanghai and the rest of the world remain open? Would they be threatened by a war between an Asian country and an imperial power or between the powers themselves?

The Jews were entrepreneurial people; all the original Jewish families who settled in Shanghai were British citizens. They knew that risk brought opportunity. They believed that the protection provided by the foreign powers would provide a good environment for business. At that time, Britain had the most powerful empire and the strongest navy in the world. The Jews gambled that the ailing Qing dynasty (清朝) would not dare to take on this empire; as British citizens, they joined its global imperial enterprise.

The gamble paid off spectacularly. For nearly 100 years, until the Japanese occupation in December 1941, the foreign concessions of Shanghai remained under western control. They developed into the most important industrial, commercial and trading centre in China and one of the most modern cities in Asia.

In the 1930s, Shanghai accounted for more than half of China's foreign trade and about 40 per cent of the country's manufacturing output. By

1940, the population had reached about five million, compared to around one million in 1910. Over that 100-year period, the city provided foreign businesses, including those owned by Jews, with social and political stability they could not find in many cities in Europe and Russia.

"In Shanghai, huge wealth was made and many opportunities were available," said Sir Michael Kadoorie, who is now head of what was one of the major Jewish families in Shanghai. (Note 1)

"Huge fortunes were made and lost in Shanghai. Jewish people do well with opportunities. Shanghai was the biggest city in the world and called the Paris of the East. Every day many poor people came into the city. In the morning, the bodies of the dead were collected."

In January 1943, in recognition of the enormous sacrifices made by China and its people in the war against Japan, Britain and the U.S. signed treaties with the Nationalist government to return their concessions to China. In 1946, France followed suit. That spelt the end of the 100-year history of the concessions.

The original Jewish residents of Shanghai were Sephardic, from Baghdad. After them came others, mostly Sephardic Jews from Iraq, Iran and India; many of them were British nationals. They were a close-knit community and provided help and welfare to the many Jewish newcomers. Then came European Ashkenazi Jews, mainly via Harbin.

The residents built synagogues and schools and helped later arrivals, like

Jews from Europe. They supported the Zionist (錫安主義) cause and funded colleges and settlements in Palestine; some emigrated there. They persuaded the Chinese government – and Dr Sun Yat-sen (孫中山) – to support the Zionist project.

To protect their own business and political interests, they engaged actively with Chinese politics; these were complex and constantly changing, especially after the overthrow of the imperial dynasty in 1911.

Before and during World War Two, Shanghai became a global centre of Jewish refugees; it accepted about 30,000. Between 1937 and 1939, it was one of the few cities in the world they could enter without a visa, job offer or financial guarantor. They lived among Chinese people who accepted them without prejudice and treated them well. The Japanese who controlled the whole city from December 1941 until the end of the war in August 1945 resisted pressure from their Nazi allies for "the final solution".

Following the Empire

The first Jew to arrive in Shanghai in the modern era was probably a British army officer named Gordon, according to the *Eye on History* magazine. (Note 2) He was member of a British military contingent who arrived there on June 17, 1842 during the First Opium War. They stayed for a week and sent a vessel up the Huangpu River to near Suzhou (蘇州). Gordon concluded that Shanghai had good business potential and sent this message to fellow Jews in India; he advised those with intelligence and ability to go there to take advantage of it.

In 1845, the first Jews arrived in Shanghai and Hong Kong in the wake of the First Opium War, which opened both places to foreign trade and settlement. They were Sephardic, originally from Baghdad. By the 18th century, the Jewish community in Baghdad numbered 5,000-6,000. Most were very poor; a small number were rich. Because of their skills in finance, the city often appointed a Jew as its treasurer, a post frequently held by a Sassoon, the most prominent Jewish family.

But in 1821, the Ottoman Sultan appointed a new governor to the city who initiated anti-Semitic policies; leading Jews were arrested and executed. David Sassoon decided to leave; he moved to Bombay (now Mumbai), part of British India. In 1832, he took British nationality and founded David Sassoon and Sons Company, which exported opium and cotton textile goods to China; opium was then considered to be a medical remedy to many illnesses. They became one of the wealthiest families in India.

David sent his second son Elias to Guangzhou to take charge of China operations; in 1841, the company opened its first office in Hong Kong. Four years later, it opened an office in Shanghai. Business there grew rapidly; its trading activities spread to Japan, Thailand, Southeast Asia and the Middle East, as well as India and other parts of China.

Opium and skyscrapers

The most profitable product of the Sassoon Company was opium. Trading in it became legal after the Second Opium War from 1856-1860; with branches well established in India, the firm became the largest dealer of the commodity in Shanghai. According to *Eye on History* magazine, its average annual shipments at the end of the 19th and early 20th centuries were more than 5,000 crates worth 38 million taels (海關両), sold through more than 50 sales agents in Shanghai. (Note 3)

Pan and Wang estimated that, between 1840 and 1914, the firm earned from opium a profit of 140.6 million taels, an annual profit of nearly two million taels. (Note 4)

The price of opium in Shanghai's International Settlement peaked at 9,012 taels (両) per bale in November 1915. By then, the trade was dwindling; it was hit by increased production in China and a prohibition movement driven by the Chinese government, civic groups and foreign missionaries.

In 1918, Sir Ellice Victor Elias Sassoon (who would be known as Victor), the fourth generation of the family, inherited the New Sassoon company; he had been educated at the elite Harrow school and Cambridge University in England.

With the fall in the opium trade, the company turned to other imports, especially cotton yarn and cotton and wool garments. By the 1920s, these had replaced opium as its most important products. The company also exported a wide range of Chinese goods, including tea, silk, eggs and vegetable oil.

In 1925, Japanese-invested cotton yarn factories in Shanghai were badly hit by a boycott of Japanese goods by Chinese consumers; they were unable to sell their output, which stockpiled in the warehouses. The price fell below that of cotton yarn in India; Sassoon bought much of the stock and exported it to England.

Tallest buildings outside the U.S.

For the Sassoon family, like other large Jewish companies in Shanghai, property was a very important sector. They were pioneers of the city's real estate market, investing in the International and French concessions. This international city became a haven for Chinese, wealthy and poor, during the country's many upheavals during the second half of the 19th century.

When the army of the Taiping Rebellion conquered Nanjing in the spring of 1853 and a triad society (小刀會) occupied the Chinese-controlled area of Shanghai in September that year, thousands of people poured into the foreign concessions.

The Sassoons set up their property business in 1877. By 1922, it had acquired 29 properties covering an area of 300 mu (20 hectares) worth more than 13 million taels. Its annual income from property was more than 500,000 taels, an annual return of 24 per cent – lower than the return from opium, but good nonetheless.

The company constructed many of Shanghai's best-known buildings, including the Cathay Hotel, Hamilton House, Metropole Hotel, Cathay Mansions and Grosvenor House. In 1923, Victor Sassoon decided to move the headquarters of the family empire from Bombay to Shanghai; he was fearful of the rise of the Indian independence movement.

He transferred millions of dollars from Bombay and invested them in the property market of the booming city. His companies invested in many other sectors – insurance, finance, lumber, building supplies, breweries, food, laundries, tramways and bus lines; they owned the city's bus and tram companies. His timing was perfect; Shanghai's most prosperous period was between the two World Wars.

Real estate became his most important investment. In April 1925, Sassoon began work on his most ambitious project, Sassoon House, on the corner of Nanjing Road (南京路) and the Bund (外灘), then as now the centre of the city. It took four years and five months to complete and cost 5.6 million taels; it had 13 storeys, was 77 metres high and had a built-up area of 36,317 square metres. (Note 5)

It was the highest structure in Shanghai and the Far East. The top floor housed Sassoon's personal penthouse, his downtown pied-a-terre; the ground floor was the main hall of the Cathay Hotel and space rented to two foreign banks. The second to fourth floors were office space, the fifth to seventh hotel rooms, the eighth a bar and dance floor and Chinese restaurant and the ninth a restaurant and night club.

It was the most desirable location in the city; the two foreign banks on the ground floor each paid a monthly rent of 1,354 taels. The hotel rooms had Deco glasswork and original Arts and Crafts furniture. It became the centre for the rich and famous of Shanghai to meet, eat, drink and party.

Sassoon's large investments in real estate helped to create a boom that produced the first high-rise city in the Far East; it had the tallest buildings in the world outside the United States. In the pre-war period, Shanghai had 28 buildings of more than 10 storeys; Sassoon owned six of them.

The Art Deco Grosvenor House, which was completed in 1934, remains one of the most desirable residential addresses in Shanghai today; it has spacious rooms with high ceilings, large bathtubs, servants' quarters and – a rarity for that time – elevators. It is now part of the Jinjiang Hotel and remains an upmarket apartment building. U.S. President Richard Nixon stayed in it and signed the Shanghai Communique there during his ground-breaking visit to China in 1972.

Overlooking Suzhou Creek, Sassoon's Embankment House, the largest building on the coast of China, had a frontage of a quarter mile; it housed those who worked for him. After 1949, the apartments were given to high-ranking members of the Communist Party; since 2000, the wealthy, both Chinese and foreigners, have been able to buy its apartments.

Victor himself lived in Villa Eve (the name coming from his first three initials), a large Tudor-style home on the outskirts of the city, with a big estate. Now the site houses the Sassoon Villa Hotel and the Shanghai Zoo, which used to be Sassoon's favourite golf course.

According to Pan and Wang, the Sassoon company was the biggest property company in Shanghai before the Communist takeover. In January 1941, its real estate assets were worth 86.89 million legal tender

Sir Victor Sassoon (seated, centre) with his associates.

Sir Victor Sassoon and a lady friend.

(法幣), more than six times their value, 13.3 million, in 1921. It remained number one until the eve of the Communist takeover, with 540,000 square metres in nearly 100 sites. (Note 6)

A member of the Sassoon family was on the provisional committee that founded the Hongkong and Shanghai Banking Corporation in 1864.

According to Pan and Wang, the footprints of the Sassoon business empire were evident all over China. "By the late 19th century, the Sassoon group was trading opium, cotton yarn, cotton cloth, kerosene, arms and other commodities in north, northeast and northwest China. It had branches and investments in all parts of the country, with buyers even in border regions." (Note 7)

To protect his business interests, Sassoon maintained close relations with the different sources of power in China – the Beiyang Government (北洋政府) in Beijing, the warlords that controlled different regions and the Kuomintang government (國民黨政府) that united much of the country in 1927.

After World War One, he several times bought large stocks of scrap steel and weapons left over by the combatants in Europe and sold them to the KMT government and warlords in Sichuan, Guangdong and Manchuria; the profits were substantial. After the KMT government was set up in 1927, he bought in London and Shanghai bonds worth 200,000 sterling and 100,000 yuan; the money was to be used for construction of railways. It was a public vote of confidence in the new administration.

Victor Sassoon was a close friend of Song Zi-wen (宋子文), Finance Minister of the Nationalist government, and met him frequently.

He and other leading Jewish businessmen played an important role in the government of the foreign concessions. David Sassoon, the Kadoories and Silas Aaron Hardoon served as members of the councils which ran the International and French Concessions. Most of them held British nationality.

Property empire and Buddhist scriptures

With the Sassoons, the biggest opium and property magnate in Shanghai was Silas Aaron Hardoon. The two families were closely linked.

Hardoon was born in 1851 into a poor Jewish family in Baghdad; his family left for Bombay, where he was educated at a charitable school funded by David Sassoon. In 1873, he too went to Shanghai, where the Sassoon Company employed him as a rent collector and watchman at its opium warehouse.

He showed a flair for the property business and climbed through the ranks of the firm. In 1882, he left and set up his own brokerage trading cotton; it did not prosper; in 1885, he rejoined E.D. Sassoon and Company as its branch manager in Shanghai, investing in real estate and trading opium.

That year he earned the firm more than five million taels in the property market; a war between China and France led to an exodus of people and a plunge in prices. Hardoon's wife begged him to take refuge in Hong Kong. But he ignored her; believing the downturn temporary, Hardoon invested heavily in real estate that had suddenly become cheaper. Unexpectedly, the two countries signed a peace treaty in April 1885; prices recovered rapidly as a result. Hardoon continued to work for E.D. Sassoon; at the same time, he invested on his own account in property in the International Settlement.

The property boom in the city convinced him to try again on his own; he left his employer in 1901 and, this time, made the right bet. His greatest success was to buy sites along Nanjing Road. At the end of the 19th and early 20th century, the city's commercial centre was Guangdong Road and Fuzhou Road, near the old area of Shanghai; Hardoon correctly forecast that the expansion of the International Settlement would move this centre west along Nanjing Road, rather than on a north-south axis; he used his influence in the municipal councils to this end.

In 1905, he spent 600,000 taels of his own money to build the city's most modern road from the Bund to what is now Xizang Lu (西藏路) or Tibet Road; this was to encourage people to use the road. In 1906, the city's first tram went east-west along Nanjing Road, making it the most convenient route for travel.

Shops sprang up on both sides, including several multi-storey department stores that were pioneers of the retail business in China; they had restaurants, coffee shops, dance floors and entertainment as well as a wide array of merchandise, Chinese and imported. They attracted thousands of visitors a day. Two of the city's four big department stores – Wing On (永安) and Xin Xin (新新) – rented properties owned by Hardoon. The area became the centre of Shanghai's commerce, shopping and entertainment, a role it still enjoys today.

For him as for Sassoon, opium was a key commodity. "Under pressure from all quarters of society, the Qing government in 1906 issued an edict (詔書) that the opium business, both at home and abroad, would be completely abolished. Hardoon judged that, because the government was so desperate for the revenue from opium taxes, this edict was simply empty talk. Other traders sold in large quantities, driving prices down. He continued to buy at low prices and stock up. The result was as Hardoon anticipated. Due to the interference of the imperial powers, the grand anti-opium movement soon came to nothing and the opium price rose 30 per cent. Hardoon made a killing." (Note 8)

Both he and the Sassoon company invested much of the money made from opium into the property market.

To protect his business interests, Hardoon maintained relations with different warlords that controlled areas around Shanghai and other parts of China after the 1911 revolution; several gave him awards in recognition of his support and the substantial charity donations made by him and his wife.

Hardoon's power and influence was reflected in the public positions he held. In 1887, he was invited to be director of the Municipal Administrative Council (公董局) of the French Concession, a post he held until 1901. From 1900, he was also a director in the Shanghai Municipal Council (公共租界工部局董事) that governed the International Concession. This made him the first – and the only – man to hold positions in both councils at the same time. In 1893, he became a member of the Shanghai Club, the first choice of the city's British elite. He spoke English with a strong Arabic accent and drank whiskey. He never renounced his Iraqi nationality; according to the Jewish Telegraph Agency, the Foreign Office in London accepted him as a British subject in 1925. (Note 9)

Wang Jian, deputy dean of the Centre of Jewish Studies in Shanghai (上海猶太研究中心副主任王健), said that, between them, Sassoon and Hardoon accounted for 60-70 per cent of the opium trade. "Initially, there was a huge trade deficit between China and the outside world. China did not need foreign goods, except textiles.

"When opium was banned, the two stopped trading in it. While other foreigners took their money out, they re-invested it in Shanghai in property, finance, manufacturing and public utilities. They took a long-term view. Three generations of the Sassoon family invested here. Today Lord Sassoon, a member of the family, is chairman of the China-Britain Business Council." (Note 10)

Breaking a taboo

In one important respect, Hardoon was different to his fellow Jews.

Instead of choosing a wife from the Sephardic community, he married Luo Jialing (羅迦陵); she had been born Lisa Roos in 1864, daughter of a French sailor and a Chinese mother. Shortly after the birth, her father returned to France; when she was six or seven, her mother died and she was brought up by relatives.

While she had limited formal education, she was quick and intelligent and learnt French and English on her own. It was while she was working as a domestic maid that she met her future husband. She was a woman with a powerful personality, and a devout Buddhist who saw herself as a Chinese; she had a great influence over her husband. They married in September 1886. In the tight-knit world of Baghdadi Jews, it was taboo to marry a non-Jew, especially a Eurasian who was a devout Buddhist.

She introduced her husband to a Buddhist monk named Huang Zong-yang (黃宗仰); from 1898, he became a close adviser to the family. They invited him to design the new house and estate they built from 1904 on 20 hectares of land in the Puxi district, at a cost of 700,000 taels.

After its completion in 1910, it was the largest and most luxurious private residence in the city; they named it *Aili Yuan* (愛儷園), the "Garden of the Loving Couple".

In the house, the family served both western and Chinese food, with knives and forks set beside the chopsticks. Monk Huang designed it in the style of a traditional Chinese garden, with lakes, hills and pavilions; some said it was based on Da Guan Yuan (大觀園), the house in the Chinese classic novel, *Dream of the Red Chamber* (紅樓夢).

The garden included a Buddhist temple and a retreat for Buddhist nuns. For the next 30 years, it was one of the most important centres of Buddhism in China; the family hosted a large number of monks from all over the country.

Mindful of how her poverty had deprived her of a formal education, Lisa set up a boarding school in the grounds, with all the costs paid by the family. The curriculum included study of ancient Chinese characters and works of art; the family invited famous scholars to teach the courses. They also sponsored scholars of Chinese bone inscriptions.

More than 1,600 students passed through the school. In 1909, Lisa gave 200,000 taels for the reprinting of a complete set of a major Buddhist scripture Tripitaka (in Chinese, *Da Zang Jing* 大藏經); under the direction of Monk Huang, the project took four years to complete and ran to 8,416 scrolls (卷).

Lisa said prayers every day and spent enormous sums on the repair of Buddhist temples and the support of monks all over China. Hardoon and his wife gave generously. In 1910 and 1917, Hardoon gave more than 10 million yuan to victims of serious flooding in Jiangsu and Henan provinces.

They also donated large sums to charity, relief and educational causes in China, including five schools to train working people to read.

Hardoon's wife and the world she moved in meant that, in his social and personal life, he was different to his fellow Jews and the majority of expatriate residents of Shanghai. He played little part in the religious life of the Jews in the city, although he funded construction of the Beth Aaron synagogue in 1927 on Museum Road (now Huqiu Road, 虎丘路). He learnt the customs and practices of Chinese society and had close relations with many Chinese people; most of his fellow Jews, on the other hand, preferred a social life among their own kind and with the British community.

Wang Jian said that, unlike most wealthy Jews, Hardoon spoke fluent Shanghainese. "The early arrivals had little direct contact with ordinary Chinese, other than their servants. Sassoon identified himself as British more than Jewish: Hardoon liked Chinese culture and Buddhism."

Hardoon had close relations with many segments of the Chinese elite, including the Imperial dynasty and those trying to overthrow it. In August 1923, he and his wife visited Beijing and met the last Emperor Pu Yi (溥儀), who had abdicated in 1911.

For many years, he also maintained good relations with Sun Yat-sen, Cai Yuan-pei (蔡元培) and other revolutionaries. As early as 1903, when he found that Sun did not have the money to leave from Hawaii, he sent funds to him. When Sun returned in triumph after the success of the revolution on Christmas Day 1911, Hardoon sent monk Huang to meet him on his behalf at the Wusong pier (吳淞碼頭). Huang escorted Sun to Hardoon's house where other leaders of the revolution were waiting to

Silas Aaron Hardoon

Lisa Roos, also known as Luo jialing (羅迦陵, the Eurasian wife of Silas Aaron Hardoon.)

The Beth Aaron synagogue on Museum Road (now Huqiu Road, 虎丘路), built in 1927 with funds from Silas Aaron Hardoon.

celebrate with him.

The house was often used for secret talks between warring factions in China, including those held immediately after the Xinhai Revolution (辛亥革命) of October 11. Representatives of north and south met there and reached an agreement – it avoided a civil war between the two sides. After Sun become president of the new Republic of China in January 1912, he invited Hardoon and his wife to stay with him in Nanjing. After Sun left office in April that year, he often visited Hardoon in Shanghai; Hardoon sometimes gave funds to Sun. Few other Jews – or foreigners – had such close relations with the Chinese elite.

The Hardoons had no children of their own. Instead, they adopted 21 children; 11 were foreign and carried their father's name and 10 were Chinese and carried their mother's name.

Hardoon died on June 19, 1931, at the age of 80. Several thousand people attended his funeral. In its obituary, the English-language *North China Daily News* reported: "The couple lived together very happily for 45 years and were devoted to each other. The deceased treated the lady in all respects as his wife and always spoke of her as 'my wife'. She went to the synagogue as his wife, perhaps three times a year. Mrs Hardoon gave presents to the children at the synagogue, the children interested her very much."

In its obituary published on July 3, 1931, the *Shanghai Evening Post and Mercury* reported: "Mr Hardoon was one of the richest men in the Far East, but his wealth acted only as a foundation for his enigmatic character.

His fortune was reputed to be 100,000,000 taels. He spent millions of dollars for a whim and yet his office, where he worked alone, was often unbearably cold in the winter."

He was buried according to Jewish rites in the family compound; the family imported marble from Italy to build a mausoleum.

Pan and Wang said that, as of his death, Hardoon owned 44.23 per cent of the properties on Nanjing Road and a total of 1,387 buildings, including apartment blocks, office blocks, hotels and warehouses. (Note 11)

Contemporary accounts put the value of his assets at US$35 million. According to the *Global Times*, by the 1920s, the value of his properties in Shanghai exceeded that of the Sassoons'. (Note 12)

In his will, he left all his estate to his wife. But members of his family in Shanghai, Basra, Baghdad, Bombay, Jerusalem and other places contested the will. They argued that, since Luo was a Buddhist who had never converted to Judaism, her marriage to a Jew was not legal. They produced testimony from the Baghdad Beth Din (Jewish rabbinical court) that their marriage was illegal and not valid. The family was supported by the Government of Iraq that said that, since Hardoon had never renounced his Iraqi citizenship, the case should be tried by Iraqi law. (Note 13)

After a long and bitter legal fight, the court awarded in favour of the widow.

Following her husband's death, Luo was broken-hearted; she struggled to manage family affairs in the face of the many competing claims. She suffered from kidney problems and became blind in 1938; she gravitated even further toward Buddhism. She died at home on October 3, 1941 and was buried on November 12 – the birthday of Dr Sun Yat-sen – in the grounds of *Aili Yuan*; the funeral was conducted according to Buddhist rites and cost 200,000 yuan; she was buried next to her husband but not in his mausoleum.

After her death, a second battle ensued over the Hardoon estate, involving the children, associates and relatives from Iraq. It was complicated by the Japanese occupation of the city from December that year until August 1945, then the Chinese civil war, the hyper-inflation of 1948 and the Communist takeover. By the early 1950s, nearly all the Hardoon children had left China. The dispute was finally settled by Shanghai courts in 1956, the same year that the Hardoon company ceased to keep accounts.

During the Japanese occupation of the foreign Concessions from December 1941, the family residence was used by the Japanese military. It was severely damaged by several fires. The new government in 1949 took it over; it demolished what remained and built on the site the Sino-Soviet Friendship Building (中蘇友好大廈); it is known today as the Shanghai Exhibition Centre (上海展覽中心) and is used for meetings and exhibitions.

Marble Hall

Another imposing home was built by the Kadoories, who, along with the

Sassoons and the Hardoons, made up the three most prominent Jewish families in the city. The Kadoories were the major shareholder of the Shanghai Gas Company, established about 1865, and also invested heavily in real estate.

The family had the "Marble Hall" built between 1920 and 1924; they were away for two and a half years in Europe. The house had a floor area of 4,700 square metres on a land area of 14,000 square metres, at a cost of one million taels; it earned its nickname the "Marble Hall", because it used 250 tonnes of marble imported from Carrara in Italy.

"It was 220 feet long and had 12 bedrooms upstairs," said Sir Michael Kadoorie, the head of the family who now lives in Hong Kong. (Note 14)

"There was space for 3,000 people in the ballroom. The dining room could seat 72 when extended and 42 when shortened." It had 18-foot chandeliers and was the first house in Shanghai to have air conditioning. The grand ballroom was 80 feet long and 65 feet high and had 3,600 electric bulbs in different colours that could turn the room from pink to blue to red. It became a centre of the city's social life and employed more than 40 servants. Among the guests were senior British army officers, prominent Zionists and Bengali poet Rabindranath Tagore; the house could handle up to 1,500 guests.

Sir Michael said that, during World War Two, his father, uncle and grandfather were interned in the stables of the house and that Chinese friends brought food to them. "My father used to listen to a short-wave radio in the basement, which was dangerous. The Japanese protected the house which they saw as the home of the puppet governor of the city after their victory. Since it was well preserved, it became the Allied headquarters after the Japanese surrender." It remains standing today, with a garden, and is a Children's Palace (少年宫).

Coffee shops and Siberian Fur

Trading and property were only two of the many sectors in which Jewish businesses in Shanghai were active. Jewish interests extended into banking, insurance, industry, shipping, warehousing, buses and trams, gas, hotels, department stores, restaurants, coffee shops, cinemas and a wide range of retail businesses.

Many were owned by Russian Ashkenazi Jews who had moved to Shanghai. They came from Harbin and other cities in Manchuria and north China; some had arrived in the country in the early years of the 19th century, others after the Bolshevik Revolution of 1917.

One such business was the Siberian Fur Store, founded by Gregori Klebanov in 1925; it started with one main shop in Shanghai and opened two branches in the city. He had begun in the trade in Heilongjiang and Inner Mongolia before moving to Shanghai. The departure of Jews from Manchuria accelerated after the Japanese occupation in 1931.

By the early 1930s, there were nearly 6,000 Jews living in Shanghai; they included the Sephardic who came first and the Ashkenazi from

Marble Hall, home of the Kadoorie family in Shanghai, in the Jing An district (靜安區).

After 1949, Marble Hall became a Children's Palace. (Credit: The Hong Kong Heritage Project)

Russia who arrived later. Most of the newcomers lacked the capital and connections of the well-established Sephardic companies and ran small-scale businesses, like shops and restaurants. They helped to turn Avenue Joffre, now Huaihai Lu (淮海路), into the city's second shopping district, with western restaurants, bars, bread shops, tailors, bars, toy shops, coffee houses and clothes shops.

Like Hardoon's Nanjing Road, Huaihai Lu remains one of Shanghai's most expensive streets, especially for retail and commercial space. Some of the shops established by the Russian Jews remain today, under Chinese owners.

"The Russian Jews liked French culture and lived in the French concession," said Wang Jian. "They owned 70 per cent of the shops in Avenue Joffre, such as coffee and bread shops, pharmacies and tailors. Because they lived and worked together with Chinese, they learnt Shanghainese and Mandarin. Also, the Shanghai people learnt English and German. The language of commerce was English. There were evening classes for the German and Austrian refugees to learn English." (Note 15)

From Crimea to Nanjing Road – "Happiest years of my life"

One of the Ashkenazi arrivals was Sioma Lifshitz whose life illustrates the extraordinary odyssey of Jews during the 20th century. (Note 16) He was born in 1902 in the Crimean Peninsula, the son of a teacher who educated him at home. In 1915, while the First World War was raging in Russia, the family moved to Harbin, where the young man worked as a delivery man in a department store. After the Bolshevik Revolution, he worked on the China Eastern Railway.

When conditions became more chaotic in Manchuria, he and his parents took a British steamer to Shanghai in 1922. There he changed his name to Sam Sanzetti, which was easier to pronounce. After he learnt Mandarin, he chose the Chinese name Shen Shi-di (沈石蒂); both names remained with him for the rest of his life.

Like many Russian Jews, he arrived in Shanghai with only the clothes on his back. He found a job shining shoes outside a photographic shop run by an American. His boss liked him and invited him inside the shop to become an apprentice. He learnt English and Mandarin in addition to his native Russian.

In photography, he found his passion in life. After learning the craft, he set up his own studio in 1928, on the second floor of 73 Nanjing Road, above a jewellery and watchmaker shop. His first customers were foreigners; then rich and famous Chinese came. Sanzetti was hard-working and sociable; he mixed well with all kinds of people. Business boomed; he opened new branches, hired a car and driver and lived in a hotel.

This is how, in an interview with an Israeli paper in the 1970s, he described the city during the 1920s and 30s: "Shanghai was a very abnormal city, always noisy and always changing. It was a city of bright lights and bustling crowds. There were frauds, pickpockets, prostitutes and sex slaves. It was a city of many colours and many odours, full of chaos and full of beauty. Everything was interesting and made you curious. I did not sink into this dream world but put my heart in what I wanted to do."

The war badly hurt his business, as it did everyone else's. As a holder of a Soviet (Russian) passport, he was more fortunate than American or British Jews who were interned or the stateless ones who were moved into a segregated area in Hongkou (虹口) in February 1943.

After the war, he remained in the city and continued his photographic business; he married a Chinese lady named Nancy more than 20 years his junior. In 1955, he was forced to sell his shop to a Chinese, when the Communist government took over private business.

Sanzetti taught English at a school for two more years, before emigrating to Israel. After 35 years in Shanghai, he was very reluctant to leave; there were only about 100 Jews left in the city by that time. Nancy did not go with him; marrying a foreigner at that time was politically unwise and she may have been denied an exit visa. Since China and Israel did not have diplomatic relations, Sanzetti did not dare to write to her.

Life in his new country was hard; he rented a small apartment in Tel Aviv and worked as a photographer. His years in Shanghai were the happiest of his life; he loved to meet Chinese visitors and practice his Mandarin with them. He died in Tel Aviv on June 29, 1987.

Seven synagogues

The Jewish community in Shanghai built synagogues, associations, clubs, schools, old people's homes, cemeteries and newspapers.

The first Sephardic synagogue, Beth El, was built in 1887 and a second in 1900. In 1920, David Sassoon funded construction of Ohel Rachel synagogue (拉結會堂), in memory of his wife, in Seymour Road, now Shaanxi North Road (陝西北路).

One of the largest synagogues in the Far East, it had two storeys and space for 700 people; its ark held 30 Torah scrolls. It included a library, a ritual bath and a playground. The Jewish Achdut (Unity) Club opened in the synagogue compound in 1921. Shanghai would have a total of seven synagogues; today only two of them, including the Ohel Rachel, survive.

Living apart

The Jewish community largely lived apart from their Chinese neighbours. The vast majority married within their community and had their social and cultural life within it. Few learnt Mandarin or Shanghainese, the dialect spoken by most residents of the city. About a third of the 1,000 Baghdadi Jews held British nationality, having been born in British India or having lived for a long time in a British possession.

They identified with and felt part of the British community; they sent their children to English schools and spoke English with a standard British accent. The Chinese they met were servants, shopkeepers and, in the course of business, staff and compradors. So, they paid little attention to Chinese life and politics. Their most intense relationships with Chinese were with their servants. The colonial world was very stratified; the Jews of Shanghai wanted to find the best place for themselves within it. Silas Hardoon was the exception; through his wife, he integrated with Chinese society and it left him little time for a religious life.

"From the early period in Shanghai, there were misunderstandings between wealthy Jews and poor Chinese," wrote Pan and Wang. (Note 17) "But there never existed in China anti-Semitic ideology or movements."

In 1935 and 1938, newspapers in the city published by Germans and Japanese said that many of the Jews were Communists or Communist sympathisers. But these accusations did not come from Chinese.

"In China, there was no religious prejudice such as existed in Europe. The Jews living in China had a sense of ease and stability. Shanghai was the most European city in China. On the basis of Chinese tradition, it had attracted European customs and practices, creating the best conditions for the Jews of Europe to live and do business." (Note 18)

As we saw in chapter two, Harbin was also a European city, like Shanghai.

"The Jews of Shanghai were different to those who had lived in Kaifeng," said Wang Zhijun and Li Wei. (Note 19) "They did not become Chinese citizens. They kept their identity and lifestyle as foreigners and were not Sinicised. Chinese culture and ways of living had basically no impact on them. Apart for business dealings and relations with staff in the house, they basically had no interaction with Chinese people. A few Jews, like

Hardoon, married Chinese. They maintained their national traditions, lived with other members of the community and built their own synagogues, cemeteries and schools, forming a Jewish society."

Zionism

Unlike their brethren in Kaifeng, the Jews of Shanghai and other cities of China who had arrived since the 1840s kept close contact with the global Jewish community. In Shanghai as in Harbin, Jews took a keen interest in Zionism; they did not know how long they would be able to live in China.

In 1900, three years after the World Zionist Congress held its first meeting in Basel, Switzerland, the Palestine Foundation Fund in Shanghai was set up, with Elly Kadoorie as chairman. It collected money to help fund a Hebrew University in Jerusalem; the institution was founded in July 1918, 30 years before the state of Israel, and is the second oldest in the country. The foundation also funded the Beth Sepher Kadoorie Agricultural School in Palestine.

A group founded the Shanghai Zionist Association (SZA) in 1903; its leaders were Nissim Elias Benjamin Ezra and Elly Kadoorie. It was one of the three earliest Zionist organisations in Asia, together with those in Iraq and Turkey. A Baghdadi Jew, Ezra was born in 1883 in Lahore, then part of British India and now Pakistan, who later settled in Shanghai. In 1903, the SZA sent a delegation to the Sixth Zionist Congress in Basel, Switzerland.

In 1904, Ezra founded the movement's official newspaper, *Israel's Messenger*; he served as its editor-in-chief until his death in 1936. This English-language paper was one of the oldest Jewish periodicals in China; it also circulated in the United States.

In March 1905, the SZA had about 100 members; Elly Kadoorie gave generously to it and became its chairman in 1915. Many Sephardic Jews in the city held British nationality. During the First World War, they supported the Franco-British Allies. On November 2, 1917, the British Foreign Secretary Arthur James Balfour issued the Balfour Declaration, expressing the support of his government for a Jewish national home in Palestine. This greatly encouraged the movement.

Ezra used his newspaper to champion the Zionist case and lobby governments in Asia to support it. He was more successful than he expected – China, Japan and Thailand expressed their support. On December 14, 1918, China's Vice Foreign Minister Chen Lu (陳籙) sent a letter to Elly Kadoorie, chairman of the SZA, as follows: "My government has the same opinion as the British government toward the aspiration of your association (to set up a Jewish state in Palestine)."

Ezra did even better 17 months later when he received this letter from Sun Yat-sen, father of the Republic of China. "I have read your letter and the copy of *Israel's Messenger* with much interest and wish to assure you of my sympathy for this movement, which is one of the greatest movements of the present time. All lovers of democracy cannot help but support and welcome it with enthusiasm, the movement to restore your wonderful and historic nation which has contributed so much to the civilisation of the world and which deserves an honourable place in the family of nations."

With the support of one of the world's leading imperial powers, the dream of a Jewish state suddenly became more feasible. So, after the Balfour Declaration, more members joined the SZO.

In 1920, they established a colony of Jews in Palestine called the China Jewish settlement. In 1922, they organised a large meeting in Shanghai to hear a speech by world-famous scientist Albert Einstein in support of its ideal.

And in 1929, Ezra and the new chairman of the SZO, Mrs Raymond Elias Toeg, were invited by the government to the burial of Dr Sun Yat-sen in Nanjing (南京). This showed the good relations the Jewish community enjoyed with the government.

From the late 1920s, the Zionist movement began to splinter, as it did in the rest of the world. The main dispute was over how far to co-operate with the British administration that controlled Palestine, especially after a White Paper in October 1930 by Colonial Secretary Lord Passfield (Sidney Webb). It said that sales of land to Jewish settlers there should be restricted and found that Zionist policy damaged the economic development of the Arabs.

The "Revisionists", led by Vladimir Jabotinsky, called for strong opposition, including violence, against the British. The "Moderates", under Chaim Weizmann, advocated continued co-operation with Britain

Israel's Messenger, newspaper of the Shanghai Zionist Association.

1940 annual of the Tientsin Jewish School

Sir Elly Kadoorie (Credit: The Hong Kong Heritage Project)

as the power which controlled the Holy Land.

In 1923, in Riga, Latvia, Jabotinsky set up Betar as a youth movement to train Jews in his version of Zionism and receive military training. A Shanghai branch of Betar was set up in 1931; within a year, it had grown to nearly 100 members and, by 1936, 400-500. In 1934, the branch's founder L. Kotovitch, emigrated to Palestine. In 1932, its members formed the first Jewish unit in the Shanghai Volunteer Corps (SVC), a multinational unit set by the Municipal Council to defend the foreign concessions against attack; the SVF existed between 1853 and 1942. The Betar branch was the first Jewish military company in China.

Guarding the President

One of the most remarkable Jews in China during the Republican period was Morris Abraham Cohen; he became the personal bodyguard of President Sun Yat-sen and his wife and helped to train his army. He was intensely loyal to the Republic of China.

Cohen was born in 1887 in Radzanow, a Polish shetl not far from Warsaw. At the age of three, he joined his father Joseph who was operating a sewing machine in a garment workshop in the East End of London, like thousands of other Jewish immigrants. He had changed the family name from Miaczyn to Cohen, to make it easier for the English to pronounce.

The young Morris was a rowdy boy who preferred boxing to study; he spent time at a reform school and an industrial school. Eager to reduce the number of mouths at the family table, his parents sent him in 1905 to Saskatchewan in western Canada; he worked as a farmhand and learnt to shoot at beer barrels with a gun in each hand – hence his nickname – and to cheat at cards.

He moved to Saskatoon, in Saskatchewan, where he met Mah Sam (馬三), owner of a Chinese restaurant. It was a friendship that changed his life. He gambled on behalf of Mah's restaurant and split the winnings with him. Late one night, he attacked a man who was trying to force Mah to hand over the diamond ring on his finger – the act of a white man helping a Chinese was unheard of and won him the confidence of the close-knit Chinese community in Saskatoon.

Mah was a strong supporter of Sun Yat-sen, a fellow Cantonese, and his revolutionary movement; he told Cohen about it. In 1912, with Mah's support, Cohen joined the Calgary branch of Sun's Tong Meng Hui (同盟會), together with 200 Chinese and took an oath of allegiance "pledging to devote his life to the service of Sun Yat-sen and the liberation of the Chinese people".

During World War One, Cohen served in the British Army in Belgium and worked with the Chinese Labour Corps of 135,000 men sent to support the British and French armies on the western front. In 1922, Sun invited Cohen to his house in the French concession in Shanghai to discuss the building of a railway from Guangzhou to Wuhan; at their meeting, he persuaded the President to hire him as his bodyguard.

He trained Sun's other bodyguards to box and fight and negotiated the purchase of foreign arms for the Chinese government he also helped to organise and train Dr Sun's army. An ardent Zionist, he used his influence to persuade Sun to favour a Jewish homeland in Palestine. After Sun's death in March 1925, he continued to work for the government, including as the guardian of the reserves in the Central Bank.

He was also involved in the Jewish community in Shanghai. After the Japanese conquest of Nanjing in 1937, he moved with the government to Chongqing. In 1941 in Hong Kong, he served as bodyguard for Song Qing-ling (宋慶齡), Sun's widow; wherever she went, giving speeches and raising money for the war effort, he accompanied her. She had complete confidence in him.

While she was airlifted to Chongqing in 1941, Cohen chose to remain in Hong Kong; he was captured by the Japanese after their victory and was sent to an internment camp in Stanley with other Allied prisoners. Previously overweight, he became wafer-thin because of the minimal rations. In August 1943, as a Canadian prisoner-of-war, he was exchanged and taken on a Red Cross ship to Goa.

In April 1945, he attended the first conference of the United Nations in San Francisco as part of the Jewish delegation; it aimed to ensure the British honour their promise of a Jewish homeland in Palestine. Senior members of the Chinese delegation greeted Cohen as an old friend – his presence helped to win their support. In January 1946, he returned to China looking for a niche. He remained fiercely loyal to the Nationalists:

"Communism is an aberration in the Chinese character," he said. Events proved him wrong.

In November 1966, the new government in Beijing invited him for an official visit to mark the 100th anniversary of the birth of Sun Yat-sen. Chairman Mao had launched the devastating Cultural Revolution three months before – Cohen was the only Westerner on the podium.

In 1970, he died in Manchester, England, aged 83, and was buried in the Jewish cemetery in Salford. Madame Sun paid for his tombstone. She dictated the inscription in English and Chinese via the Chinese embassy in London: "This is the tomb of Ma Kun inscribed by Song Qing-ling, vice chairman of the People's Republic of China." (馬坤先生之墓　宋慶齡題) Ma Kun was Cohen's Chinese name.

Few foreigners, if any, had the close personal relationship Cohen enjoyed with Sun Yat-sen and his wife. His loyalty to them and to China was inspired, perhaps, by a common sense of being an outsider; just as China was battling great odds to become an independent republic, so Israel was fighting many enemies to become a sovereign state. (Note 20)

Gamble paid off

For a century, the city of Shanghai offered remarkable economic opportunities to the Jews who chose to settle there. Their gamble paid off handsomely. They had correctly calculated that the Chinese government, both the Qing dynasty and its Republican successor, would not challenge the foreign powers that controlled the International settlements. Many prospered; some made a fortune. They had been able to enjoy a Jewish religious, educational and social life denied to their brothers and sisters in Russia and many countries in Europe. But now the years of plenty and good harvests had come to an end – and the years of famine and exile had arrived.

Notes

1   Sir Michael Kadoorie, Fireside Chat 16/12/2008 from the library of the Jewish Community Centre, Hong Kong.

2   *Eye on History* magazine (看歷史), by Mao Jianjie (毛劍傑：十里洋場的猶太印記), April 2012.

3   *Eye on History* magazine, by Liu Dong (劉棟：新沙遜洋行：舊上海的地產生意), April 2017.

4   *The Jews and China* (猶太人與中國) by Professors Pan Guang (潘光) and Wang Jian (王健), Shishi Publishing Company (時事出版社), 2009, page 75.

5   *Eye on History* magazine, April 2017.

6   Pan and Wang, page 82.

7   Pan and Wang, page 101.

8   Pan and Wang, page 75.

9   Report of Jewish Telegraph Agency, 8/6/1932.

10 Interview with Professor Wang Jian (王健), 14/12/2016.

11 Pan and Wang, page 84.

12 *Global Times* (環球時報), 26/7/2006.

13 Report of Jewish Telegraph Agency 8/6/1932.

14 Sir Michael Kadoorie, Fireside chat.

15 Interview with Professor Wang Jian.

16 Section on Sam Sanzetti from *Sanlian Shenghuo* magazine (三聯生活周刊), 2011, number 49.

17-18 Pan and Wang, pages 35-36.

19 *Harbin Jews in Early 1900s: Their Political and Religious Lives* (20 世紀上半期哈爾濱猶太人的宗教生活與政治生活), by Wang Zhijun (王志軍) and Li Wei (李薇), People's Publishing House (人民出版社), April 2013, pages 296.

20 "The Extraordinary Adventures of Two-Gun Cohen", by Sara Jo Ben Zvi, *Asian Jewish Life*, issue 12.

Chapter Four

World War Two –
Escape from Hell

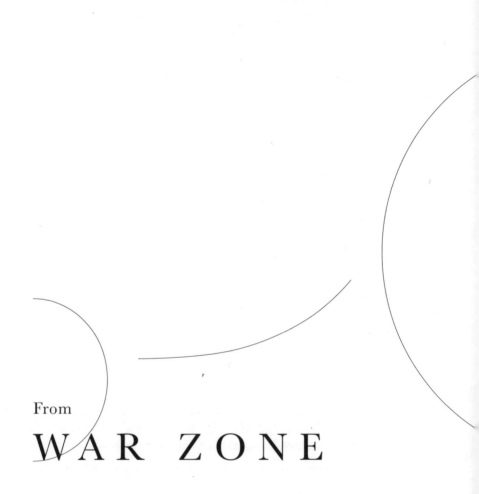

From

WAR ZONE

S E G R E G A T E D   A R E A

The city of Shanghai occupies a special place in Jewish history as a sanctuary during the Holocaust – not only for the 6,000 living there at the start of the 1930s but also for the 30,000 who escaped from Europe between 1933 and 1941.

By the time of the Japanese attack on Pearl Harbor in December 1941, 25,000 Jewish refugees were living in Shanghai. The Jews who found refuge there were more than those admitted by Australia, Canada, New Zealand, South Africa and India put together.

During the four years after Pearl Harbor, about 1,000 died, mainly of illness, shortages of food and medicine and harsh living conditions. In a U.S. air raid that mistakenly attacked the Jewish area in July 1945, 31 were killed and 250 injured. But, compared to their brothers and sisters in Nazi-occupied Europe, the Jews of Shanghai were blessed.

The Japanese who controlled the city between December 1941 and the end of the war resisted pressure from their Nazi allies for the "final solution"; but they used harsh measures to control the Jewish refugees. The Chinese residents – many themselves refugees – mostly shared the same residential quarters as the refugees; they treated their Jewish neighbours with kindness and provided them with food and medical care.

Door closes in Europe

By the early 1930s, Shanghai had nearly 6,000 Jews, most of them Sephardic from the Middle East and the rest Europeans; it was a well-established community with synagogues, schools, hospitals, old people's homes, cemeteries, commercial and political associations, newspapers and magazines. While Jews in Russia and Eastern Europe had suffered pogroms and persecution in the late 19th and 20th century, the community in Shanghai was able to develop peacefully and prosper during this period. The existence of the community meant that the city became a place of refuge for Jews elsewhere in the world.

After Adolf Hitler became Chancellor of Germany on January 30 1933, systematic persecution of Jews began. At that time, the doors of other countries were still open, so the number who chose to come to Shanghai – a city on the other side of the world – was small. They were able to take a ship directly from Germany. Those who came had relatives, links to German firms or had lived there before. In 1933, the first group of arrivals consisted of 12 families of about 100 people. (Note 1)

Between 1933 and Japan's all-out war on China launched in July 1937, about 1,000-1,500 German Jews came; most were trained professionals, like doctors, lawyers, teacher and entrepreneurs, and brought financial assets. They were able to find work and enjoyed a middle-class life in one of Shanghai's two foreign concessions.

Between August and November 1937, the Japanese fought one of the biggest battles of World War Two in China for control of Shanghai. The foreign concessions were not affected, because, at that time, Japan did not wish to confront the western powers. A million soldiers were involved on the two sides; the Chinese lost an estimated 250,000 and the Japanese side about 40,000. After three months of bitter fighting and heroic resistance by the less well-equipped Chinese, the Japanese took over the Chinese-controlled areas of the city. As a result, the two foreign concessions became an "island" accessible to the outside world only by sea.

For the 24 months from August 1937 to August 1939, Shanghai was a "visa-free zone", one of the few such cities in the world. New arrivals required neither a visa, nor financial guarantee, job or good-conduct permit from the police. This was a godsend for many Jews from Europe who had been stripped of their nationality by the Nazis and had no identity papers. They came from Germany, Austria and Eastern Europe.

As each month passed, so the outlook worsened. Fearful of a flood of refugees, countries in Western Europe and elsewhere restricted entry, even Britain and the U.S., which both had large Jewish populations. On the night of November 9/10, 1938, Kristallnacht, Nazi militia and German civilians attacked and looted Jewish-owned stores, buildings and synagogues in Germany and Austria and murdered dozens of Jews.

Fearful that the Arabs would side with Germany in the war it expected soon, Britain in May 1939 restricted Jewish immigration to Palestine. During this 24-month period, about 21,000-22,000 Jews reached

Shanghai, most without identity papers. A majority went via Italy, where they boarded a ship; others went to France, Belgium and Holland and took ships there; a smaller number left through the Balkans. They arrived in Shanghai with no more than they could carry; some were wealthy people who had left everything behind. (Note 2)

By 1940, there were 40,000-50,000 Jews in the whole of China, of whom half were refugees from Europe. The largest communities were in Shanghai, Hong Kong, Harbin and Tianjin. There were also communities in the Manchurian cities of Manzhouli, Hailar, Qiqihar, Shenyang and Dalian, as well as in Qingdao and Beijing.

Why was the door open?

This "open door" to Shanghai was due to the policy of the councils who ran the two foreign concessions. They were controlled by foreigners who were not anti-Semitic and were running a city, not a country. They did not expect to be there for a long time, especially as a war between Japan and the West looked increasingly probable. For years, Shanghai had been an international city, open to people from many countries; the councils regarded this as one of its strengths. In addition, those running the councils had personal friends among the Jewish community who were urging them to keep the doors open. There was no public opposition to admitting Jews.

The Jewish community in the city mobilised quickly to help their brothers and sisters. In 1934, the German Jews in the city set up a Relief Fund.

On August 8, 1938, an International Committee for Granting Relief to European Refugees was set up, with Paul Komor, a Hungarian Jew, in charge. Sir Victor Sassoon provided the giant Embankment House as a reception centre; there was also a public kitchen.

Other relief agencies were set up, with finance from home and abroad, and the community also received help from non-Jewish groups, including the city's Young Men's Christian Association. A small number of the refugees arranged passage to a third country, like the U.S., Australia and South Africa; this required a sponsor and financial guarantees that most were unable to find. They were the lucky ones – they would spend the war outside the range of artillery and air raids.

Most of the new arrivals settled in Hongkou (虹口), a district outside the international concession, to the north. It would later be called "the Jewish ghetto". Rents were 30 per cent lower than in other areas of the city and 75 per cent lower than in the international and French concessions. Life was very difficult – 30-50 people lived in one room, sometimes up to 200. It was hard to find a proper job or anything close to what they had done in their former life. They delivered coal, repaired electrical appliances, baked bread and sold newspapers. Some set up stalls or small shops in Hongkou. If and when their financial situation improved, they moved to a nicer area. (Note 3)

But, by the summer of 1939, the numbers had become so large that the residents of the concessions expressed their opposition; they feared social chaos and deterioration of their conditions of life. So, in August 1939, the

International and French concessions and Japanese military authorities announced conditions for a Jewish refugee from Europe to land – he or she must obtain a landing permit which required a US$400 deposit for an adult and US$100 for children below 13: he must have relatives or a job in the city or be planning to marry a city resident.

Shipping companies could refuse those without a permit. Despite these restrictions, the flow continued, if more slowly, thanks to the help of Jewish organisations around the world. Over the 10 months up to June 1940, 2,000-3,000 came, from Germany and Austria and also Poland, Czechoslovakia, Hungary, Romania and the three Baltic states.

Meanwhile, events in Europe were moving rapidly, all for the worse. In September 1939, Germany and the Soviet Union invaded and occupied Poland, home to Europe's largest Jewish population of more than three million. In June 1940, Germany obtained the surrender of France, home to 330,000 Jews. Italy declared war on Britain and France and the war spread to the Balkans and North Africa.

With the Axis powers taking over continental Europe, the Jews there lost the sea routes to Shanghai; the only option left was by rail or road across Siberia, Manchuria, Japan or Korea. It could take months and was full of danger. Nonetheless, despite all the obstacles, during the 12 months after the fall of France, an estimated 2,000 Jewish refugees made it to Shanghai. (Note 4)

In June 1941, the Nazis invaded the Soviet Union; that cut this final land route. Over the next six months until the attack on Pearl Harbor, the only new arrivals – about 2,000 – were of Jews from Poland and Lithuania who had already left and were living in the Soviet Far East, Manchuria or Japan.

Among them were more than 400 rabbis and scholars of the Mir Yeshiva, founded in 1815, in the then Polish town of Mir, which was part of Tsarist Russia. Mir is now in Belarus. A yeshiva is a Jewish institution that focuses on the study of traditional religious texts.

In the summer of 1940, they received transit visas from Chiune Sugihara, the Japanese vice-consul in Kaunas, Lithuania. Each paid US$200 for a ticket on the trans-Siberian railway to Vladivostok and then boarded a ship to Tsuruga (敦賀), Japan. (We will describe the story of Chiune Sugihara in detail in the next chapter).

In March 1941, the yeshiva re-opened in Kobe, Japan. That summer, the Japanese moved them to Shanghai, where they occupied the Beth Aaron synagogue built by Silas Hardoon. After the end of the war, the members moved to Palestine and New York. It was the only yeshiva of occupied Europe to survive the Holocaust.

A Jewish homeland in southwest China

In February 1939, Sun Ke (孫科), chairman of the Republic of China's Legislative Yuan (中華民國立法院長), proposed two areas of settlement for Jewish refugees on China's southwest border. (Note 5)

They were to be in the southwest province of Yunnan, one close to Burma and the other close to Vietnam. Sun was the first son of Sun Yat-sen (孫中山) and a member of the ruling National Defence Committee (國防最高委員會), as well as chairman of the Parliament.

He said that these areas in Yunnan would relieve the pressure of arrivals that Shanghai was finding it hard to bear and was in line with his father's support for oppressed minorities. Another motive was to arouse the sympathy of the public in the U.S. and U.K; these were the countries with the world's strongest Jewish communities and which China needed most in her life-and-death struggle with Japan. Thirdly, the Chinese believed that Jews had considerable economic means and talents which would be useful for China.

As we mentioned in Chapter Three, Sun's father had in 1920 declared his support for the Jews and a homeland in Palestine. Sun Ke embraced his father's opinion; in the spring of 1928, he visited the vibrant and growing Jewish community in Palestine. The visit only strengthened his support for Zionism.

Sun's idea and the Fugu Plan of the Japanese (to settle Jewish refugees in Japanese-occupied territory) were driven by similar motives. Both saw the global Jewish community as wealthy, powerful and talented. Yunnan was, like Manchuria, a remote region rich in natural resources but sparse in population; neither China nor Japan had the capital to develop them – both looked to the overseas Jewish community to provide funds. Both had a strong resemblance to Josef Stalin's idea for an "autonomous Jewish region" in Siberia.

For Tokyo, settling Jews in Manchukuo was a way to receive large sums of money from the well-to-do Jewish communities in America and improve control over the new colony and develop its economy – just as Britain and France had introduced Indians, Chinese, Lebanese and other foreigners into their colonies in Africa and the Caribbean.

On March 7, the National Defence Committee approved the idea in principle and ordered five government departments to draw up detailed plans. These included allowing entry to Jews and permitting them to apply for Chinese nationality. One condition for this was that they must obey China's laws and refrain from politics or ideological activity; but they would enjoy the same rights and responsibilities as a Chinese citizen and not be subject to racial or religious discrimination.

"Our country is in the stage of construction and needs skilled people in many fields, such as scientists, engineers, doctors and machinists," the plan said. Accordingly, ministries should draw up a list of professions that required manpower and send them to China's embassies abroad; people with desired skills would be given preference. The embassies should ask the League of Nations and international charitable bodies to help find applicants.

General Long Yun (龍雲), chairman of the Yunnan provincial government, sent a telegram of support to the central government in Chongqing, saying that he welcomed the Jews to help cultivate the land: "Yunnan is a large area with a sparse population and fertile soil. The Jews are concentrated in Shanghai. They have rich knowledge and abundant financial resources. If they could settle in Yunnan and cultivate the empty land, it would bring benefit to everyone."

The support of General Long was essential. After serving in the army of the provincial warlord of Yunnan, he overthrew him in a coup in 1927. Soon afterwards, he became Commander of the Nationalists' 38th Army; so, he held tightly both civilian and military power in Yunnan.

The war was bringing economic benefits to his remote inland province; factories, universities and government departments had moved there from areas in the east conquered by the Japanese. Yunnan was the corridor by which supplies came from Burma and India to supply military bases in all parts of China. Long's army had an important role, to defend the country from Japanese forces in Burma.

The areas proposed for the Jews were in Tengchong (騰沖) in the west of Yunnan, close to Burma, and Mengzi (蒙自) in the southeast, close to Vietnam. For the well-educated, urban and middle-class Jews refugees in Shanghai, Tengchong was not a first choice for settlement. The city is more than 1,600 metres above sea level and suffers from frequent earthquakes. Its economy was agricultural – tobacco, tea, grain and oil-bearing crops; it was also known for its geothermal springs and as a centre for the sale of jade and amber. Digging the land on a kibbutz in the Holy Land was one thing – but planting tobacco on the slopes of a remote Chinese mountain something else.

The Jewish community in Shanghai warmly welcomed the proposal, in part because it was going to relieve the congestion and free the city from the burden the refugees brought. They held several rounds of talks with the Chinese government; it offered places for 100,000 Jews – an astonishing figure given the plight of the Jewish people in the world.

The biggest obstacle to creating a new home was money – the refugees had been stripped of their assets before leaving Europe and China was in the middle of a devastating war, so the capital would have to come from the Jewish communities abroad. The logistical obstacles were also formidable – the Japanese military controlled many of the major ports of China and had the most powerful navy in the South China Sea. How were the Jews of Shanghai or elsewhere to reach Yunnan and build new lives there? They would have first had to go to Thailand or Burma, then under British control.

The plan was never implemented. The Chinese government was weak; it had lost its capital, Nanjing, and the main industrial areas of the country to the Japanese military. It did not have the military, logistical or financial resources to put the plan into practice. And, even if the transport lines had been open, how many European Jewish refugees wanted to settle in this remote rural corner of China? Their hope was to wait out the war and move to countries with established Jewish communities. The only "migrants" were 10 Jews who arrived in Yunnan in 1939 to work as drivers and in the provincial salt management bureau. (Note 6)

Cut off from the world

After its attack on Pearl Harbor on December 7, 1941, the Japanese military quickly occupied the foreign concessions of Shanghai; it had overwhelming superiority over the limited forces of the Allied countries there. So the entire city came under the control of the Japanese. Shanghai was cut off from the rest of the world and no new arrivals were possible. The 25,000 Jewish people in the city could not leave; whether they lived or died rested in the hands of the new masters of the city.

Their situation worsened. The relief provided by the Jewish community of the U.S. and other Allied countries stopped because Shanghai had become "enemy" territory. The Japanese arrested nationals of "enemy countries", including Britain, the U.S. and Holland. Many of the 1,000 Baghdadi Sephardic Jews held British citizenship; they were put into internment camps and lost many of their assets. The wealthiest members of the community, they could no longer give the same help as before to the arrivals from Europe.

More fortunate were the Jews from Russia, who held Russian passports and whose country was not at war with Japan; they were not interned and were able to carry on their lives as before. Tokyo was resisting strong pressure from the Nazis to invade the Soviet Union. The Russian Jews set up a Central European Refugee Committee, which supported 600-700 poor children. (Note 7)

The "Final Solution"

In July 1942, Colonel Josef Meisinger, chief representative of the Gestapo in Japan, visited Shanghai and proposed the "Final Solution" for the Jews of the city. He was known as the "Butcher of Warsaw" for his brutality in the mass execution of Poles and Jews in Poland in 1939 and 1940. From April 1941 to May 1945, he was Gestapo liaison at the German Embassy in Tokyo. Like other Nazi leaders, he assumed that, now it had become an ally in a global war against the Allies, Japan would follow the racial policies of the Third Reich. The plan was top secret; Meisinger transmitted it to Japanese military and civil officials only verbally, with no written record.

He proposed a plan with several steps. First, arrest all the members of the community when they were celebrating the Jewish New Year with their families. Then dispose of them in one of three ways – put them on board ageing ships which would be set adrift in the East China Sea, where they would die of hunger or drowning: put them to work in abandoned salt mines on the Huangpu River where they would die of overwork and exhaustion: or set up a concentration camp in Chongming Island, where they could be used for medical experiments.

The Japanese authorities refused to implement this policy. Why was this? As we described in Chapter Two, the Japanese cabinet had on December 5, 1938 adopted the Fugu Plan to settle tens of thousands of Jews in areas of China it controlled. The plan was never realised; but it reflected the majority view within the government and the army that the Jews were a wealthy and talented people whose skills should be used to benefit the

Japanese empire.

Absent, in Japan as in China, was the historical anti-Semitism of Europe. The rare examples of it in Shanghai came from White Russians and Germans, not Chinese. Japanese officials and those of the Chinese puppet government in Shanghai had no interest or motive to carry out such a policy. Indeed, after Mitsugi Shibata (柴田付), Japanese vice-consul in Shanghai, learnt of the Meisinger plan, he quickly informed the city's Jewish leaders about it – despite the fact that he was leaking a state secret. This enabled the Jewish leaders to organise a lobbying campaign against it. Unfortunately for Shibata, someone revealed the leak to his Japanese colleagues; he was detained for several weeks and sent back to Tokyo in disgrace.

For Japan, there was no military or diplomatic benefit in killing the Jews; to do this would be a serious diplomatic mistake. Japan wanted to maintain neutrality with the Soviet Union because it did not want a war in addition to the one it was waging with the U.S.; eliminating the Jews would mean killing many Russians. Within Japan was a lobby which advocated peace with the U.S.; treating the Jews of Shanghai well was essential to keeping good relations with Washington.

Another reason why Meisinger's plan was not implemented was lobbying by leaders of the Jewish community in Harbin and Kobe of Japanese officials they knew. After Shibata's briefing, the leaders in Shanghai informed Dr Abraham Kaufman in Harbin; he raised the issue with Norihito Yasue, one of the architects of the "Fugu Plan", who was based in Dalian.

While he was not as influential as he had been three years before, Yasue retained good contacts at the top of the Japanese government. He argued against implementing the plan. On March 7, 1947, Meisinger was executed in the Mokotow Prison in Warsaw, after being found guilty of Nazi crimes in Poland.

Building a ghetto

In February 1943, the Japanese announced a concession to the Nazis – establishment of a segregated zone for stateless Jewish refugees, 2.68 square kilometres in size. Many called it a "ghetto", because those living within it needed permission to leave. An article in the Xin Shenbao, a pro-Japanese newspaper (新申報), in February described how the Sassoons and other Jewish families had made large sums of money out of opium and said that they were "typical examples of international Jewry".

On February 18, the media published the details of the new zone, in the Hongkou district; it said that stateless people who had arrived in the city from Europe after 1937 would have to move there before May 18, taking their businesses with them. Without a permit, other people were not allowed to live in the zone. It was next to an area with a prison, wharves, a fuel dump and a large radio transmitter; the Japanese expected that the Americans would not bomb the ghetto – and so spare these adjacent facilities. The area was already densely populated, with 100,000 Chinese residents. The Jewish community was full of foreboding; they feared that it would be like the ghettoes of eastern Europe.

Between 14,000 and 18,000 people in 2,800 families had to move there. On the evening of February 23, Tsutomu Kubota (久保田務), the city's Director of Jewish Affairs, told a meeting of the Ashkenazi Association that the new zone was not a result of anti-Semitism among Japanese but because of serious shortages of food and housing in Shanghai: he said it was necessary to exercise control over several thousand stateless people. He called on the Russian Jews to co-operate with the Japanese. (Note 8)

Jewish refugees from Poland who were ordered to move into the ghetto argued that they were Polish citizens with Polish passports and therefore, like their Russian brothers, should be free to live outside and without restrictions. Several demonstrated against the Japanese decision; the army executed five of them. This zone existed between February 1943 and the end of the war in August 1945. Conditions there were very difficult, with overcrowding, poor sanitation and lack of food, but the vast majority of its residents survived.

In 2008, the city opened a Shanghai Refugee Museum at 62 Changyang Road (長陽路) in what had been the ghetto area. The museum used to be the Ohel Moshe Synagogue (摩西會堂); founded in 1907, it was the first Ashkenazi synagogue for Orthodox Russian and German Jews in the city; it moved to its current site in 1927. It ceased operating as a synagogue after 1949.

The museum guide said that living conditions for the Jews in the segregated area were extremely crowded, with a family of four or five having 2-3 square metres. The museum has reconstructed a typical room with a wooden table, chair, a bookshelf, fan, clock and radio. At night, the family slept on the floor below the table. On a wall in the courtyard is engraved a list of more than 14,000 Jews in Shanghai during the war.

"When they left German-occupied areas, they were allowed to take a maximum of 10 Reichsmarks," the museum guide said. Next to the museum are Zhoushan (舟山路) and Huoshan Roads (霍山路), with rows of three-storey residential homes built in the 1920s and 1930s; many refugees lived packed into these homes. (Note 9)

The area was surrounded by barbed wire and patrolled by guards (保甲自警團) under the supervision of the Japanese military; Chinese and foreign men from the ghetto, they wore armbands and ensured that those who went out had the necessary permits. The man in charge of permits was a Japanese official named Kano Ghoya (合屋); a photograph of him hangs on the wall of the museum. The guide said that Ghoya was a mean, evil man who liked to extract a price in exchange for a permit. For example, she said, the daughter of a rabbi asked for a permit in order to see a doctor; in exchange, Ghoya demanded that her father rest his chin on a table so that he could cut off his beard – a symbol of his wisdom and authority.

One of the inmates was Ernest Heppner, a German Jew who escaped to Shanghai with his mother in February 1939; he has given a vivid description of the zone in *Shanghai Refuge* published in 1995. "The

Shanghai Jewish Refugee Museum in Hongkou district; it opened in 2008 in what had once been the Ohel Moshe synagogue.

A room inside the museum formerly used for religious events.

ghetto was governed by a brutal, sadistic Japanese named Ghoya. He was paranoid, he was a psychopath and he called himself 'the King of the Jews'…The ghetto was surrounded by barbed wire and we were under a volunteer service under the Japanese. They wore armbands and had to be at the ghetto exits and entrances to guard against anybody leaving who was not authorised."

Liang Min-hong (梁民閎), a retired teacher from Shanghai, was visiting the museum. This was his comment on the exhibits: "The Japanese looked up to westerners and despised other Asians. That is why they did not kill the Jews but killed so many Chinese."

Keys to survival

"Between February 1943 and August 1945, the Jewish refugees in this designated area endured extremely difficult conditions, but the vast majority survived," said Professors Pan Guang and Wang Jian. (Note 10)

"There were three major reasons – their spirit and determination and mutual help. Many were intellectuals and people with special talents, like doctors, teachers, engineers, architects and many medical professionals, including 200 physicians."

At the end of 1938, they set up a medical clinic and, in March 1939, the first hospital for refugees with 60 beds. By 1940, it had grown to 120 beds, with X-ray, dentistry, ophthalmology and gynaecology. Teachers provided classes to children and adults: editors and reporters produced

The Japanese head of Hongkou Ghetto distributing passes to refugees.

Certificates of inoculation given to Jewish refugees by the Public Health Department of the Shanghai Municipal Council.

Licence to rent stall given to Jewish refugees by the Shanghai Municipal Council.

newspapers and magazines in German, Polish and Yiddish: artists and musicians performed, including the first Yiddish play in Shanghai.

"Overall, there was remarkable unity among the refugees. They arranged an orchestra, football games and artistic events, a mobile library and a place to exchange books – spiritual food." (Note 11)

Refugees opened groceries, pharmacies, bakeries, coffee shops, other retail outlets and even small factories; Zhoushan Road became known as "Little Vienna".

The second reason was the aid the refugees received from many quarters, including wealthy families like the Sassoons and the Kadoories. The Kadoorie family, for example, set up a free school, the Shanghai Jewish Youth Association School, for about 700 children of refugees who could not afford school fees.

After Pearl Harbor, the Jews holding British, Dutch and American nationality were interned and most of their assets confiscated. So, it fell to the Russian Jews to help; less wealthy than their Sephardic brothers, they provided food, clothing and other support to those in the restricted area.

Aid from Jewish organisations overseas was also important, including those in Kobe, Palestine, Stockholm, Lisbon and the United States. Much of it arrived via the help of the Jewish community in Hong Kong.

The most important of these organisations was the American Jewish

Joint Distribution Committee (JDC), which set up a Shanghai office in Huoshan Road in 1938 and gave monthly donations averaging US$30,000. After Pearl Harbor, its representative in Shanghai, Laura Margolis, was put into a camp by the Japanese. She succeeded in obtaining her release at the end of 1943 and returned to the U.S. She and others successfully lobbied her government to lift its ban on paying money to "enemy-occupied territories".

From March 1944, the JDC was able to send US$25,000 through Switzerland. In the face of inflation, this was increased to US$100,000 per month in January 1945 and remained at this level until the end of the war.

The third factor was the support provided by Chinese residents of Hongkou. "They overcame all kinds of difficulties to vacate their rooms to put up refugees. Before the hospitals for Jewish refugees were set up, Chinese hospitals treated a great number of Jewish refugees and saved many lives." (Note 12)

In her book *Four Decades of My Life* (Note 13), Lilli Finkelstein recalled her days in Hongkou: "The Chinese in the neighbourhood behaved very well toward us. They knew how precarious our situation was and they did not take advantage of it. They let us live our life unmolested."

After the American bombing raid on July 17, 1945 that mistakenly hit the segregated zone, Chinese residents helped to carry the wounded refugees to emergency clinics and brought food and money to them. More remarkable is the fact that many of the Chinese were themselves refugees

A street in the Hongkou district of Shanghai looked like one in Vienna.

A street in the ghetto of Hongkou district where Jewish refugees lived.

from their homes in other places who had fled the Japanese military; unlike the Jewish refugees, they did not enjoy the support of relief money sent from abroad and were themselves living on the edge of survival.

Professor Wang Jian said that the arrival of so many refugees meant less living space for Shanghai people. "But the Jewish relief organisations were very active on their behalf, providing 70-80 per cent of their funds. They rented empty rooms and factories for them and encouraged them to become self-supporting, with small loans. Less than one third relied on aid, mostly the old people; some had help from relatives here and the overseas funds. They did not take over the homes of Shanghai people." (Note 14)

Did Japan save the Jews?

Neither in Manchuria, Shanghai or other cities in China under their control with a Jewish population did the Japanese implement the "final solution" despite the pressure of their Nazi allies. During the war, the Jewish refugees in Shanghai died of disease, malnutrition and other causes. In a report in 1943, the International Red Cross put their death toll at 130 in 1940, then 167, 320 and 311 respectively in the next three years. Thousands of Chinese died of similar causes during that terrible period.

Does this mean that the Japanese saved the Jews? "We cannot say that," said Professor Wang Jian. (Note 15) "The International Concession, the French concession – all these saved the Jews. The Japanese did not kill them."

Wang divided Japan's policies into three phases. One was between 1931 and 1937, when Tokyo allowed the Jews to enter areas of China it controlled; it encouraged their settlement in Manchuria to promote the economic development of the region. Its aim was to influence the U.S. and the Soviet Union to be more favourable to Japan; but it failed to achieve either objective and did not attract capital from U.S. Jews for the settlement of their brothers and sisters in China.

The second stage, Wang said, was to control the arrival of Jews into Shanghai. In 1938, the Japanese restricted their entry into Hongkou, a district under its control that bordered the International Concession.

The third stage, after the attack on Pearl Harbor, was to treat the Jews like citizens of other "enemy countries", like Britain, the U.S. and Holland. "In the end, the Allies won the war. But what if the Axis powers had won? What would Japan have done with the Jews then?" Wang said.

German historian Heinz Eberhard Maul said that Japan's policy toward the Jews was greatly influenced by the progress of World War Two. "In the summer of 1942, when Germany was winning major victories in the Soviet Union, the Japanese began to consider the Nazi plan to eliminate the Jews. But, after the (German) defeat at Stalingrad (July 1942-February 1943) and Japan's refusal to attack the Soviet Union, Tokyo's attitude changed. It finally set up the segregated area. Whether (or not) to save the lives of the Jews was not a result of the magnanimity of the Japanese but (was) a reflection of changes in the progress of the war." (Note 16)

As we explained in Chapter Two, among the Japanese military and civilian leadership, there were different opinions on the Jews. Most favourable were those like Norihiro Yasue, the colonel in military intelligence and one of the architects of the Fugu Plan. His influence diminished after Tokyo signed the Tripartite Pact with Germany and Italy in September 1940. But he remained in Dalian as an adviser to the Manchukuo government and kept his close contacts with the Jews of Harbin and of Shanghai.

He and his associates played an important role in lobbying his government not to accept the Meisinger Plan in 1942. In August 1945, after the Soviet invasion of Manchuria, he refused the option of escaping to Japan, said goodbye to his family and allowed himself to be captured by the Soviet forces in Dalian on August 23. He told his family that all his generation was to blame for the war and its consequences; it was therefore dishonourable for them to flee their responsibilities. He died in 1950 in a labour camp in Khabarovsk.

Nightmare ends

On May 8, 1945, Nazi Germany surrendered and the war in Europe was over. American bombing raids on Japanese targets in China intensified. On August 9, the Soviet Red Army invaded Manchuria. On August 6 and 9, U.S. planes dropped nuclear bombs on Hiroshima and Nagasaki.

When they heard this news, the Jews of Shanghai knew that the war would soon be over. Emperor Hirohito announced the surrender on August 15, setting off scenes of unbridled joy among the refugees and their Chinese neighbours. They set off firecrackers, danced and sang in the street and took photographs together. Some were afraid of chaos before the arrival of the Allied forces. But the streets were calm.

By September 3 and 4, the U.S. Seventh Fleet docked in Shanghai, bringing American, British and other Allied soldiers to the city. The Marines invited residents to see films they had brought with them; after months without female company, they whistled in admiration at the ladies of Shanghai.

The Chinese guards who used to patrol the perimeter of the Hongkou segregated area disappeared suddenly, as did the barbed wire fences that surrounded it. Fearful of reprisals, the Japanese soldiers hid themselves from public view.

The refugees began to learn from newspapers and documentary films of the fate of their brothers and sisters in Europe; they began to realise that, however difficult their life had been in the segregated area, it had been a haven of safety compared to Europe. "The Jews did not want to stay in Shanghai," said Wang Jian. (Note 17) "They wanted to go to the U.S. and other countries. The conditions of life here were very difficult and hard to bear. Only after World War Two, when they found out what had happened elsewhere, did they realise how valuable Shanghai had been to them."

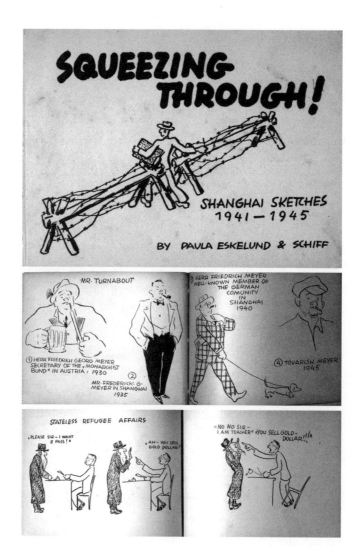

Sketches by Paul Eskelund and Friedrich Schiff showing the life of Jews in Shanghai during World War Two.

Learning the violin

One of the refugees was a boy named Heinz Gruenberg, who arrived in 1938, at the age of five, with his mother on a ship from Italy. He did not waste his 11 years in Shanghai – he acquired his first violin and learnt the skills that enabled him to play for 30 years as a soloist with the Vienna Symphony Orchestra. "They were the decisive years of my life and it was the place where I started my profession," he said during his first return visit in 50 years. (Note 18) "I feel as I had never left."

He and his parents lived in a tiny apartment in Zhoushan Road. His father was a textile expert who had tuberculosis; his mother earned a meagre income as a seamstress. "The Chinese treated us well, no differently from anyone else."

Gruenberg was able to live a normal life, attend school, play in the park and study the violin with a Jewish master who had also fled there. He stayed in Shanghai until January 1949 when he returned to his native Vienna and began his distinguished musical career. "The Nazis killed 40 of my family. But my parents and I and a few of our relatives found our refuge in Shanghai."

His story was the subject of a 60-minute documentary film *Escape to Shanghai* (逃亡上海) directed by Chen Yifei (陳逸飛), a Shanghai painter and film-maker; it premiered in Israel in 1999.

The idea for the film came to Chen when an elderly Jewish woman approached him in a New York art gallery in 1990 and addressed him in the fluent Shanghainese she had learnt during the war. Chen began to visit former Shanghai Jews in different cities in the world and chose Gruenberg as his subject. The soundtrack for the film is the violin music the young man learnt in Shanghai; it ends with a performance of *Ode to Joy* by Beethoven, which Gruenberg gave with the Shanghai Symphony Orchestra. "(Oskar) Schindler took 9,000 Jews and Shanghai 25,000," said Chen. (Note 19) "Schindler used them for his own profit and Shanghai got no benefit. The Chinese people were very generous. It is something we should be proud of. I hope many people will see my film and learn of a story that few know about."

Notes

1   *The Jews and China* (猶太人與中國) by Professors Pan Guang (潘光) and Wang Jian (王健), Shishi Publishing Company (時事出版社), 2009, pages 38.

2   Same, page 39.

3   Same, page 41.

4   Same, page 43.

5-6   *Escape and Rescue, Jewish Refugees and Shanghai in World War II* (逃 亡 與 拯救：二戰中的猶太難民與上海), by Wang Jian (王健), Shanghai Jiaotong University Press (上海交通大學出版社), 2016, pages 221-233.

7   Pan Guang and Wang Jian, page 47.

8   Visit by author to Shanghai Jewish Refugee Museum, December 2016.

9   Pan and Wang, page 48.

10   Same, page 50.

11   Same, page 48.

12   Same, page 50.

13   *Four Decades of My Life*, by Lilli Finkelstein, page 163.

14-15   Interview with author, 14/12/2016.

16   *Warum Japan Keine Juden verfolgte, Die Judenpolitik des Kaiserreches Japan wahrend der Zeit des National-sozialismus 1933-1945*, by Heinz Eberhard Maul, Iudicium Verlag GmbH, 2007.

17   Interview with author, 14/12/2016.

18-19   Article by author in *The South China Morning Post*, 2/5/1999.

5

Diplomats –
Those who saved
the Jews

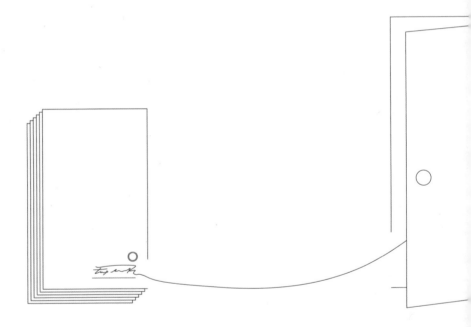

From

DIPLOMATS

In 1953, the Israeli Parliament, the Knesset, decided to create the title of "Righteous Among the Nations" to honour Gentiles who saved the Jews during the Holocaust. It entrusted this mission to Yad Vashem (YV), the World Holocaust Remembrance Centre set up that year. It is located on the western slope of Mount Herzl on the Mount of Remembrance in Jerusalem, 804 metres above sea level.

A Supreme Court judge chairs a committee of public personalities who make the judgement using the following criteria – the person acted entirely at his own discretion: in territories controlled by the Germans or their collaborators: at the risk of their freedom, safety or lives: and received no reward or remuneration as a precondition for their help.

As of January 1, 2017, the YV website listed 26,513 people who have been so honoured; among countries, Poland ranks first, with 6,706, followed by Holland with 5,595 and France with 3,995. There are two from China and one from Japan.

Of the total, nine are diplomats. There are three criteria for recognizing them as "Righteous Among the Nations". "The situation of diplomats – official representatives of foreign governments – was unique since danger to their

To SAVIOURS

person was significantly less than to others who aided Jews. The criteria are that they acted against explicit orders from their superiors: risked their careers: and extended help to a sizable number of people."

The one from Japan and one of the two from China are diplomats. Most of the Jews they helped spent the war in China, mainly Shanghai. This chapter will describe the lives of those three individuals, and two others in China and Japan who helped Jews during World War Two.

In a booklet called *Visa for Life: Diplomats who rescued Jews*, the Israeli Foreign Ministry had this to say about the nine diplomats who have been honoured. "Diplomats enjoyed a special status in the countries where they served and were in a unique position to extend significant help to refugees. Many used every nuance of the regulations to keep Jews from entering their countries. Yet a few shine as beacons of light in the vast darkness, lone lighthouses guiding refugees past the lethal rocks and deadly minefields of the Holocaust ... They truly stand as beacons of light for us all." (Note 1)

Mission boy who saved thousands

Ho Feng-shan (何鳳山) is one of the two Chinese honoured at Yad Vashem. He was consul-general of the Nationalist government in Vienna from April 1938 to March 1940; during this time, he gave Shanghai-destination visas to thousands of Jews seeking to escape persecution by the Nazis. He did this in defiance of orders from his superiors and at a time of worsening persecution by the German state against the Jews.

While his diplomatic status gave him a certain protection, it was not absolute, especially against attacks by individual Nazis. He did not carry a weapon or have bodyguards.

Ho was born in 1901 into a poor family in Yiyang, Hunan province (湖南益陽) and lost his father when he was seven. He was taken in by the Norwegian Missionary Society in Yiyang, which gave his mother a job and him an education through middle school. "My father believed that it was the chance for an education that made him the man he was," said his daughter Ho Manli (何曼禮).

An outstanding student, he obtained a scholarship at the age of 19 to the College of Yale-in-China, a school established in Changsha (長沙), Hunan, by the Yale-China Association of the United States. He brought his mother and younger sister to Changsha, where he taught English to pay living and study costs.

After graduating in 1926, he obtained a fellowship for doctoral studies at Munich University in Germany. He graduated magna cum laude with a Ph.D in political economics in 1932 and joined the Foreign Ministry in 1935, with his first posting to Turkey.

In 1937, he was transferred to serve as first secretary at the Chinese legation in Vienna. Because of his fluent German, he became the public face of the Chinese legation, giving speeches on Chinese culture. After Japan's all-out invasion of China in July 1937, he drummed up support for the Chinese cause, wrote articles for the city's main newspaper against the invaders and engaged in a fierce debate with his Japanese counterpart.

In April 1938, one month after the Anschluss, the union of Austria and Nazi Germany, the legation became a consulate-general and Ho was appointed consul-general. (Note 2)

"After the annexation of Austria by Germany, the persecution of Jews by Hitler became increasingly fierce," Ho wrote in memoirs published in 1990. "The fate of Austrian Jews was tragic. Persecution was a daily occurrence."

He described a meeting between Adolf Hitler and the foreign diplomatic corps. "He was a short little man. He had a ridiculous mustache. He was an unspeakable martinet."

In April 1938, the first Austrian Jews were sent to Dachau and Buchenwald concentration camps. They were told by the Nazis that, if they emigrated from Austria immediately, they would be released. The news of the deportations spread alarm and panic among the 180,000 Jews in the country, the third largest community in Europe.

In July 1938, representatives from 32 Western countries attended a conference in Evian, France to consider the plight of Jewish refugees. The only countries that expressed willingness to accept a large number of Jews at a price were the Dominican Republic, and later Costa Rica. The major Western countries were unwilling to change their immigration policies. China and Japan were not represented at the conference. When they heard the outcome of the conference, the Jews of Europe were filled with despair and foreboding. The world had closed its doors to them.

It was against this background that Ho took the decision to issue visas to Jews in Austria. "There were American religious and charitable organisations which were urgently trying to save the Jews," Ho wrote in his memoir. "I secretly kept in close contact with these organisations. I spared no effort in using any means possible. Innumerable Jews were thus saved. I knew that the Chinese visas were to Shanghai 'in name' only," he later recalled. "In reality, it was a means for them to find a way to get to the United States, England or other preferred destinations."

Several visas went to the family of Fritz Heiduschka, who was arrested in April 1938. His wife obtained the visas and presented them to the Nazi authorities; within hours, her husband was released and the family was able to leave Austria. They found shelter in Manila in the Philippines.

Eric Goldstaub, then 17, went to consulates all over Vienna but could not obtain visas for himself and his family. Ho provided 20 for them all. In November, Goldstaub and his father were arrested but let out after two days because they had the visas to China. The family boarded an Italian ship and sailed for Shanghai, where they lived for 10 years.

Word of Ho's generosity spread among the Jewish community; an enormous queue formed in front of the consulate. People had to wait outside for days, while Nazi hooligans harassed them. On the morning of November 10, Ho went to the home of Jewish friends, the Rosenbergs, to see them off. He found that the Gestapo had arrived a little earlier and detained the father of the household. Because of Ho's intervention, Mr Rosenberg was released and the family was able to leave Vienna for Shanghai.

In the nearly two years following the Anschluss, Ho issued 500 visas a month on average to Jewish refugees, sometimes as many as 900 and, on a least one occasion, 100 in a single day.

His superior, Chen Jie (陳介), the Chinese ambassador in Berlin, learnt of what he was doing. Fearful that this mass issuance of visas would harm China's good relations with Germany, he called Ho and ordered him to stop. When Ho did not, Cheng sent his subordinate to Vienna unannounced to investigate any wrongdoing, but nothing was found.

In the meantime, in contravention of the Geneva convention on diplomatic extra-territoriality, the Nazis confiscated the consulate building on the pretext that it was Jewish-owned. Undaunted, Ho moved into much smaller quarters, paying the rent out of his own pocket when the home government refused to cover the costs, and continued to issue the visas. Some of the recipients went to Shanghai; others used the visas to go to Portugal, Palestine, North and South America, the Philippines, Cuba and other countries.

By the time Ho left Vienna in the spring of 1940, he had established Shanghai as a refuge of last resort for Jews fleeing Nazi persecution and some 18,000 European Jews fled there. No-one knows exactly how many visas he issued; the number was in the thousands.

Following his posting in Vienna, Ho worked in the United States for the Chinese Military Commission in Washington DC before returning to China, where he rejoined the Foreign Ministry as head of the Information Section. After the war, he had postings in Egypt, Mexico, Bolivia and Colombia before he retired in 1973.

During his last posting as ambassador to Colombia, a disgruntled subordinate alleged that Ho had misappropriated some US$300 in embassy expenses and US$8 in car inspection fees. Despite submitting evidence of his innocence four separate times, Ho was nevertheless impeached in 1975 – nearly two years after he had retired – by the Control Yuan, the watchdog for public officials in Taiwan, and denied his pension for 40 years of service. Ho never returned to Taiwan and spent the last years of his life in California, where he died on September 28, 1997, at the age of 96.

Despite repeated appeals over the last two decades by his family of what they see as a grave political injustice, Ho has yet to be exonerated and his name restored by Taiwan authorities.

Ho also never saw again any of the Jews he had helped. Toward the end of his life, he wrote a memoir *Forty Years of My Diplomatic Life* (外交生涯四十年), published in 1990 by the Chinese University Press in Hong Kong. In this 700-page memoir, there were only 70 characters on the rescue effort.

"There is very little in his memoirs about his rescue activities in Vienna and certainly no details," said his daughter Ho Manli. "He did not talk about it during his lifetime. Not even we, his family, really knew the full extent of his work." (Note 3)

She remembers her father as a traditional Chinese intellectual who named his son Monto (曼德) and daughter Man-li after the Confucian precepts of "De" (德) meaning virtue and "Li" (禮) meaning decorum; these were qualities he wanted in his children. Fearful that life abroad would deprive them of their roots, he insisted that they speak and write Chinese at home.

After her father's death, Manli, who was trained as a journalist, wrote an obituary in a San Francisco newspaper, which briefly mentioned what Ho had done in Vienna. The obituary was read by a Jewish impresario named Eric Saul, who contacted Manli to see if he could add her father to his photo exhibition on diplomatic rescuers of Jews. "Somehow his asking for information propelled me to embark on this odyssey to uncover my father's work. I had to reconstruct the events of more than 60 years ago by looking for survivors and documentation. It was a daunting task!" Manli recalled.

"My father thought it only natural to feel compassion and to want to help those in need. If it is something that is natural to any human being, why warrant particular praise or mention?" Manli said. "It is for this same reason that he said so little about his rescue activities during his lifetime. He adhered to his unwavering standards of integrity and compassion

Dr Ho Feng-shan, the Chinese consul in Vienna from 1938 to 1940. (Credit: Manli Ho)

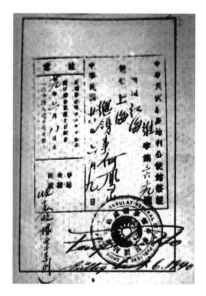

One of the visas issued by Consul Ho.

Dr Ho in later life with his daughter Ho Manli. (Credit: Manli Ho)

throughout his life. He had the courage of his convictions and refused to renounce his principles for the sake of either political expediency or even personal safety, and he bore the consequences without complaint."

In 2000, the Israeli government awarded Ho the honour of "Righteous Among the Nations". He met the criteria set by Yad Vashem – he risked his career and possibly his life to save the life of Jews, without monetary recompense, and did so against the orders of his government. Manli and her brother Monto went to Jerusalem to receive the honour at a ceremony in January 2001.

"My father was never reunited with any of the people he had helped," said Manli. "He was unknown to most of them. It has been my good fortune to find some of the beneficiaries of those visas. It is very special of me to meet survivors and hear their stories. My father is gone, but he lives on through them."

Chinese worker in Kharkov saves Jewish girl

The other Chinese to be honoured at Yad Vashem is Pan Junshun (潘均順) Born in 1889, he moved to Russia in 1916 in search of work. He went to Moscow and became a labourer. After the Bolshevik Revolution of 1917, he found it impossible to go home, so he settled in Moscow. He married and had two sons.

In 1936, he moved to the Ukrainian city of Kharkov, one of the most important industrial and arms production centres in the Soviet Union.

His wife died before the outbreak of World War Two in 1939. Their two sons were drafted into the Red Army and never returned; Pan presumed that they had been killed in the fighting.

After the Wehrmacht captured Kharkov in October 1941 following an intense battle, the Nazis rounded up a group of Jews in a tractor factory. They housed them in old huts and gave them no food or water; they were forced to eat snow. Among them was Yelisaveta Dvorkina and her children. The Germans announced that they would transport the children; in fact, they planned to kill them en route. Fearful of what would happen, Dvorkina bribed the compound guards with jewellery to allow her children to escape.

Her daughter Ludmilla succeeded in reaching the family home. Their neighbours included several Chinese, of whom Pan was one. He had lost his wife and two sons; he decided to look after Ludmilla. With the help of three neighbours – also honoured as Righteous Among the Nations – Pan hid the girl in his home from January 1942 until the re-conquest of Kharkov by the Red Army on August 23 1943. He continued to look after her and arranged her education; she later married. Pan died in 1974. Yad Vashem honoured him on January 19, 1995. He was the first Chinese to be so honoured. (Note 4)

The forgotten Chinese Schindler?

Wang Ti-fu's (王替夫) name is not mentioned at Yad Vashem. But perhaps it should be. He was a diplomat in the foreign service of

Manchukuo (滿洲國), the state established by Japan in Manchuria after it conquered the region in September 1931. A fluent German speaker, Wang was sent to the Manchukuo legation in Berlin, where he worked until 1941, He was one of the few Chinese who met and conversed with Adolf Hitler. According to a biography of Wang published in October 2001, three months after his death, he issued 10,000 visas, some for more than one individual, to Jewish people between spring 1939 and June 1941, enabling a total of 12,000 to escape the Holocaust.

But Wang had the misfortune to serve a government that was a puppet of the Japanese. As a result, after the war, he was regarded by the Chinese, both Nationalist and Communist, and the Soviet Union as a collaborator and traitor.

In 1945, the Soviet army arrested him; he spent 12 years in labour camps in Siberia and Kazakhstan. In 1956, he returned to his home in Harbin, northeast China. In the early 1960s, he was sent to a village outside the city and did not return until after the Cultural Revolution having been exiled for a total of 22 years.

In March 1992, he joined the Heilongjiang Literature and History Research Museum and trained more than 1,000 students in foreign languages. He died on July 13, 2001, at the age of 91. The biography, based on extensive interviews with Wang, was published in October that year. The title is *The Personal Statement of a Manchukuo Diplomat* (一個偽滿外交官的人生告白). After a life of official disgrace, Wang wanted people to know his account of history before he died. Because he was a "black" person, it made it very difficult for anyone, within China or abroad, to do the extensive investigation required to earn him a place at Yad Vashem. A search of his name on its database found no information.

Wang was born on June 29, 1911, in a suburb of Jilin city (吉林市) in Jilin province. From a young age, he loved languages and learnt English and Russian. He went to the Harbin University of Law and Politics (哈爾濱法政大學) where he studied Japanese, Russian, English and German. During his time there, he probably met Jewish people, either on the faculty or in his wider social life.

Wang was in his third year, in 1931, when the Japanese took over Manchuria. As a patriot, he and other students collected money and clothes for the soldiers of a Chinese general Ma Zhan-shan (馬占山) who was resisting the invaders.

But the Japanese soon captured Harbin, a city without a wall, and arrested the 20-year-old student; at once they recognised that his language skills could be of use to the new state. They also arrested his family and warned that, if he did not co-operate, they would be harmed. After deep reflection, he decided that he had no alternative but to join the government of Manchukuo.

In December 1932, he was sent to work in its consulate in Chita, in Siberia. In May 1932, Germany recognised the new state of Manchukuo; it set up a legation in Berlin.

Because of his fluency in German, Wang was sent to Berlin as a secretary in the legation, which opened in January 1939. On March 1 that year, he and his colleagues went to present their credentials to the Fuhrer at his new Chancellery, an imposing building that had just been completed at enormous cost, with the aim of inspiring awe and dread among all who entered it.

Wang and his colleagues walked the 220 metres through the rooms to Hitler's reception gallery, which was itself 145 metres long. Hitler's own office was 400 square metres in size and equipped with a large marble-topped table.

"After a wait of half an hour, accompanied by Foreign Minister Joachim von Ribbentrop, Hitler entered the enormous hall. Everyone got up as a sign of courtesy and clapped to welcome this dictator who had carved up Europe and shaken the world … He was only 5 feet 9 inches, with a broad bottom and legs thin and long. He was the image of an ugly man. Wang was 1.9 metres tall; to shake Hitler's hand, he had to lean forward and look down into his shallow blue eyes. These eyes were complicated, both savage and warm."

The visitors were given a tour of the building, including Hitler's enormous office and a basement floor three storeys below ground, complete with offices containing equipment to send secret messages, an air raid shelter and a command centre. This is where Hitler and his wife Eva Braun would kill themselves on April 30, 1945.

The guests were given lunch; Wang sat three places away from Hitler, with his two superiors in between. In his speech, the German leader spoke of the many resources of Manchukuo, especially soybean, which could be used as grain and in oils, leather, textile fibre and in the chemicals industry.

"So I urgently wanted to establish relations with Manchuria, because I badly need your soybean … The people of Asia are intelligent and talented. Six centuries ago Genghis Khan had the ambition to conquer the world. He reached Turkey and the Balkans – how extraordinary! Then a man from Asian steppe could reach Europe. Now why cannot a great man from Europe reach Asia?" (Note 5) Wang's heart trembled when he heard these words and the boundless ambition of Hitler.

From the three-storey legation in a historic building in the city centre, Wang had a ringside view of the extraordinary events unfolding in Berlin, a view available to few Chinese. His job was not so busy; the real interaction was between the Nazi government and the Japanese embassy, not that of Manchukuo. So, Wang had the opportunity to hear Hitler's speeches to the Parliament and attend mass military parades; he saw Jews beaten and killed on the streets of Berlin. All this enabled him to understand clearly what was going on and the fate of the Jews of Germany.

One day in August, his Foreign Ministry ordered him to the German border close to Poland to meet colleagues from the consulate in Warsaw. They told him that the Nazis had massed large numbers of tanks, armoured vehicles and solders on the border in preparation for the

Wang Ti-fu, a diplomat of the Manchukuo government in Berlin, and his wife: picture taken in Berlin in 1938.

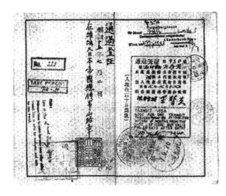

A visa issued by Wang Ti-fu, a diplomat of the Manchukuo government in Berlin, to a Jewish person in 1940.

invasion. After the war broke out, he sent his wife and four children, aged between several months and 10 years, back home. After travelling by ship from Germany, they arrived safely in Dalian and from there onto Harbin.

The war intensified and Hitler's rhetoric became more manic; Wang found him both comic and terrifying, in part because everyone believed what he was saying and in his promise of victory. "Wang was very clear, that one day Germany would collapse and, with it, Japan and Manchukuo would cease to exist. He dared say this to no-one, not even his wife. He knew he had to help those who needed to be helped. He would not regret it. He did not know how long he would be able to do this nor the risk he was running." (Note 6)

In 1939, Wang's superior, Lu Yi-wen (呂宜文), Minister of the Legation, was summoned to the German Foreign Ministry; it demanded that he issue visas to the Jews to get them out of the country and said Moscow had given its approval for them to transit the Soviet Union. Lu realised that this was also the order of the Japanese; he told Wang to start work, which he did on June 10. By August, he had issued 7,000 such visas. Through this process, Wang came to know many Jews and become sympathetic to them.

But, in October 1939, the German policy changed. Lu was summoned again to the German Foreign Ministry and told to stop issuing the visas; after its swift and successful invasion of Poland, the Nazi government had decided on another way to "solve the Jewish question".

Lu informed Wang of this new policy; by now, Wang was pro-Jewish and decided to continue issuing the visas in secret, without the Germans finding out. He sent his German secretary to the Jewish Association in Berlin to collect the passports of the applicants; in the evening, he stamped them with the visas and his secretary returned them to the association the next day, before taking the next batch. Finally, in the spring of 1940, the Legation received an order from the Manchukuo Foreign Ministry to issue no more visas to Jews; so, he could not do so any more. Between October 1939 and May 1940, Wang had issued 5,000 visas – making a total of more than 12,000. (Note 7)

Between 1941 and 1943, he served as a diplomat in Denmark, Romania and Bulgaria; in 1944, he returned to Changchun to work in the cabinet office of the Manchukuo government.

After the war, he was arrested by the Soviet Army which had invaded Manchuria; it sent him to a labour camp in Siberia. He returned to Harbin in 1956. In the 1960s, his past in the Manchukuo government was revealed and he was arrested again. He spent a total of 22 years in rural exile.

His superior in Berlin, Lu Yi-wen, was also arrested after the war and sentenced to death by a High Court in Kunming, Yunnan; he succeeded in escaping execution, but, in October 1950, was killed by a unit of the People's Liberation Army in Yunnan during operations against the Nationalist soldiers still operating in the mainland.

After a Calvary of 34 years, Wang finally returned to Harbin to rejoin his children. During the last years of his life, he worked in the archives of the Heilongjiang provincial government and taught foreign languages to more than 1,000 students. But, even then, he was not spared punishment; in his 70s, he was designated a bell-ringer (打更人) during the night for 10 years. This required him to sound a bell at 19:00, 21:00, 23:00, 01:00 and 03:00 every night, so that people in the neighbourhood knew what time it was.

He rarely spoke about his experiences during the war, except to Chen Ming, the writer who wrote his biography. Wang died on July 13, 2001. On July 30, the then Israeli ambassador to China, Itzhak Shelef, arrived in Harbin, hoping to seek him; he came two weeks too late.

In their book *Harbin Jews in Early 1900s, Their Political and Religious Lives*, Professors Wang Zhijun and Li Wei said that, because of complex historical reason, it was extremely difficult to find records of Wang's help toward the Jews.

"We can confirm that Wang Ti-fu assisted Jews but we do not have the evidence to say how many. We cannot confirm or deny what he said himself, in issuing visas to so many Jews." (Note 8)

What they meant was that Wang's remarkable humanitarian work for the Jews in Berlin was, for China, overshadowed by the fact that he was an official of a Japanese puppet government. More than 70 years after the end of the war, the mainland government refers to Manchukuo and those who worked for it in the most derogatory terms.

So how could he be considered a hero? From reading his biography, his motives in issuing the visas were in part a desire to help those at risk of death and in part to assuage his own guilt, as he discovered the true nature of the regime for whom he was working and its allies. "When Wang considered that he had saved more than 10,000 lives, he knew that he could die a hundred times and his life was worthwhile." (Note 9)

Wang wrote in the preface: "This life of a man does not entirely belong to him. If he knows he has committed wrong, then he must seize the moment to do good things."

The modest Japanese

The only Japanese in the Righteous Among the Nations is Chiune Sugihara (杉原千畝), who was, like Dr Ho, a diplomat in Eastern Europe during the war. As consul in Kaunas, Lithuania from August 1939 to September 1940, he issued an estimated 6,000 transit visas to Jews, enabling them to escape from Europe. After collecting testimony from hundreds of survivors, Yad Vashem declared him a "Righteous Among the Nations" in 1985.

Chiune Sugihara was born on January 1, 1900 in a small town named Mino-shi (美濃市) in Gifu Prefecture (岐阜縣) in central Japan. He was the second son of six children, in a middle-class family. His father was frequently moved by his employer, the tax bureau. The young Chiune spent his early years in different places before studying middle school in Nagoya (名古屋). In March 1918, he entered the prestigious Waseda University (早稻田大學) in Tokyo to study English and stayed for one year. In 1919, he passed the exam to enter the Foreign Ministry. (Note 10)

The ministry sent him to study Russian in Harbin in northeast China. As we described in Chapter Two, this city had a large Russian and Jewish populations. "As a student, my father won a scholarship to study Russian in Harbin," said his son Nobuki (杉原伸生). (Note 11)

"He studied there for three years in a Russian language school (Harbin Gakuin – 哈爾濱學院) run by the Japanese Foreign Ministry. He spoke Russian better than Russian people."

Sugihara spent the best part of 16 years in Harbin. He married a Russian woman, whom he later divorced. He led negotiations, which lasted nearly two years, with the Soviet government to buy the branch of the Chinese Eastern Railway that crossed Manchuria; this was a very strategic railway. In 1933, the year after the foundation of Manchukuo, this was renamed "The North Manchurian Railway" (北滿鐵路).

"He was a very strong negotiator," said Nobuki. "In 1935, he left his position in Harbin because he did not like the behaviour of young officers in the military, 21-23 years old, who were ruling Manchuria. Then the Foreign Ministry assigned him to the embassy in Moscow and he went to Helsinki, to wait for his entry permit.

"But the Soviet Union remembered his work as a negotiator in Manchuria and refused a visa. Instead, he was sent to Lithuania to collect information on a possible German invasion of the Soviet Union. Japan did not trust Germany. He was vice-consul in Kaunas, the temporary capital of Lithuania."

The appointment was at the end of August 1939, a few days before the German and Soviet invasions of Poland. Kaunas was the largest and most industrialised city in the country; it had a Jewish community of 35,000-40,000, about 25 per cent of the total population. They began settling there from the second half of the 17th century. They accounted for much of the city's commercial, artisan and professional elite. Kaunas was a centre of Jewish learning, with 40 synagogues, many schools, a Jewish hospital and dozens of Jewish-owned businesses.

In the modern era, Lithuania had only gained its independence in February 1918, after 120 years as part of the Russian empire. Kaunas had been the temporary capital since 1920. When Sugihara arrived there, the country's independence was under threat by the Soviet Union to the east and Nazi Germany to the west. In June 1940, the Soviet Union occupied and annexed Lithuania under secret protocols of the Molotov-Ribbentrop Pact, which it had signed with Nazi Germany in August 1939.

After the occupation, many Jews from Lithuania tried to acquire exit visas but could not find countries willing to issue them. They were joined by Jews from Poland, under Nazi occupation since September 1939. So, it was that, at six o'clock in the morning of July 18, 1940, Sugihara woke up and peered through the curtains of his bedroom window onto the street; he saw dozens of people lined up and pushing against the iron railings of the consulate fence.

He sent the first of three cables to his superiors at the Foreign Ministry in Tokyo, asking for permission to issue transit visas.

"From Tokyo, the orders were to issue transit visas only to people with US$5-7,000 and a guarantor in Japan – this meant, in effect, issuing no visas," said Nobuki. "In July 1940, he negotiated an agreement with the Soviet government, under which Jews would have permission to travel to Moscow and Vladivostok and then on to Japan. He signed this agreement on July 25, 1940. On July 27, he started to issue the visas, at the rate of 100 per day for the next six weeks, until September 2. His wife and two children moved into a hotel in Kaunas, so as to avoid the pressure. His wife supported what he was doing and brought him lunch and dinner."

He later wrote in his memoirs that he signed so many visas that his fingers were calloused and every joint from his wrist to his shoulder ached. Occupied by the Red army, Lithuania ceased to be an independent country and became part of the Soviet Union; on August 3, foreign governments were given a month to close their missions. Sugihara continued to issue the visas, even after moving into a nearby hotel, until the morning of September 4, when he left with his family for Berlin.

He was even writing visas in transit from his hotel and after boarding the train at Kaunas Railway Station, throwing them out of the window into a crowd of desperate refugees as the train pulled out. The Simon Wiesenthal Centre estimates that he issued transit visas for about 6,000 Jews – including family visas which would enable several people to use one – and that 40,000 descendants are alive today because of what he did.

Most used the visas to travel to Vladivostok and then to Kobe, Japan, which had a Jewish community. They were well treated in Japan and allowed to stay until they could arrange onward passage.

"The visas he issued were for a maximum of two months," said Nobuki. "Those who received them went by train to Moscow and Vladivostok and from there by boat to the port of Tsuruga (敦賀) in Japan. In Tsuruga, Jewish groups supported them, with US$100-500 for living costs. Some went from Kobe and Yokohama to the U.S., Australia, South Africa and Palestine. Those who had no relatives in these countries and could not obtain visas went to Shanghai, where there was a large Jewish community.

"In September 1940, my father went to Berlin and was then sent to Prague, where he issued 80 transit visas to Jews, for six months," Nobuki said. "Then he was sent to Konigsberg in East Prussia (now Kaliningrad in Russia). It was a major naval port for the Germans who were preparing the invasion of the Soviet Union. The Nazis did not like him because he was too diligent in collecting intelligence, so they declared him persona non grata.

"Then he was sent to Bucharest, the capital of Romania, until the end of the war. The Soviets imprisoned him and his family for two years. He was

Chiune Sugihara (centre, seated) with other diplomats.

Chiune Sugihara (centre, seated) with his wife and two children in the consulate in Kaunas.

repeatedly interrogated over what he had done in the previous 20 years. He was released after two years.

"In 1947, the Foreign Ministry asked him to give his resignation because of his disobedience. He was bitter about that. After that, life was difficult for us, as it was for everyone in Japan. There was not enough food. My father did not regret what he had done but had a bitter feeling. He shut himself off from that world and did not want to approach government or ministries.

"He opened a small shop to sell valves to farmers; it was not successful. He held different jobs – broadcasting news in Russian on NHK and teaching Russian in schools. In 1960, he got a job as the representative of Kawakami (川上) Trading Company in Moscow. He stayed there until 1977, returning every year for a few weeks to see the family; his wife and the children stayed in Japan. He was happy in Moscow, since he loved the language, the culture and the music."

Sugihara wrote his memoirs in 1983.

Like the children of Ho Feng-shan, Nobuki and his brothers and sisters did not know of their father's heroism, "My parents did not speak of what they had done in the war. In 1968, an Israeli diplomat arranged a meeting with him and I went along. He was the son of a survivor and showed us the visa with my father's signature on it. I heard of their life in Lithuania and the journey of the Jews."

Chiune Sugihara died in July 1986.

So why did he help the Jewish refugees?

"During his one year in Lithuania (1939-40), he travelled often to Berlin to report to the embassy there. When he passed through Poland, he found out what was happening and believed that Lithuania would be next. He was prepared. He was not religious, not Christian nor Buddhist. But he believed that there was a God, a God for everyone. He felt protected by God or Love, the Love of humans. He was a very warm person. He told everything directly, unlike a Japanese. He took care of the family; that was the most important."

Those saved by Sugihara lobbied for him to be included in Yad Vashem. After the necessary research, he received the honour in 1985. He was too ill to travel himself, so his wife Yukiko and Nobuki, their youngest son, accepted the honour on his behalf.

He and his descendants were given perpetual Israeli citizenship. There are streets named after him in Kaunas and Vilnius in Lithuania, Tel Aviv and Netanya in Israel and a park named after him in Jerusalem. Posthumously, he was awarded honours by Poland, Lithuania and the Japanese Canadian Cultural Centre.

In 1985, when asked about his motivation in an interview, Sugihara said: "I felt at that time that the Japanese government did not have any uniform opinion in Tokyo. Some Japanese military leaders were just scared because

Nobuki, son of Chiune Sugihara.

Jewish people waiting outside the Japanese consulate in Kaunas, Lithuania, in the hope of obtaining a visa, on July 7, 1940.

of the pressure from the Nazis, while other officials in the Home Ministry were simply ambivalent … I knew that somebody would surely complain about me in the future. But I myself thought this would be the right thing to do. There is nothing wrong in saving people's lives."

"In 1990, when Lithuania regained its independence, the Japanese Foreign Ministry wanted to make some kind of apology," Nobuki said. "It made a plaque of my father – but put it in a storage room, where no-one would see it. Among those he saved were 500 from the Mir Yeshiva in Poland. After the war, some went to Brooklyn and some went to Jerusalem. I was told by these yeshivas that, today, there are between 250,000 and 500,000 descendants of those he saved around the world."

Linked to Israel

His father's heroism created a strong link between Nobuki and Israel. He received a scholarship from Hebrew University in Jerusalem. "When I went there, I could not speak English," Nobuki said. "I studied Hebrew. I stayed at the university for two and a half years but did not graduate. I met a Japanese diamond buyer and translated for him. I liked it and got to know the business. I stayed in Israel for 15 years working in diamonds; I went to Japan each month. I liked the Jewish way of doing business – there is no written contract, but a verbal agreement and the goods are delivered. Then I moved to Antwerp and set up my own company. My wife is half-Belgian; we have four daughters." Since 1990, he has lived in Antwerp.

Japanese professor who converted

Sugihara was not the only Japanese who actively helped the Jews during World War Two. Another was Setsuzo Kotsuji (小辻節三), a professor who was at that time the only Japanese who could read and speak Hebrew. His contribution was to lobby his government successfully to extend short-term visas given to Jewish refugees, enabling them to stay for up to eight months.

During 1941 and 1942, he travelled all over Japan to give lectures that presented a positive picture of the Jews and countered the anti-Semitism of the media and parts of the government. He was arrested by the military police and interrogated about his role in the "Jewish plot to take over the world".

Kotsuji was born on February 3, 1899 in Kyoto (京都) into an upper-class family. His father, a prominent Shinto priest, descended from a long line of priests and hoped his son would follow this vocation. When the young man was 13, he found in an antique bookshop a copy of the Tanakh, the Hebrew Bible, which had been translated into Japanese. He was fascinated by what he read and stopped attending the Shinto rituals.

Despite the strong opposition of his father, he went to study theology at Meiji Gakuin University (明治學院大學), a Christian institution. He became a Protestant minister and was sent to a church in Hokkaido (北海道). In July 1927, with his new wife and young daughter, he went to California Pacific university in the United States to study Hebrew and the

Old Testament; during his four years of obtaining a doctorate there, he turned increasingly toward Judaism.

After obtaining a doctorate, he returned to Tokyo. After one year teaching at a university, he resigned for reasons of ill health; his daughter, seven, passed away and his wife fell ill. Then he set up a research institute on the Old Testament; he became known as one of the few Japanese scholars who was knowledgeable about the Jews. But, after three years, he had to close the institute for want of financial support.

In 1938, the South Manchurian Railway Company (SMRC) (南滿洲鐵道株式會社) hired him as an advisor on Jewish affairs. That October, with his family, he moved to Dalian (大連) on the southern tip of Liaoning, where the company had its headquarters.

During his two years in Manchuria, he came to know many Jewish people closely in the course of writing reports for the president of the SMRC. In Harbin, he met for the first time Orthodox Jews who followed traditional laws and customs, including Rabbi Aharon Moshe Kiselev. They made a deep impression on him. He gained a detailed knowledge of the tragedy of the Jews in Europe and how and why they had been forced to flee to the other side of the world.

At the second meeting of the Far Eastern Jewish Council in Harbin in 1938, as we described in Chapter Two, he gave a speech in Hebrew. He felt increasingly close to those he had come to know during those two years.

It was on his return to Japan, at the end of 1940, that the thousands of refugees given visas by Chiune Sugihara began to arrive in the western Japanese port of Tsuruga. They walked off the ships, exhausted and fearful after their long journey across the Soviet Union and the Sea of Japan; they had arrived in an unknown country with no idea of what would happen next.

Fortunately, the city's residents sympathised with them and provided food; owners of bath-houses opened their facilities on the day of the week that they were normally closed, so that they could wash away the dirt and smell of their long journey.

Most then left for Kobe, the city in Japan with the largest Jewish community. How would it deal with his mass arrival of people, whose visas were for only two weeks? One of the Kobe Jews remembered Kotsuji from his speech in Harbin and asked him to come and help; he went at once.

Among the refugees were rabbis and students of the Mir Yeshiva; he was very touched by them. After understanding their situation, he returned to Tokyo and called on the Foreign Minister – the same man who had been his boss as president of the South Manchurian Railway. The minister explained that power to extend visas rested with the security forces and that he himself could not authorise it.

So Kotsuji borrowed money from a wealthy brother-in-law and used it to bribe senior members of the Kobe police force. Thanks to his efforts, the visas were extended for eight months from the original two weeks. By the summer of 1941, the government was becoming anxious about having so many Jewish refugees in Kobe, a major port and military base. In the autumn, it moved them to the port of Yokohama (横濱). Those with the necessary connections left for the U.S., Canada and other countries; the majority went to Shanghai. Only Jews who had lived in Kobe before the arrival of the refugees were allowed to stay.

It was in 1941 that official anti-Semitism was at its strongest in Japan, in part because of the victories of the Wehrmacht (German army) on the Soviet front. The media carried articles on the "global Jewish conspiracy" and published insulting cartoons. To counter this, Kotsuji published a book *The True Character of the Jewish Nation*, in which he presented them in a positive light and denounced the Nazis.

He travelled across the country delivering lectures with this message and asking his audiences to assist the Jews. He acted as mediator and translator in meetings with the representatives of the refugees and government officials.

At the end of 1942, the Japanese military police Kempeitai (憲兵隊) arrested Kotsuji and accused him of helping the Jewish "global conspiracy". The interrogators demanded he reveal his role in it. In reply, he said that the "conspiracy" was a figment of the imagination of the anti-Semites. The officers refused to believe him and continued their interrogation; they beat him unconscious. At that moment, a high-ranking colonel in the military arrived at the prison; a close friend of Kotsuji, he was astonished to see one of the country's most famous scholars being imprisoned on false charges. He demanded that the professor be released; he walked free and the charges against him were dropped.

But Kostuji remained on the radar of the Kempeitai. On June 7, 1945, when the war had turned irrevocably against Japan, he and his family were shipped back to Manchuria. Suddenly, he found himself in a situation similar to that of the refugees he had helped. On August 9, the Soviet army invaded Manchuria and quickly conquered it. It arrested many Japanese people, military and civilian, and deported them to labour camps in Siberia.

For Kotsuji, fortunately, the good he had done was rewarded. A Jewish friend protected him from discovery by the Soviet forces; he and his family were able to return to Japan.

After the war, Kotsuji remained in close contact with his friends from the Kobe period, including the rabbis of the Mir Yeshiva. He became increasingly religious and decided to convert to Judaism. In 1959, he went to Jerusalem for this purpose. After circumcision in an ultra-Orthodox hospital and the approval of a rabbinical court, he was converted on August 9, at the age of 60, and given the Hebrew name Avraham.

Those whom he had helped in Japan hosted a meal in his honour. Chaim Shmulevitz, a rabbi of the Mir Yeshiva in Jerusalem, said: "We will never forget what you did for us in Japan, nor how you risked your life to save us," the rabbi said. "The merit of that self-sacrifice is what stood in your stead and led you to seek shelter under the wings of the 'Divine Presence' and to become a genuine member of the Nation you helped so much". Kotsuji was very moved to be thanked in person by so many people; he wept with joy.

He passed away on October 31, 1973; in his will, he asked to be buried in Israel. Just six days before, Israel had finished fighting in the Yom Kippur war against a coalition of Arab states. The family contacted Zerach Warhaftig, the Minister of Religions in the Israeli government; he and his family had received visas from Chiune Sugihara, which enabled them to escape from Lithuania to Japan in 1941. Despite the exceptional demands of the war, the minister arranged for Kotsuji's body to be flown to Israel. He went to the airport in person to meet the airplane and gave the oration at the funeral; it was attended by several hundred people. The Minister said that Kotsuji had always remained in the hearts of those he had helped. "We greatly respect him. I did all I could to welcome him to the land he loved and bury him in this holy place." (Note 12)

Notes

1   *Visa for Life, Diplomats who rescued Jews*, published by the Israel Ministry of Foreign Affairs.

2   *Global Times* (環球時報), 4/2/2000.

3   Correspondence between Ho Manli and the author.

4   Yad Vashem website (https://www.yadvashem.org/).

5   *The Personal Statement of a Manchukuo Diplomat* (一個偽滿外交官的人生告白), by Chen Ming (陳明), Chun Feng Wenyi Publishing Company (春風文藝出版社), October 2001, pages 133-138.

6   Chen Ming, page 185.

7   Article in *Changchun Evening News* (長春晚報), 14/6/2014.

8   *Harbin Jews in Early 1900s: Their Political and Religious Lives* (20 世紀上半期哈爾濱猶太人的宗教生活與政治生活), by Wang Zhijun (王志軍) and Li Wei (李薇), People's Publishing House (人民出版社), April 2013, pages 320-321.

9   Chen Ming, page 191.

10 *Japan Times*, 11/7/2015.

11 Author's interview with Nobuki Sugihara in September 2016.

12 The International Foreign Students Association, of Japan and "The Japanese Convert" by D. Sofer in www.aish.com, 20/11/2004.

Leaving China, going 'home'

Chapter Six

From

CHINA

The surrender of Emperor Hirohito (昭和天皇) in August 1945 brought immeasurable joy and relief – the end of the Japanese occupation of China, three months after the fall of the Nazi regime. It gave the Jewish refugees in China the chance to go "home". But, for those who had made their home in China, it brought new challenges – what was their future there? What kind of country would it be and would it welcome them?

With the re-establishment of links with the outside world, the Jews learnt the catastrophic news of what had happened to their brothers and sisters in Europe. They went to the Red Cross and other international agencies in search of news of their family members. They could make contact with Jewish communities around the world, links not possible since the attack on Pearl Harbor.

Jewish and Zionist organisations resumed their activities; the community published newspapers and magazines in English, Russian and German. Many activities were held in the Jewish Club on Avenue Pichon in the French Concession.

The situation of the three groups of Jews – refugees, Ashkenazi and Sephardic – was different. For the refugees, Shanghai was a temporary home; they did not

To ISRAEL

want to stay for the long term. During the war, they had lost contact with their family and friends; their priority was to find them and decide where to make a new life. Did they want to return to the country they had left in Europe? Would there be a Jewish state in Palestine where they could go? If neither of these, then which country did they wish to go to and would it accept them?

The coming of the Allied forces meant the arrival of food packages, blankets, clothing and other relief items from Jewish agencies and individuals in the United States and other countries as well as from U.N. agencies. In 1946, the United Nations Relief and Rehabilitation Agency (UNRRA) set up an office in Shanghai. Its mission was to give material aid to countries with a large number of refugees and help those displaced to go home. Its programme in China was the largest of any of country in the world; it received US$581 million, ahead of Poland with US$478 million. There were 260 million Chinese who had been living in areas controlled by the Japanese military.

The next six years saw the departure of the vast majority of the Jews in China – not only the refugees but also the long-term residents. A devastating civil war, hyperinflation, labour disputes and the Communist revolution persuaded them that they had no future there.

According to Chinese estimates, about 25,000-28,000 Jews left Shanghai between 1946 and 1951. In 1946, the number departing was about 3,000-4,000: then 8,000-9,000, 5,000, 5,000-6,000, 2,000 and 2,000 in the succeeding years. The vast majority were refugees from Europe. The four main destinations were the U.S., Canada, Australia and Israel, followed by South Africa and Latin America. Less than 1,000 returned to Europe. Among them were nearly 300 members of the German Communist Party and other left-wing people who wanted to join the establishment of the new Socialist state of East Germany; one of them later became its first ambassador to the People's Republic of China. (Note 1)

Where to go?

Those wishing to leave had to find a country to accept them. Every Jew had the right to go to Israel – but the country was re-established only in May 1948. Before that, the British authorities who controlled Palestine restricted the entry of Jews. For other countries, the Jews of China needed a visa. To enter the U.S., for example, an applicant needed an affidavit from a relative or a Jewish organisation and to pass a rigorous health test.

One who succeeded was Ernest Heppner, who had escaped to Shanghai with his mother from Breslau in Germany in 1939. He has given a graphic description of his life in *Shanghai Refuge*, published by the University of Nebraska in 1993. In 1947, he left Shanghai on board the *General Gordon*, a ship which arrived to carry Jewish people to the United States.

He went with his wife, whom he had met and married in Shanghai. He arrived in his new country with US$11 in his pocket. This is how he described his feelings on arrival. "We had been living in limbo, in an alien world. No matter how many friends I had made among the Chinese, ours had been an artificial existence. We had struggled to survive the murderous climate ... after our liberation, all Illo [his wife)]and I could think of was getting out of China to the U.S. After all, Shanghai was supposed to have been a temporary stopover until our quota number was called ... Yet the closer we came to New York, the more apprehensive I grew ... How would I find a job and what kind of job? Would I be a labourer for the rest of my life?" (Note 2)

Australia was another important destination. Between the end of the war and 1954, over 17,000 Jews arrived in Australia from Shanghai and Europe. In 1945, Australia established a Department of Immigration for the first time. But the door to Jews was only partially open. Before the war, it had a "White Australia" immigration policy that aimed at migrants being 98 per cent Anglo-Celtic; this continued in a modified form until 1973.

Anti-Jewish sentiment was strong and expressed in public, in newspaper articles and cartoons. As a result, the country limited the immigration of Jews. "Charles Glassgold, representative of the American Joint Distribution Committee in Shanghai in 1949, quoted the Australian consul in the city as saying: "We have never wanted these people (Jews) in Australia and we still don't want them. We will issue a few visas to those who have relations there as a gesture."

The consul was Major General O.C. W. Fuhrman; he ordered a limit of 25 per cent on Jewish passengers on all ships and later on planes. He described the Jews as the criminal element of Shanghai.

The Australian government introduced a quota system and various measures to limit Jewish refugee and survivor migration. The aim was to ensure that Jews, who constituted only a tiny minority before 1933, would continue to remain as a very small percentage of the population.

"A gentleman's agreement" in January 1949 set the quota for Jewish immigrants to 3,000 per annum ... The 'Iron Curtain Embargo' in December 1949 effectively excluded Jews who originated from countries under Soviet rule; and [there were] special discriminatory policies towards Jews of Middle Eastern origins, including India." (Note 3)

It was a similar story in Canada, another country seen by many refugees as a desirable destination. During the 12 years of Nazi rule from 1933 to 1945, it had accepted only 5,000 Jewish refugees. The Prime Minister from 1935 to 1948 was Mackenzie King, who regarded the acceptance of a large number of Jewish immigrants as a threat to Canadian society because he believed they would not assimilate nor change their religious and cultural beliefs. His views were shared by much of the Anglophone and Francophone elites.

"Even when the war ended and the full evidence of the death camps became clear to all Canadians, there was no immediate lifting of the immigration barriers for the survivors," wrote Michael R. Angel in *Manitoba History*. "Canada now was looking for new immigrants, but a 1946 opinion poll showed that only the Japanese were more unpopular as immigrants than Jews – even Germans fared better, presumably because of their Teutonic background." (Note 4)

Most fortunate were those with family members in another country who could apply for visas for them: those with links to Jewish organisations abroad who could sponsor them: and those with money and connections who could hire lawyers and consultants to facilitate the migration process. The unfortunate were those with no such links and no money to pay for help: those who were stateless and could not obtain the necessary papers: also the old, infirm, ill and physically handicapped who could not pass health examinations mandatory for many countries.

Another constraint was a shortage of transport. The post-war period was a time of mass movement of people around the Pacific – Allied soldiers returning to their countries, Japanese soldiers and civilians being repatriated and tens of thousands of others going home or migrating as a result of the war. All this put great pressure on availability of ships.

A secret agreement between the new Chinese government and the Israeli government at the end of 1949 established an office of "Aliyah – immigration of Jews to Israel" in Shanghai, where an Israeli representative issued letters of travel to Israel to all the stateless refugees as well as to any Jewish person who needed a paper to a new destination.

For Chinese people, the end of a war that had lasted 14 years was a time of enormous hope. It gave millions the chance to return to the homes from which they had been driven out. But the hope was short-lived. The war with Japan had merely postponed a civil war between the Nationalist government and the Communist People's Liberation Army (PLA) that had begun in the 1920s. Peace talks between the two in the autumn of 1945 produced no results. In November 1945, fighting broke out in Liaoning province over control of Manchuria; in June 1946, it became a full-scale civil war that lasted for three years.

Russian Jews

The situation of the Russian Ashkenazi Jews was slightly different to that of the refugees. During the war, as citizens of a neutral country, the Soviet Union, they had fared better than other Jews; Stalin only declared war on Japan on August 8, 1945. Until then, the Russian Jews had been able to carry on their lives and run their businesses in Harbin, Shanghai and other cities.

"At the time the war ended, the vast majority of the Russian Jews wished to settle in China. Some were preparing to take the good opportunities of (post-war) reconstruction," according to Pan Guang and Wang Jian. (Note 5)

"But, from 1946, the civil war forced many of them to give up hope. The wealthier ones followed the European Jews in emigrating to North America and Australia. In 1948, when relations between the Moscow and the Nationalist government deteriorated, a small number returned to the Soviet Union and the majority went to other countries."

Nonetheless, some Russian Jews stayed in Harbin and Shanghai. In August 1949, two months before the PRC was established, Harbin had 1,600 Russian Jews, down from 2,000 at the end of the war four years earlier. "In October 1949, many of the Russians Jews in Shanghai had not left." (Note 6)

But the situation was not as rosy as they described. Most of the Russian Jews lost their passports after the Bolshevik Revolution of 1917 and de facto became stateless. When the Japanese army in Harbin established the BREM, a White Russian office under their influence, most Jews refused to get new passports there. Without a Russian (Soviet) passport, one could not be employed or enjoy other benefits.

Sephardic Jews

During the war, the Sephardic Jews of Shanghai suffered greatly. The Japanese attack on the city in 1937 had severely affected its trade with the outside world. After Pearl Harbor, those holding British or American nationality were interned and their assets confiscated by the Japanese. After the end of the war, they were able to recover some of their assets and consider how to rebuild their businesses. But the Shanghai of 1945 was a different city to what it had been 10 years before.

In the autumn of 1942, Britain and the United States agreed to give up their extra-territorial rights in China, including those in Shanghai.. France signed a similar agreement in February 1946. This meant that, like other foreigners, the Jews no longer enjoyed legal privileges nor worked in a city under foreign administration.

The surrender of Japan had not brought peace but the resumption of the civil war between the government and the Communists. From 1946, the major Jewish businesses began to move their capital out of the city, mainly to the British colony of Hong Kong, and change their assets into Hong

Kong dollars.

In 1949, Sir Victor Sassoon moved the headquarters of his New Sassoon Company to Nassau, capital of the Bahamas in the Caribbean, and continued to liquidate his assets in Shanghai. "A range of factors determined this choice," said Maise Meyer in her book *Shanghai's Baghdadi Jews*. (Note 7) "Distance from the Communists, minimum income tax and death duties, excellent communications with the rest of the world, a good climate and a vibrant horse-racing circle."

"Sucking the blood and sweat of Chinese"

In *The Sassoon Group in Old China*, published in 1985, two Chinese scholars, Zhang Zhongli and Chen Zengnian (張仲禮、陳曾年), detail how the Sassoon company took its money out. They said that the withdrawal began as early as the 1930s after Japan occupied Manchuria in 1931 and especially after it launched its all-out war in July 1937. The company exchanged assets into sterling that could be easily moved.

"By 1938, this sterling investment had reached 1.15 million pounds. Before the start of the Pacific War (in December 1941), the firm had moved out more than 7.15 million pounds," they said. This money was mainly raised from the sale of shares; it retained most of its Shanghai property. The withdrawal accelerated after the end of the war.

Sir Victor Sassoon gave an interview in Bombay in September 1945 to the Central News Agency (中央社), the official news agency of the

Nationalist government; he said that the era of major development of business in China was over. "In the future, foreigners will only play a helping role. The business will be done by Chinese, not foreigners."

So, from September 1945 until May 1948, tenants of his Shanghai properties had to pay rents to designated foreign banks in U.S. dollars or British pounds; the firm earned US$3 million in rental income during this period. The firm moved its Shanghai businesses to Hong Kong and shifted the capital into HK dollars.

After 1948, this withdrawal accelerated, through sales of shares, factories and property; for example, three prime sites in Shanghai sold to Chinese businessmen raised US$1.28 million. Sassoon sold Villa Eve, his personal villa in Hongqiao Road (虹橋路), for US$120,000

"Because of the speed of the Chinese people's liberation war, the company could not sell all its property shares," Zhang and Chen said. They estimated the company's total profits in China over 100 years at more than 270 million taels (両). Before 1921, it was 140 million taels from trading opium and 22.19 million taels from property. After 1921, it was 108 million taels from property. Sassoon moved earlier and more decisively than other foreign businessmen to move his assets out. (Note 8) For his part, in public statements, Sassoon estimated his losses in China at about 20 million pounds.

This is how Zhang and Chen summarised the century of investment by the Sassoons in China. "The Sassoon group played an important role in the foreign capitalist economic invasion of China. It stuck to the body of China and made itself fat by sucking the blood and sweat of Chinese and devastated the Chinese economy." Through its opium trading, "it devastated the physical and psychological health of China, decaying the body of Chinese society. Its evil influence was unprecedented. It successfully ran away with the vast majority of its income and took it abroad. Most of its investment was not productive ... It introduced very little advanced technology or management or stimulated the development of the commodity economy."

Published in 1985, this book received an award for scientific excellence from the Shanghai City Philosophy Society. It reflected the Marxist view of foreign investors during the pre-1949 period. With an outlook like that, no wonder the new Communist government did not want to pay compensation to these investors.

It also explains why there are no statues of Sassoon in Shanghai or anywhere else in China; on the other hand, many of his buildings were so sturdy and well-designed that they are, in effect, his memorials.

The new Communist government imposed new taxes on owners of property, including a large land tax. It forced foreign companies, such as the Sassoons, to pay by refusing to allow their staff to leave China until they had paid all their bills.

Sir Victor's cousin, Lucien Ovadia, the manager of ED Sassoon & Co, was not able to leave until 1953. "He got an exit permit only after he made final arrangements for paying the government a huge sum for giving them the Cathay Hotel ... in 1958, Sir Victor's extensive holdings in Shanghai were written off, including his three Shanghai hotels which the new government now used as offices." (Note 9)

One carpet and six brandy glasses

In 1948, as a Communist victory looked increasingly probable, the sell-off accelerated. Mao Zedong saw the Soviet Union as the model for his new state: the government controlled the economy and allowed little or no place for private business, especially that owned by "foreign imperialists".

Like the Sassoons, the Kadoorie family moved to Hong Kong. "From 1948, the Communists came," recalled Sir Michael Kadoorie, the current head of the family. "Many lost everything. My family came out with one carpet and six brandy glasses." (Note 10)

The Kadoorie family was better placed than most, because it had long-established businesses in Hong Kong, especially in hotels and electric power. It received no compensation from the new government for its extensive assets in Shanghai; these included office blocks, schools and apartment buildings, as well as the palatial family home, the Marble Hall.

After the victory, the home was used as the Allied headquarters, with senior American and British officers staying there; it also housed diplomats and visiting dignitaries. Following the Communist takeover, Song Qing-ling, widow of Dr Sun Yat-sen, asked Lawrence Kadoorie if he would donate the mansion to the new government. Without much alternative, he said yes. It has now become a Children's Palace, where young people are trained in arts. Lord Lawrence Kadoorie graciously said later: "It is pleasing to know that this house, of which my father was particularly fond, is now used by thousands of happy children benefitting from the classes provided." (Note 11)

Despite their substantial losses, the family has since 1949 been careful to maintain good relations with the PRC. In 1985, its China Light & Power (CLP) Company invested in a joint-venture nuclear power plant in Daya Bay, close to Hong Kong; it was the first nuclear station in China and one of the earliest and largest joint-venture projects under the "open door" policy. CLP owns a stake of 25 per cent.

Lord Kadoorie played a role in the Sino-British negotiations ahead of Hong Kong's return to China in 1997. In 2009, the Peninsula Hotel opened in Shanghai, a brother to the one in Hong Kong. Its location at the top of the Bund (外灘) – a prime site – seemed to many a recognition by the government of the support the Kadoorie family had given over the years.

Hyperinflation and strikes

What drove the Jews and other foreign business people out was not only the intensifying civil war but also the hyperinflation and labour disputes that resulted from it.

Immediately after the war, industry in Shanghai recovered. Factories seized by the Japanese were returned to their original owners. After years of shortages, the domestic market needed many goods, as did markets in Southeast Asia.

But, in 1947, in order to curb an outflow of foreign exchange, the government introduced restrictions on industry. Inflation carried over from the war began to climb in 1946. Taking September 1945 as the base, wholesale prices in Shanghai had increased five-fold by February 1946, 11-fold by May and 30-fold by February 1947.

In 1946, there were 1,716 strikes and other labour disputes in the city; the Communists had infiltrated many unions and encouraged strikes. Factories had to pay increasing amounts of money to buy raw materials and pay wages indexed to inflation. To pay for a war it was losing, the government printed more and more money.

Inflation worsened in 1948: taking May 1947 as 100, the wholesale price index in Shanghai reached 2,100 in May 1948 and 11,100 in July. In August, a standard large sack of rice weighing 171 pounds (western equivalent) cost 63 million yuan. Hyperinflation killed investment and production; the economy turned to barter and hoarding. In 1948, manufacturers began to move their operations to Guangzhou and Hong Kong. This hyperinflation and the increasing likelihood of a Communist victory persuaded many business people, Chinese and foreign, including Jews, that they had no future in the mainland.

The model for the Chinese Communist Party was the Soviet Union; on taking power, the Soviets had nationalised private business and confiscated foreign companies and factories, without compensation. That was what most business people expected Mao's party to do.

Despite their 100 years in the city and contribution to many sectors of its economy, the Jews could expect treatment no different to other foreign business people. In late May 1949, Shanghai fell to the People's Liberation Army after only token resistance. The better off were those who left early and got something in exchange for their assets; many lost all they had.

Palestine

The hope for many Jews in China, as in other countries, was a new homeland in Palestine.

In 1946, Zionists in Shanghai founded a branch of Irgun, a paramilitary organisation set up in Israel in 1931. Their aim was to drive the British out of Palestine. Edward Nissim, a prominent member of the Sephardic community, provided a building and compound in the French Concession of the city for meetings and training. In April 1947, unwilling and unable to control an increasingly chaotic and dangerous conflict between Jews and Arabs in Palestine, the British government asked the General Assembly of the United Nations to take over.

In November that year, the General Assembly accepted a plan to partition the Holy Land, with separate states for Jews and Arabs. The British finally withdrew in May 1948.

On 14 May 1948, the day the last British forces left from Haifa, David Ben-Gurion proclaimed the establishment of the state of Israel. The next day the armies of five Arab states invaded the new country. The Jews in China followed these developments with the same intensity as their brothers and sisters around the world. In September 1948, members of the Shanghai Irgun boarded a Dutch airline to Marseilles; they later arrived in Israel, where they took part in fighting the Egyptian army in the Negev desert.

The government of Israel moved quickly to help the Jews of Shanghai come to their new country; it desperately needed new citizens as soldiers and to build the state in the face of its many enemies.

In December 1948, Moshe Yuval, Israeli vice-consul in New York, moved to Shanghai as representative of the Ministry of Immigration; he had the power to issue visas. It was a matter of urgency. That month the Jewish Agency chartered two ships *Wooster Victory* and *Anna Salem* to carry people to Israel; they were the first vessels to go from Shanghai to the new state. The Jewish Agency in Jerusalem also transported people in aeroplanes.

Thanks to these efforts, several thousand Jews from Shanghai made *aliyah*. "The majority of the Jewish community left Shanghai during 1948-49 and about 20 per cent of them came to Israel," it said. (Note 12)

The Israeli representatives in Shanghai issued an estimated 7,000 Israeli passports and visas; 4,000 to 5,000 people actually emigrated to Israel, mostly Russian Jews and refugees from Europe. (Note 13)

With this rapid decline in the community, its leaders closed the facilities it had used for many decades. On February 1, 1949 the committee of stewards of the Jewish Club donated the club to the government of Israel. On May 4, it was also given ownership of the Ohel Moshe synagogue in Shanghai.

Under the Red Star

On October 1, 1949, Mao Zedong (毛澤東) proclaimed the People's Republic of China from the Tiananmen (天安門) gate in central Beijing, in front of the former Imperial Palace. His revolution had defeated the Republic of China that had replaced the Qing dynasty in 1911.

Mao vowed to build a new country on the model of the Soviet Union, in which the state controlled the economy, and to eliminate the foreign capitalists who had dominated much of it for the previous 100 years. The new government proclaimed atheism as its ideology, calling religion "the opium of the people", in the words of Karl Marx.

The new government recognised only five religions – Buddhism, Taoism, Islam, Protestantism and Catholicism – and created official institutions to manage them, led by government-appointed leaders. Judaism was not one of the five.

Our Life, a Russian-language Jewish magazine published in Shanghai.

Tagar, biweekly magazine, in English and Russian, of the Beitar movement in Shanghai from 1946-1948.

In October 1950, Mao ordered Chinese forces to cross the Yalu River to join with the North Korean military in its war with the South and its U.N. allies; it marked the start of a cold war and trade embargo with the West that lasted nearly 30 years. It was in these western countries that a majority of the world's Jews lived; and it was with these countries that Jewish companies in China had done most of their trade.

The atmosphere in China became increasingly anti-western. Mao launched terrifying political campaigns against landlords, "counter-revolutionaries", "rightists" and secret religious organisations. In 1956, the state took over all private businesses as part of its "transformation' into a Socialist economy. Was there a place for Jews in this new world?

The answer was very little, except for a small number of those who had joined the Communist revolution and devoted themselves to its service. Jewish entrepreneurs could no longer run their own companies and factories; finance and trade with the outside world was tightly controlled by the government. So they decided to make their future abroad.

According to Professors Pan and Wang, there were between 5,000 and 10,000 Jews in China in 1949, the majority of them Russian Jews; many held passports of the Soviet Union. Over the next 10 years, they left once they could find a place in a new country. According to the Council of the Jewish Community of Shanghai, 364 Jews left China in 1952, of whom 99 went to Israel; in 1953, the figure was 301, 201 for Israel; in 1955, it was 169, 49 for Israel and 87 for the Soviet Union. At the end of 1955, the Jewish Club in Shanghai closed and donated its more than 3,000 books to the Israeli Ministry of Education and Culture. In July 1956, the community sold its synagogue on Route Tenant de la Tour and donated its holy scrolls and other religious items to the Israeli government.

In Harbin, at the end of 1953, there were 453 Jews; some left for the Soviet Union and, by the end of 1955, there were less than 100 left. The remnants of the once thriving Jewish community were forced to sell the New Synagogue that was opened in 1921 to representatives of the government. Between 1958 and 1962, the old Jewish cemetery was being demolished. Out of approximately 3,300 graves there, about 830 tombstones were relocated to a new site at the Huangshan Public Cemetery at the outskirts of the city.

In 1960, the Old (Main) Synagogue had no rabbi or religious ceremonies and closed. The Podolsky family was the last to leave Harbin. They obtained papers and were able to emigrate to Israel, marking the end of more than 60 years of Jewish life there.

Political events in China further accelerated the departure. One was the Great Leap Forward (1958-1962), which provoked a Great Famine in which up to 36 million died of hunger. Another was the Sino-Soviet split of 1960; this made it difficult for Jews holding Soviet passports to remain.

The final blow was the Cultural Revolution which broke out in 1966; all foreigners had to leave China. "In New China, there was no anti-Semitism as there was in Europe," said Pan & Wang. (Note 14) "The Chinese government and people maintained friendly relations with the Jews in the country and actively helped them go to the country of their choice, assisting them in the procedures."

Others put it in a different way – "foreign cleansing": there were no Jews in China, so there was no anti-Semitism.

Three generations in Harbin

The Soviet army occupied Harbin from 1945 to 1947. Synagogues remained open to serve the dwindling Jewish community. In 1949, the Chief Rabbi of Harbin and the Jewish Communities in the Far East, Aharon Moshe Kiselev, passed away at the age of 63; a learned and charismatic leader, he had served in the city since 1913.

The Communist revolution had a profound impact on the Jews, as it did on everyone else in China. The new government promoted atheism and officially recognised five religions; Judaism was not one of them. It nationalised private business, the main economic activity of the community. So most of the Jews of Harbin left for Israel, the U.S., Australia and other countries.

The Moustafines had been in Harbin since 1909, when the first member of the family arrived from Byelorussia, according to Mara Moustafine, an Australian. (Note 15) The family stayed on during the post-war period and after the establishment of the PRC.

"In 1956, my family started to make concrete plans to leave Harbin,"

Mara Moustafine said. "With one campaign being rolled out after another, like many other Russians, they found it difficult to adapt to life in Harbin with an increasingly Maoist flavour. By that time, my parents, both graduates from the Harbin Polytechnical Institute's new faculty of Oriental Studies and fluent in Mandarin, had spent several years as technical interpreters working with the Sugar Refineries Construction Bureau. They had resisted first the invitation, then pressure to repatriate to the Soviet Union as part of Khrushchev's 'Virgin Land' campaign. Now they were at risk of being sacked from their job. Even so they refused to contemplate the proposition of taking me to the Soviet Union to build the 'socialist paradise'."

To pre-empt the nationalisation of private business, her grandfather, Motya Zaretsky, and his partners had sold their meat and livestock businesses. In 1951, he had become director and manager of cash transactions at the Jewish Bank in Harbin; he later took on the additional role of performing the kosher slaughter of animals for the dwindling Jewish community.

"Our exit options were twofold – Israel, where some of the Zaretskys had gone on aliyah, or Australia, which was one of the few countries taking Russian refugees at that time. It took a while to obtain visas, co-ordinate the exit and entry permits required and conclude all formalities."

The family played its role in the Great Leap Forward; it fed scrap metal into the neighbourhood furnace and clattered saucepans on the roof to eliminate sparrows.

"By the time we departed for Sydney in 1959, the Russian community in Harbin had dwindled to a couple of thousand and a couple of hundred Jews. Some of our relatives, unable to secure visas earlier, left China in 1964, bearing the repercussions of the breakdown of relations between China and the Soviet Union in the early 1960s."

In 1958, the Jewish cemetery that had opened in 1903 had 3,173 graves; that year the city government decided to move it to a new site in Huangshan in an eastern suburb, with 836 square metres of space and 677 spaces. It is administered by the city's Civil Affairs Bureau. According to the *NHH* magazine, "today it is the most complete and best preserved Jewish cemetery in the Far East."

The tombstones have Hebrew inscriptions. "In 1940, there were only 2,800 Jews in Harbin. After the founding of 'New China', the members continued to leave, the synagogues closed one after another and the Jewish residential area ceased to exist. They left behind Jewish buildings in the European style, including hotels, hospitals, school, businesses and apartments." (Note 16)

The last member of the Harbin community was Hannah Agre, a musician, who died in 1985, aged 76. Her father had fled pogroms in the Ukraine in the early 20th century, married a Siberian woman and settled in Harbin, where he worked on the railroad and later in a factory.

Hannah was born in the city and lived there her whole life. But she never learnt Chinese; she spoke Russian and Yiddish. In an interview with *The*

New York Times in February 1983, she said that she had worked for a wealthy family with a big house; she married a Russian sailor in 1938, but the two later separated.

For more than 20 years, she lived in the same room; during the Cultural Revolution, she endured harassment by the Red Guards. "I do not want to go to Israel or the Soviet Union and, 20 years ago, turned down an offer to resettle in Denmark," she said. "I am officially 'stateless'," she said. (Note 17) Her passing marked the death of the last Jew in Harbin.

"Friends of China"

A very small number of Jews stayed throughout the tumultuous first three decades of the Communist state. They strongly supported and participated in the revolution and dedicated their lives to it. Today Beijing remembers them with affection and respect, especially because they remained and suffered during periods of intense xenophobia; some spent years in prison.

One of them was Sidney Shapiro, who was born in Brooklyn, New York in December 1915. He graduated from St John's Law School and practiced as a lawyer in New York for four years. He was disturbed by the great inequalities of the U.S. during the Depression. During World War Two, the Army recruited him to study Mandarin. Before he could use his skills, the war ended; he moved to Shanghai in April 1947 to work as a lawyer.

He met and became sympathetic to the revolutionaries and secretly helped

A letter of recommendation by the Tientsin (Tianjin) Hebrew Association for one of its employees who is leaving the city to emigrate to Israel, dated 31/5/1949.

the underground members of the Communist Party in the city. He met and fell in love with Feng zi (鳳子), an actress, author and Communist sympathiser; they married in May 1948. He edited an English-language magazine promoting land reform and helped break a government blockade preventing medicines entering areas controlled by the Communists.

The two moved to Beijing just before it fell to the PLA; they were invited to attend Mao Zedong's proclamation of the new state at Tiananmen Gate on October 1, 1949. Sidney Shapiro became a Chinese citizen in 1963, thanks to the approval of Premier Zhou Enlai (周恩來); he was one of the very few foreigners to receive this honour. He and his wife had three children and he later wrote that, living in revolutionary China, he had finally found a sense of purpose.

He became a translator of Chinese poetry, novels and short stories into English; he translated more than 20. He served on the Chinese People's Political Consultative Conference, also a rare honour for a foreigner. During the Cultural Revolution, his wife was sent to perform forced labour outside Beijing in 1969 and only allowed occasional visits home before her release in 1975. He himself succeeded in avoiding imprisonment; in 1971, he visited his family in the U.S. for the first time. His wife died in 1996.

"He was always very opposed to U.S. capitalism, hypocrisy and inequality and he got disillusioned as China got more that way," said Ted Plafker, a Beijing-based journalist and long-time friend. He died on October 18, 2014, aged 98. (Note 18)

Sidney Shapiro and his wife Feng zi

Israel Epstein was born on April 20, 1915 in Warsaw, capital of Poland, then under Russian control. His parents were Jewish Socialists, both members of the Bund, the Jewish Labour Alliance. His father, Lazar, was arrested five times and imprisoned by the Tsar's police for leading a labour uprising; his mother was arrested at the age of 16 and exiled to Siberia. She managed to escape, all the way to Paris, where she was reunited with Lazar.

They returned to Poland where they married. After the outbreak of World War One, his father was sent by his company to develop business in the Pacific. As the German Army approached, his mother fled the city with her baby son in her arms.

After a reunion, the two and their 18-month-old son made Harbin their home for almost two years; then they settled in Tianjin. At the age of 15, he began his career as a journalist, working for an English-language newspaper; he covered China's war with Japan for United Press International and other western news media and was often near the front line. He covered the battle of Taierzhuang (台兒莊) in April 1938; it was the first major Chinese victory of the war which broke the myth of Japanese military invincibility. The Japanese lost more than 11,000 men; the Chinese captured 31 pieces of artillery, 11 armoured cars, eight armored fighting vehicles, 1,000 machine guns and 10,000 rifles.

In Hong Kong, Epstein met Song Qing-ling (宋慶齡), the widow of Sun Yat-sen. In 1944, she arranged for him to visit the base in northwest China where Mao Zedong and his comrades were leading their revolution.

Epstein later said that long conversations in a cave with Mao changed his life. Between 1944 and 1949, he lived in the U.S. where he published *The Unfinished Revolution in China*; it was well reviewed. In 1951, he accepted the invitation of Song Qing-ling to return to China to edit a magazine called *China Reconstructs*, later called *China Today*. He was editor-in-chief until his retirement at 70.

In 1957, he became a Chinese citizen and in 1964 joined the Communist Party. During the Cultural Revolution, he and his British-born wife were jailed for five years, on charges of "plotting against (Premier) Zhou Enlai"; he was kept in solitary confinement. He was released in 1973, given a personal apology by Zhou himself and restored to his previous post.

Every year he met and held talks with Chairman Mao. He served on government and party committees. In 1996, he told the British *Observer* newspaper: "My basic ideas have not changed. I see no reason to change them." He wrote a book *My China Eye*, published by Long River Press of San Francisco in 2005; it recounted his extraordinary life. "At the end of the day, I remain a Marxist," he wrote on the concluding page. (Note 19)

Epstein died on May 26, 2005, aged 90, and was buried in the Babaoshan (八寶山) cemetery in Beijing, a place reserved for senior members of the Communist Party. Of his 90 years, he lived 82 in China. Like Shapiro, he remained loyal to the country and the party he had joined, despite all the things it had done to hurt him and its people during his lifetime.

A third was Sidney Rittenberg. He was born on August 14, 1921 into a prominent Jewish family in Charleston, South Carolina. He attended the University of North Carolina at Chapel Hill, where he majored in philosophy. In 1942, he joined the Army and was sent to its Far Eastern Language and Area School, where he learnt Chinese; and he was sent to China in 1944.

Shortly after arrival, Rittenberg was sent to bring a cheque for US$26 to the family of a girl killed by a drunken U.S. soldier; despite its devastation, the family gave him US$6 for his help. He was deeply touched.

After the end of the war, he stayed on as part of the United Nations famine relief programme and met Communist leaders in Yenan in 1946. Like Epstein, he was transformed by the experience. He earned the trust of the leaders and worked for them as a translator, for Radio Peking, the Xinhua News Agency and translating the works of Mao. He was an active participant in the revolution.

From 1949 to 1955, he was held in solitary confinement on suspicion of being a member of a spy network; for one year, he was kept in a completely dark room. He was released as a result of the death of Josef Stalin in March 1953.

He became a prominent party propagandist and middleman with foreign journalists and VIPs. During the Cultural Revolution, he was politically active. But in February 1968, he was arrested again and held until November 1977. In March 1980, with his Chinese wife and four children, he moved back to the United States, where he worked as a professor.

Rittenberg and his wife set up a consulting firm that provides assistance to businesses that work with Chinese firms. In 1993, he wrote a book about his experiences called *The Man Who Stayed Behind*. He and his wife settled in Arizona, in the southwest.

In an interview published in the *Financial* Times in January 2013, Rittenberg gave this assessment of Mao: "China has to face the fact that Mao was a monster, one of the worst people in human history. He was a genius, but his genius got completely out of control ... He gave himself the right to conduct social experiments that involved upturning the lives of hundreds of millions of people, when he did not know what the outcome might be. And that created famines in which tens of millions died, and a revolution in which nobody knows how many died."

But Rittenberg defended the achievements of the Communist government. "The regime has lifted more people out of poverty than has ever been done before. They've solved food, shelter and clothing. The percentage of people living below that line is below that in America." (Note 20)

These three men played an important role as spokesmen for China, especially during the Cold War, when the country had no diplomatic relations with the West and travel between the two was extremely restricted.

Through their books, newspapers and magazines, they presented a positive picture of "New China". They met foreign journalists, dignitaries and other visitors and explained what was happening in language they could easily understand.

While many in the West were vilifying Communism, they described the successes and achievements of the new state. In the event, the "New China" has not turned out the way they imagined in the idealistic days of the 1940s; it has become more capitalist than the U.S. they chose to reject. But all three left a mark on history far deeper than if they had remained in their own countries.

Notes

1   *Escape and Rescue, Jewish Refugees and Shanghai in World War II* (逃 亡 與 拯救：二戰中的猶太難民與上海), by Wang Jian (王健), Shanghai Jiaotong University Press (上海交通大學出版社), 2016, pages 279-285; and *The Jews and China* (猶太人與中國) by Professors Pan Guang (潘光) and Wang Jian (王健), Shishi Publishing Company (時事出版社), 2009, page 225-226.

2   Ernest Heppner, *Refuge in Shanghai*, University of Nebraska Press, 1993, page 163.

3   "Jewish Immigration after the Second World War", by Suzanne Rutland, in the Journal of the History Teachers'Association, University of Sydney, New South Wales, 2006.

4   Article in *Manitoba History*, by Michael R. Angel, Elizabeth Dafoe Library, University of Manitoba, Number 7, Spring 1984.

5   Pan Guang and Wang Jian, page 228.

6   Pan Guang and Wang Jian, page 229.

7   *Shanghai's Baghdadi Jews*, by Maisie Meyer, Blacksmith Books, 2015, page 295.

8   *The Sassoon Group in Old China* (沙遜集團在舊中國), by Zhang Zhongli (張仲禮) and Chen Zengnian (陳曾年), People's Publishing Company (人民出版社), 1985.

9   Maisie Meyer, page 295.

10   Sir Michael Kadoorie, Fireside Chat 16/12/2008 from the library of the Jewish Community Centre, Hong Kong.

11   Maisie Meyer, page 141.

12   *The Chronology of the Jews of Shanghai*, by the Jewish Community of China.

13   Pan Guang and Wang Jian, page 228.

14   Pan Guang and Wang Jian, page 233.

15   Paper by Mara Moustafine, "My family and its city: 50 years in Harbin," given

at an international seminar on the History and Culture of Harbin Jews at the Shangri-La Hotel, Harbin on August 3 - September 2, 2004.

16   *National Humanities magazine* (國家人文雜誌), July 2016, page 123.

17   *The New York Times*, 27/2/1983.

18   *National Humanities* magazine, 1/4/2017.

19   *My China Eye*, by Israel Epstein, Long River, 2005, page 342.

20   *Financial Times*, 12/1/2003.

Courting Beijing for 42 years

7

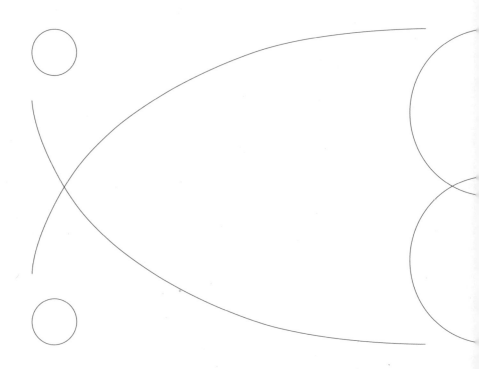

From

STRANGERS

The state of Israel was born on May 14, 1948. Within ten months, it was recognised by the Republic of China, which voted to admit it as a member of the United Nations in May 1949. But it took 42 years to set up diplomatic relations with the People's Republic of China (PRC), which was established on October 1, 1949.

Israel made great efforts to achieve this, especially from the 1980s onwards, promoting trade and people-to-people exchanges and selling arms; but, for most of that time, China was hostile and reluctant. This chapter explains why it took more than four decades for the couple to come to the altar.

Seeking Friends

When the state of Israel was created, it was immediately invaded by the armies of five Arab states. Fighting lasted a year before a ceasefire was declared. The new country desperately needed foreign friends and supporters. None was more important than the five permanent members of the United Nations Security Council – the United States, the Soviet Union, France, Britain and China. The aim of the Israeli government was to establish the best relations it could with these five nations and as rapidly as possible; it did not expect peace with its Arab neighbours to last.

TO FRIENDS

In May 1948, the Nationalist government in Nanjing – the Republic of China (RoC) – still controlled the mainland, although it was losing the civil war with the Communists.

The Jewish community had always had good relations with the RoC. As early as December 1918, the government had expressed its support for the Balfour Declaration 13 months earlier. In April 1920, Dr Sun Yat-sen, father of the Chinese Republic, wrote a letter of support for the Zionist movement. This was repeated in July 1947 by his son Sun Ke (孫科), Vice President and President of the Legislative Yuan (立法院).

There was traditional friendship between the two sides and, in China, no powerful Muslim lobby nor history of anti-Semitism, except among some Japanese and White Russians. On the critical vote at the United Nations in November 1947 on partitioning the Holy Land, the RoC abstained. On March 1, 1949, the RoC recognised Israel. On May 11 that year, it voted with a majority of members of the United Nations General Assembly to admit Israel as a member of the U.N.

In the summer of 1949, the Nationalist government fled to Taiwan; Chairman Mao proclaimed the People's Republic of China (PRC) on October 1, 1949. Countries in the West hesitated; they did not want to recognise a new Communist state and a close ally of the Soviet Union. They had backed the Nationalist side in the civil war.

But Israel had taken no position in that war and had no historical ties with the RoC; more important was recognition from foreign powers, especially large ones.

So, on January 9, 1950, Foreign Minister Moshe Sharett announced that Israel had decided to recognise the PRC as the de jure government of China, becoming the first state in the Middle East to do so. It would be six years before the second one, Egypt, in May 1956; Syria and Yemen followed that summer.

But the PRC did not reciprocate and recognise Israel. This was despite the fact that the countries had no conflict of interest; like the Nationalists, the Communist leaders had not opposed the ideals of Zionism. It was not so much a policy decision; rather, the new government had more urgent matters to address in its first months in power.

In June 1950, representatives of the two governments met in Moscow to discuss how to proceed. That same month, the Korean War broke out; the United States led military forces from allied members of the United Nations to support the southern side. In October, China sent its army to support the North.

The U.S. imposed a trade embargo against China and the Cold War froze Sino-American relations. Under heavy pressure from the U.S., Israel suspended its talks with the PRC.

Declassified Chinese Foreign Ministry documents have revealed that, by 1953, Beijing had decided to ally with Arab and Muslim countries and give up relations with Israel. In 1953 and 1954, China and Israel held

Foreign Minister Moshe Sharett, who announced in January 1950 that Israel had decided to recognise the People's Republic of China.

talks in Moscow, Helsinki, London and Rangoon, where the ambassadors of the two countries met occasionally. Opinion in Israel was divided; some feared the talks would affect the country's relations with Washington.

Non-aligned and pro-Muslim

Then came the Bandung Conference in Indonesia in April 1955, a watershed in the diplomacy of the young PRC. This was the first large-scale conference involving African and Asia countries; 29 took part, representing a combined population of 1.5 billion, with the aim of creating a movement aligned with neither the West nor the Soviet Union.

The PRC played an important role in the conference, which was attended by seven Arab countries; the participants vetoed invitations to Israel and to Taiwan. As a result, Beijing gained great acceptance from the Arab world. Its foreign policy became increasingly anti-colonial and revolutionary.

It strongly criticised Israel's military intervention in Egypt in October 1956, when it crossed the Suez Canal to support British and French forces. For the next 20 years, China's relations deepened with the Arab world. It became a hostile and virulent critic of Israel and provided the Palestine Liberation Organisation (PLO) with arms and military training.

At the same time, Israel's ties with its Arab neighbours worsened; they fought wars in 1967 and 1973. The Beijing media described Israel as "a tool of imperialist aggression" and "a Zionist entity". There was no direct contact between the two countries – neither direct trade nor postal or telecommunications links. In 1965, the Palestine Liberation Organisation opened an office in Beijing. And in October 1971, the PRC replaced Taiwan at the United Nations, in the General Assembly and the Security Council; it needed the votes of Arab states to support its diplomatic agenda.

Israel continued to try to build bridges to Beijing. In 1973, after the worst years of the Cultural Revolution, it opened a consulate in Hong Kong, as a conduit to China. But, two years later, it withdrew the consul-general due to lack of progress in Israel-PRC relations and a lack of funds. The consulate remained open, though, with a local Jewish businessman as honorary consul and supported by the local Jewish community.

Finally, the death of Mao Zedong (毛澤東) in September 1976 ended the revolutionary era and made possible a different foreign policy. Beijing praised Egyptian President Anwar Sadat for his historic visit to Israel in November 1977 and the peace treaty he signed with it in March 1979.

From 1980, Beijing published different plans to solve the Middle East crisis and create good relations between Israel and the Palestinians. It was moving from supporting only one side toward a more neutral position.

Another factor in China's change of heart was its split with the Soviet Union from 1960; Moscow turned from being Beijing's main ally to its principal enemy.

A third was the fact that the post-Mao leaders believed that the country's biggest problem was economic backwardness; this profoundly changed its foreign policy.

Military wake-up call

On February 1979, Chinese forces invaded Vietnam, to protest its occupation of Cambodia the year before. They were the first combat operations of the People's Liberation Army since the end of the Korean War in 1953. After four weeks of intense fighting, China withdrew. It announced that it had achieved its objectives – but Vietnam did not end its occupation of Cambodia.

The heavy losses of the war were a severe shock to Beijing; western estimates put the number of Chinese casualties at up to 28,000 dead and 43,000 wounded. The Chinese leaders realised the backwardness of the PLA after three decades of revolutionary rhetoric and isolation from the developed world.

They could not buy advanced weapons, equipment and technology from the U.S. and its European allies. But they could procure them through third parties. With the most advanced military industry in the Middle East and as a major buyer of American arms and equipment, Israel was a very attractive vendor. It had a unique experience of fighting Soviet weapons.

These military ties became an important factor in the improvement of bilateral relations. On February 22, 1979, an Israeli military-industrial delegation left for Beijing; it was the start of Israeli arms sales to China. These important visitors were housed in a military facility outside the capital; the Friendship Store (友誼商店), the most important shop for foreigners, had to be opened specially at night for them to make purchases, so that they would not be seen. This visit was kept secret for many years.

As Professor Yitzhak Shichor wrote: "Within a few years, China became Israel's largest arms market, a substitute for the loss of the significant Iranian market, following the downfall of the Shah in 1979 as well as for the loss of the South African arms market a few years later. Arms sales were important not only militarily but also politically as they laid the foundations and contributed to the goodwill that led, after a 42-year delay, to the establishment of full Sino-Israeli diplomatic relations." (Note 1)

The new administration under Deng Xiaoping (鄧小平) from 1978 realised how backward China was in many fields, not only the military. His open-door policy aimed to attract foreign investment, technology and management. This was another opportunity for Israel; if it could not have political relations, it had much to offer China in other fields, like agriculture, solar energy, science, technology and medicine.

The man who knew everyone

The pioneer of bilateral trade in the 1980s was Shaul Eisenberg, whose links to the Far East went back to World War Two. He was born in September 1921 in Munich to a religious Jewish family from Poland. He narrowly escaped the Nazi invasion of Holland by boarding a freighter in Rotterdam for Shanghai, with 20 florins in his pocket. Finding that the purser would not sell anything to the passengers, he bought liquor and cigarettes from him and sold them to the Chinese crew and passengers, earning US$500 by the time he reached Shanghai.

He lived there for a period; then he moved to Kobe, home to the largest Jewish community in Japan. There he fell in love with the daughter of a Japanese woman and a Viennese artist who had come to Japan before World War One and been commissioned to do portraits of the emperor; he married her and she converted to Judaism.

He had arrived in Shanghai with almost nothing; but he was extremely resourceful and made money from trading many types of goods. In Japan, he started by selling Chinese carpets. After the end of World War Two, most Jewish refugees from Europe chose to leave China and Japan; but Eisenberg stayed and earned his first fortune.

He set up a company that imported iron ore and scrap metal from the Philippines, the United States and South America to supply the giant Yawata Corporation (八幡製鐵所), later Nippon Steel (新日本製鐵株式會社). He also set up houseware factories and supplied Japanese televisions to the United States.

In the late 1950s, he moved to South Korea, where he helped to secure western financing for more than 30 development projects at a time when few foreign banks wanted to lend. For his efforts, he received the nation's highest medal. In 1968, he moved with his family to Israel; there he founded the Israel Corporation, which became one of the country's largest holding companies.

In the late 1970s, he became interested in China, then an implacable enemy of Israel and a mystery for western companies. "Shaul Eisenberg was a most unusual figure in the international business world," said Avraham Shohat, a former Finance Minister. "For decades, he was active in places where western businessmen never went."

He was one of the earliest Israeli, or foreign, businessmen to enter the China market. In 1983, he invested in Shanghai Yaohua Pilkington Glass (耀華—皮爾金頓玻璃廠), one of the first Sino-foreign joint ventures in the city.

He dealt in many commodities, including arms, vegetable oil, baby oil and fertilizer, of which Israel has large deposits in the Dead Sea; he invested in a large potassium plant in Qinghai (青海) in west China. His private Boeing 707, with its own crew, was one of the first to be allowed to land in China.

Eisenberg was an important broker for sales of Israeli arms to China in the 1980s, before such sales could be done directly. He was an ideal person for this – with good connections to government leaders in both countries but holding no official position in the Israeli government.

He was also discreet, an important virtue at a time when Beijing was in public a strong supporter of Arab causes and such sales had to be kept secret. He set up an office of his UDI trading firm in Beijing and, when he stayed there, lived in a two-bedroom apartment at the Lido Hotel (麗都酒店), next to the road to the international airport. He used a Mercedes with a driver of long standing.

"Work was his life, more important than anything," one associate told me at that time. "I do not think UDI will last a long time. It depended entirely on his personal connections. It was a one-man band all over the world. He knew all the people from ministers down. He was the only one to close the deal.

"He was not charismatic nor good at making speeches, but he had an excellent business instinct and vision. He was always thinking globally, in deals involving three or four countries. He liked difficult markets. He worked in Japan when it was closed and arrived early in China, arranging deals for other people."

Heads of state, ministers, bankers and financiers would take his calls without hesitation. He suffered from heart disease but worked until the last day. His staff described him as difficult to work with and a person who did not delegate and wanted to control everything in his office.

"He travelled the world in a private plane," one of his staff told me. "He had access to leaders of many countries. Sometimes they called him while he was flying through their airspace and asked him if he had time to land and discuss projects they wanted to present to him."

Eisenberg avoided the media and rarely gave interviews, preferring to do his business out of the public view. But once, thanks to the introduction of a Chinese friend, I was able to meet him once in Beijing, on condition that everything he said was off the record. He would not discuss his business dealings; he described his strong feelings for both China and Japan, countries which had sheltered the Jews, including himself, during World War Two.

"Chinese and Japanese admire and respect the Jews," he said. Both countries played an important part in his business success. He died in his apartment at the Lido Hotel in March 1997, aged 76. The range of his connections in China was evident from the wreaths presented to his office at a memorial service – the Foreign Ministry, the Ministry of Metallurgy, the Non-Ferrous Metals General Corporation, the Beijing city government and subway firm and the State Power Company. There were also wreaths from China North Industries (NORINCO, 中國北方工業公司), one of China's biggest arms dealers, and Zhang Aiping (張愛萍), a former Defence Minister.

Three days before his death, he had signed an agreement to establish a diamond exchange in Shanghai. He told reporters at the signing: "We picked Shanghai for this exchange because the city has very friendly relations with Israel. During World War Two, it helped many Jewish people, including myself."

Today both Yaohua Pilkington Glass, which listed on the Shanghai stock market in 1993, and the Shanghai Diamond Exchange are flourishing.

Building Taiwan's nuclear industry and defence

Beijing paid a small price for its decades of hostility to Israel. One result was to allow its enemy Taiwan to acquire advanced arms and expertise in military and nuclear power from Israel. According to the Stockholm International Peace Research Institute, between 1980 and 1992, Israel sold US$850 million worth of arms to Taiwan, accounting for 10.7 per cent of its arms imports, second to the U.S. with US$5.54 billion, 69.7 per cent.

From the 1960s, Israel supplied a wide variety of weapons, including 200 Gabriel missiles in 1979; Taiwan also bought the technology to produce them at home and, by 1992, had manufactured 523, under the name Hsiung Feng (雄風), and 77 launchers. It also bought 450 Shafrir-2 missiles to arm its U.S.-made F-100 and F-105 fighters. Other purchases included: Uzi submachine guns and Dvora-class fast patrol boats which Taiwan used as the prototype for its Seagull fast attack missile craft; LAR-160 multiple rocket launchers; Galil rifles and a variety of electronic equipment.

Israel also helped Taiwan in another important sector – the nuclear industry. Its teacher was Ernst David Bergmann, first chairman of the Israel Atomic Energy Commission. In 2016, Israeli Professor Yitzhak Shichor wrote an excellent paper entitled: "Ernst David Bergmann and Israel's Role in Taiwan's Defense". (Note 2) "Bergmann played a significant role in Taiwan's nuclear and missile programmes. In Taiwan, he maintained close relations with President Chiang Kai-shek (蔣介石) and its military-technological-scientific complex."

The Hsiung Feng missile of the Taiwan armed forces, at a military parade in Taipei; it was built with Israeli technology.

He first visited the island in 1961; Chiang wanted to use his knowledge of nuclear energy and nuclear weapons. In 1958, Israel had begun construction of a heavy-water nuclear reactor in the Negev desert, 13 kilometres southeast of the city of Dimona; it went into operation between 1962 and 1964. The government has always maintained a policy of "nuclear ambiguity" – it refuses to confirm or deny possession of nuclear weapons. Experts believe it had produced its first nuclear weapon by 1967 and may now possess several hundred.

The PRC exploded its first nuclear weapon in October 1964, a breakthrough that terrified President Chiang in Taiwan. He wanted to develop such weapons but doubted whether the Americans would allow him to. In early 1965, Bergmann paid a secret seven-day visit to Taiwan; for two days, he met Chiang and his son Chiang Ching-kuo (蔣經國) then Defence Minister. The talks were held at the Sun Moon Lake (日月潭) in central Taiwan, in an attempt to avoid the many American spies – Taiwanese as well as Caucasian – on the island.

High-level Taiwan delegations visited Israel's top scientific and military institutes and companies. In August 1968, Bergman visited Taiwan again and spent one hour with President Chiang. In 1969, he assisted the island in buying a 40-kw Canada Deuterium Uranium atomic research reactor from Canada. President Chiang died on April 5, 1975 and Bergmann one day later; Chiang's son ordered a senior general to attend the funeral and present a funeral gift (奠儀) of US$50,000 and a large and beautiful wreath.

In January 1988, Chang Hsien-yi (張憲義), deputy director of Taiwan's Institute of Energy Research and a colonel in the military, defected to the U.S. with the assistance of the CIA; he had provided the U.S. with all of Taiwan's nuclear secrets.

Armed with this information and helped by the International Atomic Energy Agency, Washington forced Taiwan to give up its programme to make nuclear weapons. In December 2016, a book was published in Chinese in which Chang explained for the first time the reasons for his defection. "I feared that ambitious politicians might use nuclear weapons," Chang said. "I believed that such people would not just be unable to foster the well-being of the Taiwan people but would also pose a safety threat to them."

The Taiwan government listed him as a fugitive for 12-and-a-half years until July 2000, when the arrest warrant expired. (Note 3) To escape detection, Chang moved with his family to the American state of Idaho, in the remote northwest. For many in Taiwan, he is a traitor.

According to the World Nuclear Association, in December 2016, Taiwan had six nuclear power reactors. It has been a significant part of the electricity supply for two decades and provides one quarter of baseload power and 16 per cent overall. In a speech on May 7, 2017 at a meeting on national security strategy, Taiwan Defence Minister Feng Shih-kuan (馮世寬), said that Taiwan had the ability to develop nuclear weapons but would not do so, despite the increasing threat posed by China. "We will never be like North Korea and develop nuclear weapons to create a nuclear crisis and use it as a card," he said. (Note 4) Professor Bergmann and his Israeli colleagues have left an important legacy.

Coming together

In 1985, the Israeli cabinet created a team to work out a China policy. In May 1986, it re-opened the Consulate-General in Hong Kong and sent a former Mossad employee turned diplomat, Reuven Merhav, to head it; he was consul-general and had the rank of an ambassador. The city became its outpost for watching China and a place to meet Chinese officials and prepare diplomats for future assignments there.

The two sides held many rounds of talks, always "unofficial" and secret; in public, Beijing still supported the Arab cause. One of Merhav's first missions was to deliver to China a container with 50,000 doses of Israeli bull sperm.

Israel used every channel to break the deadlock. Israeli businessmen were able to enter China for fairs and exhibitions and meet partners; but, since Beijing did not accept Israeli passports, they had to use ones from third countries – occasionally provided by Beijing. China was interested in tourists from Israel. Scientific and academic scholars and experts from Israel were also able to enter China for international conferences and meetings.

In September 1989, China International Travel Service opened an office in Tel Aviv with seven staff headed by a Foreign Ministry diplomat. In

June 1990, the Beijing Liaison Office of the Israel Academy of Sciences and Humanities opened. These were the first offices of each country in the other. The two sides gradually moved closer together.

Global events also pushed Beijing to set up diplomatic ties. In August 1991, the Soviet Union, the biggest supporter of the Arab world, collapsed. Its former satellites in eastern Europe recognised Israel, as did Mongolia and the Central Asian republics.

In his essay "The Crucial Year 1991", Dr. E Zev Sufott, Israel's first ambassador to China, said that events in the Middle East played a key role. (Note 5) "Despite all the slogans about the Arab-Israeli conflict as the core threat to regional peace and stability, there were other grave sources of potential conflict, as the Iran-Iraq war had earlier demonstrated. The hazards of possible Israeli involvement, whether against Iranian or Iraqi atomic plants or missiles, obligated a great power with interests in the region to seek to assure itself full access to all the regional parties, rather than abdicating influence to the declining Soviet power or the expanding U.S. hegemonism in the region.

The Gulf War (1990-1991), and the significance of Israel's restraint in the face of provocation (not responding to 39 Iraqi Scud missiles that hit civilian targets in Israel), lent new urgency to the recommendation of the PRC's influential foreign policy research institutions concerning the tempo of normalisation of relations with Israel."

In other words, if Beijing wanted to broker a solution to the Arab-Israeli conflict, it needed diplomatic relations with all the parties involved and should take a more balanced view than it had since 1949.

Sufott himself was appointed Israel's unofficial representative in Beijing in 1991 and first ambassador the next year; he had been sent to study Chinese in 1955 in anticipation of diplomatic relations – a wait of 37 years! He said that, throughout the negotiations, Chinese officials were irked by leaks in the Israeli media; they believed them to be deliberate and did not accept explanations that they were the result of a free press and free society.

Coming to the altar – finally

Finally, on January 24, 1992, the Foreign Ministers of the two countries, Qian Qichen (錢其琛) and David Levy, signed an agreement in Beijing to establish bilateral relations. It was the first ever such public visit by an Israeli minister.

Sufott said the *People's Daily* newspaper had always represented the more conservative views with the party leadership and had been constantly critical of Israel. But its editorial of January 25 "heralded the dawn of a new day in the attitudes of the *People's Daily* toward Israel. It noted the Jewish nation's diligence, wisdom and contributions to civilization and human progress, followed by expressions of the Chinese people's deep sympathy for the historic sufferings of both Jews and Arabs."

That year the two countries concluded commercial, scientific and technological agreements; in September, El Al, Israel's national airline, began a weekly charter flight to Beijing.

That same month, September 1992, Qian Qichen went to Israel, the first such visit by a Chinese foreign minister. Two months later, Israeli president Chaim Herzog reciprocated, the first visit to China by an Israeli head of state since the country was founded; he travelled to Beijing in a private Boeing jet put at his disposal by Shaul Eisenberg. It was a symbol of the special relations the entrepreneur enjoyed with the leaders of both countries.

There were no Jews in the mainland to play a role in this 42-year normalisation. But the community in Hong Kong played an important part; they had personal ties to and friendships with members of the Chinese government which were important in building bridges, especially at the beginning. Before 1991, direct trade between the two countries was banned by the Chinese side; so Hong Kong was a vital conduit.

"Jewish groups in Hong Kong played a special role in improving China's relations with western countries. From the mid-1980s, non-official relations between Israel and China developed rapidly in economics, trade, culture and between political parties; all these prepared the conditions for normalisation," according to Pan Guang and Wang Jian. (Note 6) Hong Kong played a very important part in this process.

Selling arms to the enemy

China opposes any country selling arms to Taiwan; as a condition of normalisation, Israel had to agree to stop such arms sales. Whether they are going on secretly it is hard to know. For Israel, the main issue has been China's supply of missiles and nuclear technology to Iran, one of its most bitter enemies. During the 1990s, when Israeli leaders met their Chinese counterparts, they urged them not to make such sales – to no avail.

During the last 15 years, China has become a major arms exporter. It now ranks third in the world, far behind the U.S. and Russia but ahead of France and Germany. Since the Islamic revolution of 1979, China has been supplying Iran with arms.

In November 2016, General Chang Wanquan (常萬全) went to Teheran, the first such visit by a Chinese Defence Minister, to sign an agreement with his counterpart Major General Mohammad Bagheri to increase defence and military co-operation and fight terrorism. Major General Bagheri said that his country was completely ready to expand and deepen defence-military co-operation between the two sides, including holding joint military manoeuvres. (Note 7)

Notes

1   *The World facing Israel – Israel facing the World, Images and Politics*, by Professor Yitzhak Shichor, Frank & Timme, 2011.

2   "Ernest David Bergman and Israel's Role in Taiwan's Defense", by Professor Yitzhak Shichor, in *The Asia Papers*, published by the Center for International and Regional Studies, Georgetown University School of Foreign Service, Qatar, Number 2, 2016.

3   Central News Agency of Taiwan, 9/1/2017.

4   Article in *Hong Kong Economic Journal* (香港信報), 8/5/2017.

5   "The Crucial Year 1991", by E. Zev Sufott, in *China and Israel, 1948-1998, A Fifty Year Retrospective*, edited by Jonathan Goldstein, Praeger Publishers, 1999.

6   *The Jews and China* (猶太人與中國) by Professors Pan Guang (潘光) and Wang Jian (王健), Shishi Publishing Company (時事出版社), 2009, page 248-250.

7   Mehr News Agency of Iran, 21/11/2016.

8

Return to the mainland – Shanghai, Beijing and Harbin

From **INDIVIDUAL**

To SOCIETY

The open-door policy of Deng Xiaoping from the 1980s gave Jewish people, like other foreigners, the opportunity to live and work in China. Since then, several thousands have gone there, mainly to the major cities like Beijing, Shanghai, Guangzhou and Shenzhen. An estimated 10,000 live in the mainland, with an additional 5,000 in Hong Kong.

Like their forbears in the Tang dynasty and the Sephardis in the 1850s, they have been attracted by business opportunities, a comfortable quality of life, good public order and the absence of anti-Semitism.

But, unlike the Sephardis of Shanghai in the International and French Concessions, they enjoy no special privileges or status; like other foreigners, they live and work under the terms and conditions set by the PRC government.

A majority stay for a limited period, for the term of a contract, posting or a project or until the time comes when they want their children to receive education in their home country. A smaller number have, like the Sephardis of Shanghai, made China their home; we will tell the stories of some of them later in this chapter.

Judaism is not one of the five religions recognised by

the government; the five are Buddhism, Daoism, Islam, Protestantism and Catholicism. This means that it does not have an official status. Nor has the government returned the synagogues and other properties the community used before 1949. But it has allowed them to construct new buildings or use existing ones for religious, social and community activities and permits foreign rabbis to live in China and lead these activities.

So, the community is able to have a normal religious life. For Beijing, one of the most attractive features of Judaism is that, unlike Christianity or Islam, it does not evangelise. The rabbis preach only to the members of their congregation, not to the wider Chinese public. Beijing regards with suspicion the "foreign religions" that have entered China and has a large and sophisticated system to control and monitor them; it does not need this system to supervise Judaism, although it keeps a watchful eye on it.

"We are very grateful that China respects us and gives us public space; it protects us, even though we are not officially recognised," said Shimon Freundlich, rabbi of the Beijing community, who moved to the capital in September 2001. (Note 1)

He belongs to the Chabad Lubavitch movement. Founded in 1775 in a village in what is now Belarus, it has become the largest Hasidic Orthodox Jewish group in the world. One of its missions is to send rabbis to cities around the world with Jewish communities and bring them into the Orthodox faith; it is especially active in places where a community is newly established and has no rabbi. Chabad has 4,500 such full-time *shluchim* (emissaries) around the world.

"It is wonderful how far China has come in the world in the last 35 years," he said. "Chinese really respect Jewish people and culture. During my 16 years here, I have never heard a word of anti-Semitism. The overall atmosphere and attitude is one of great admiration and respect." (Note 2)

The Jews are the kind of foreigners Beijing wants – lawyers, entrepreneurs, teachers, IT specialists, bankers and other professionals; they bring expertise, technology and capital into China and help to grow the economy. Add to this the traditional respect and admiration of the Chinese government and people toward the Jews which we have seen throughout this book – and you have the basis of a harmonious relationship.

Since 1985, the Chabad Lubavitch movement has set up at least 12 centres across China, starting in Hong Kong and later in Shanghai, Beijing, Guangzhou, Shenzhen, Chengdu and Yiwu and sent rabbis to lead them. "Chabad is the infrastructure of Jewish life in Asia," said Rabbi Mordechai Avtzon in Hong Kong, the first Chabad emissary to arrive in Asia in the modern era, in 1985. "Our unique philosophy is that no Jew is judged on his level of observance. Every Jew is welcome. We cater to the highest level of commitment." (Note 3)

"If the Messiah comes"

Given the close historical links of the Jewish people with Shanghai, their return to the city was especially significant. After 1949 and the departure of the community that we described in Chapter Six, many Jewish sites in the city were destroyed. When the Jews started to return in the 1980s, they found that only two of the seven original synagogues still survived – Ohel Rachel and Ohel Moshe; but they were no longer synagogues. For religious, social and community events, they had to use private homes and offices.

But the returnees found many of the fine structures built by their Sephardic forebears still standing, such as the Peace Hotel, Grosvenor House and Jinjiang Hotel (錦江飯店); they are used, like before, by wealthy Chinese and foreigners.

In August 1998, Rabbi Shalom Greenberg and his wife Dina arrived in the city, the first rabbi to take up long-term residence there since 1949. He belongs, like Rabbi Freundlich, to Chabad Lubavitch. He is one of 17 children – no twins or triplets – and has brothers and sisters working as *schulhim* in Michigan, Texas, Alaska, France, Odessa and other places. "My parents lived in Russia in World War Two. My father was sent to Siberia for a few years. He remained a very proud and committed Jew and wanted to live the right way.

"From 1994, our movement sent students to the mainland each summer … They came and met Jewish people here in Shanghai. In 1998, they reported back to New York that there were over 100 Jews in Shanghai and that we should consider sending a permanent rabbi. I and my wife volunteered. In our organisation, we choose our own destination. I was born in Israel and my wife in Cleveland, Ohio. We are not afraid of challenges. We jump at them. I had no prior connection with China, except for stories of the Jews

The Peace Hotel, on the Bund in Shanghai.

in Shanghai in World War Two. I was not clear of anything else. We saw the challenges, the potential and the needs." (Note 4)

Asked how long he intended to stay, Rabbi Greenberg replied: "If the Messiah comes, we will finish our mission. Otherwise, I will stay as long as the government allows. Our movement keeps people in places where they are successful. I volunteered to come here."

The early years were difficult. The rabbi and his family had tourist visas and lived in a city apartment, where they held religious services. The chef of the Ritz Carlton Hotel told them how to buy salmon and other frozen fish – as long as fish has fins and scales and is not cut, it is kosher. If it is bought from a shop that is not kosher and has been cut, it may have touched knife residue from non-kosher food. The community also had to import kosher chicken.

"The biggest challenge was to explain to the Chinese authorities what we were doing," said Greenberg. "Ours is not a recognised religion. We were not missionaries seeking to convert Chinese. The first incident occurred in 1998, when I built a *sukkah* (a tent-like or hut-like structure) on the 29th floor roof of the Ritz-Carlton; a friend had lent us the space. According to our tradition, it must be built outside, covered with branches and used for seven days. The government was not happy, thinking that it was 'an underground church'. It demanded that we take it down; we said that it was just for a week-long holiday period, to celebrate Judaism for Jews.

"This led to a dialogue that lasted for many months. The conclusion was:

'We keep one eye open and one eye closed. We know what you are doing. If you fool us, we will punish you.' During this period, there was the possibility that we would be expelled and a stamp put in our passport that we could never return. The outcome was good. We knew what we could do and not do. The officials told us that anti-Semitism had played no part in their decisions. They were proud that Shanghai had saved so many Jews during WW2. Later I learnt that this history had had an impact on the negotiations, but they did not say so at the time."

In September 1999, the city gave the community permission to use the Ohel Rachel synagogue for the first time since 1949, to hold a service at the Jewish New Year. "An official told me that, in describing this event, I could not call the building a 'synagogue' nor use the word 'prayer'. I had to say 'a historic landmark that used to be a synagogue.' The official said: 'What you do is your own business. We will help you do what you need. We will not officially break our own rules. You cannot build a Jewish centre. But you can buy the biggest residence you can find and host your friends in your own home.'

"I accept their rules and conditions. This is their country, their culture and their life. In Islamic State, if you do not convert to Islam, they will slaughter you. In 1949, China told the foreigners to leave. They could do so again. The situation we have now is of mutual benefit. China has decided that it wants to allow a foreign contribution to economic development. So, it allows Korean and Japanese schools and foreign cultural programmes; there could be an Israeli school. China accepts these as long as they do not influence China and they keep to themselves."

In the eyes of Beijing, the Jews are preferable to Christians and Muslims who wish to convert Chinese to their faith.

In 2004, there was a breakthrough. George Bohbot from Hong Kong and Max Azaria from Los Angeles each donated US$1 million toward the purchase of a US$2.8 million, four-storey residential building of 770 square metres in the Changning district (長寧區); it is an estate of upmarket villas owned by wealthy Chinese and foreigners. The community raised US$800,000 from other people. The buyer was a joint venture between Chabad Hong Kong and Chabad Shanghai.

"We had to adapt the building to our requirements," said Greenberg. "It would have been cheaper to knock it down but we could not do that. The reconstruction took a few years. Most challenging was building the *mikvah*, the ritual bath. It must be water that is collected naturally and not facilitated by humans. We had to dig deep. We use rain water."

Entry to the *mikvah* is through a side entrance next to the main building. There is an ante-room where a person takes a shower and prepares himself or herself to enter the bath; for example, a woman enters the *mikvah* before she prepares to conceive a child. Religious women, like those in Chabad, go every month at the end of their menstrual cycle; before the one in Shanghai was built, they used to travel to Hong Kong for this purpose. The building houses a synagogue, kindergarten, Sunday school, adult education classes including Hebrew, lending library, a kosher restaurant and kosher shop.

The building that serves as the centre of the Jewish community in Shanghai.

Mikvah (ritual bath) inside the building.

"We have a permanent staff of 25 in the house here. On a small scale, we have all we need, with 50-80 people here on a Friday night. To meet demand, we have opened two more centres in Shanghai – downtown and in Pudong – and one in Ningbo.

"In 2005, my brother Avraham came to be the rabbi of the Pudong centre. In total, we have 250 in the four places on a Friday night, and 800 on holidays. The Jewish community in Shanghai numbers 2,000, with large groups from Israel, France and the US, as well as people from Australia, South Africa and UK. In addition, we have thousands of business people who come for one-to-two weeks and need our services, and thousands of Jewish tourists who come to China. Most spend one or two days in Shanghai to see places connected with the Jewish past."

As a community organisation, Chabad in Shanghai is not allowed to open a bank account, receive charity or own property; its finances are run through Hong Kong or the U.S.

Thanks to years of effort, the community now has a good infrastructure for kosher food. Once a year, it brings in a container of kosher beef from Uruguay; it buys kosher lamb from Inner Mongolia and brings an authorised slaughterer to kill chickens in Beijing every two-to-three months. It imports Passover *matzah* (unleavened bread) and wine from Israel; bakeries in Shanghai, Beijing and Guangzhou can make *challah* bread (used on the Sabbath).

"We have an infrastructure in place to produce kosher food almost like a

Jewish city; this did not exist 18 years ago. We can send kosher food to people in other cities in China."

Greenberg said that, of the 2,000 Jews in Shanghai, less than half came regularly to the centre. "I feel desperate to do more. What can I do to reach out to them? I constantly think of new ideas and concepts to encourage them to come. We have many programmes and events."

Returning the synagogues?

The city of Shanghai has done much to acknowledge its Jewish heritage. It has created a Jewish Refugees Museum in the former Ohel Moshe synagogue in the Hongkou District. It has been visited by thousands of Jews from around the world, including Israeli Prime Minister Yitzhak Rabin and former U.S. Treasury Secretary Michael Blumenthal, who lived in a nearby apartment during World War Two.

In 2007, the Hongkou district provided funds for a full renovation of the building according to the original architectural drawings. The Jewish community has been allowed to hold bar mitzvahs and weddings there. The museum is one of the stops on a tour of "Jewish Shanghai" which also includes buildings where the refugees lived during World War Two and the branch office of the New York-based Joint Distribution Committee; these tours attract thousands of Jews every year.

The city is also home to The Centre for Jewish Studies, (上海猶太研究中心) under the Shanghai Academy of Social Sciences; it was established in

1988. Its director is Pan Guang (潘光); we have quoted extensively from one of his excellent books. This is the most influential research institute in China for the study of Jewish history, Judaism and Israel; Professor Pan is an important official intermediary between China and the Jewish world.

All this is evidence of how much the city values its Jewish heritage and its links with Israel and Jewish people around the world. But that does not mean it is willing to hand back the two synagogues or other pre-1949 Jewish properties, despite the fact that Judaism does not evangelise and therefore represents no "threat" to Chinese society.

In June 2006, Shlomo Amar, then Chief Sephardic Rabbi of Israel, went to Shanghai, the first such visit since Israel was founded in 1948. Accompanied by a group of rabbis, he went to the Ohel Rachel synagogue, where he led prayers; the building belongs now to the Shanghai Department of Education.

I was one of a number of reporters covering the event; we believed that this historic visit by one of the two most important rabbis in Israel portended a major announcement. In my computer in the office, I prepared a story saying that Shanghai had agreed to return the synagogue to the Jewish community after 57 years. But I was wrong; Rabbi Amar made no such announcement.

"I have come here to strengthen the community here, to aid spiritual growth, and to pray for the government to allow freedom of religion for the Jews," he said.

The former Ohel Rachel synagogue in Shanghai, consecrated in 1920. The building now belongs to the city's Education Bureau.

An official plaque explaining the history of the Ohel Rachel synagogue.

I asked Rabbi Greenberg if the community would be given back the synagogue. "There are many aspects to China returning one of its own buildings to a foreign religion. It would be a precedent. Other religions had buildings here. There is also internal pressure. The building currently belongs to the Education Bureau, which would have to find other premises. Shanghai is not willing to commit to this. We use it nine times a year. We pray for it to be returned to us. It is the historic centre of Judaism in Shanghai."

Wang Jian (王健), deputy dean of the Centre of Jewish Studies of Shanghai, said that discussions had been held over turning Ohel Rachel into a museum, to be used sometimes for religious purposes, but without result. "The community can use it for events, like Israel National Day, marriages and holidays," he said. (Note 5)

On April 24, 2017, a gathering was held in Ohel Rachel as part of the annual Holocaust memorial event. Old pictures were displayed; the event was hosted by the deputy Israeli consul general and attended by diplomats from 22 countries.

In any event, this is not a decision which Shanghai alone can take; it must be made by the central government. Before 1949, foreign and domestic religious institutions owned thousands of churches, temples, offices, houses, seminaries, orphanages and other properties across the country. Returning the two synagogues would create enormous goodwill for China in Israel and among Jews around the world; but there is no free lunch – Protestant and Catholic churches would ask for their properties back too.

If Judaism is one of the oldest religions in the world, then why is it not officially recognised as a religion in China? "The designation of the five official religions was made in the 1950s when there were no Jews in China," said Greenberg. "If the designation were changed now, it would open up new questions. We are not interested to open this issue. If we were designated an official religion, the head of it in China would have to be a Chinese. But there is no Chinese rabbi in the world." (Note 6)

The city did not do a good job in maintaining the four Jewish cemeteries with 3,700 graves that existed in 1949. In 1958, the government moved all remains of foreigners into a new 'international cemetery" in a suburb 25 km west of the centre. They were destroyed during the Cultural Revolution; local farmers used some of the gravestones as construction materials for their houses. The gravestones were scattered all over the city; some ended up on the shelves of the city's antique shops.

On September 6, 2015, city officials and members of the Jewish community opened a Jewish Memorial Park of 200 square metres at the Fushouyuan (福壽園) cemetery in the city's Qingpu district. Speaking at the dedication, Israeli Consul-General Arnon Perlman said it was very important "to remember the friendship between China and Israel and between Shanghai and Israel."

On a patch of newly laid grass, a Star of David made of stone forms the centrepiece of the park and serves as the base of a sculpture of interlocking stones with another Star of David, and a *menorah* (sacred candelabrum), at its centre.

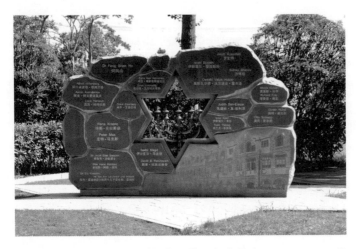

Plaque at the Jewish Memorial Park in Shanghai's Fushouyuan cemetery. It marks the contribution of Jewish people to the city.

Sculptures in the Jewish Memorial Park in Fushouyuan cemetery.

A memorial stone with names of Ho Fengshan (何鳳山) – the Chinese diplomat in Vienna who is credited with saving many Jews from the Nazis – as well as 24 famous Jewish people, who had contributed to development of Shanghai, was unveiled in the park. They include Silas Aaron Hardoon, Victor Sassoon and Elly Kadoorie.

At the opening, Pan Guang said they had built the park to commemorate the more than 20,000 Jewish people who sought refuge in Shanghai but also to show respect to the many Jewish people who contributed to Shanghai's prosperity and liberation through business, wisdom or courage.

"The park has two Jewish tombstones and hopes to collect more scattered across the city," said Pan. "The graves were badly damaged during the Cultural Revolution and it is hard to find them now. So, when Jewish people come to Shanghai and want to see the graves of their parents or grandparents, they cannot find them. That's why we want to have this park and we went to replace the cemeteries that have disappeared."

Jewish community leader Maurice Ohana said that, of the nearly 4,000 Jewish people living in Shanghai now, very few were descendants of those refugees. (Note 7)

Dentures in Paris, made in Shanghai

Ohana is one of the leaders of the Jewish community who has lived there for 20 years. A native of Morocco, he emigrated to France; after moving to

Shanghai, he sold the property he owned in France. "What has attracted Jews to China is the economic growth, the sense of dynamism, feeling of personal safety and lack of anti-Semitism. There is no example in history of the economic progress like that made in China in the past 20 years. Europe is in decline. Every Jewish person I have met liked China at once – there is the same desire to succeed. We share with Chinese the sense of family values, the love of children and the desire to do the best for them and the drive to keep our culture alive abroad." (Note 8)

Jewish people and institutions in France have been a prime target of Islamic fundamentalists; several Jews have been killed in the last several years. "Here, my son comes home at three in the morning and I do not worry. My children have never complained of a security problem," he said. "Anti-Semitism is not in the culture of the Chinese. They respect us and we respect them. They are very interested in our history and how we have survived in the world."

Ohana is the founder of the Longfield Trading Company, which handles a wide variety of commodities. One of them is false teeth. Parisians go to their dentist for a fitting of dentures; the moulds are sent by FedEx to Shanghai. "We send them to a factory in Shanghai, where workers will craft their new teeth. We send them back by FedEx to Paris. The patients collect them after a few days and never know they are made in China." No two dentures are the same.

One of the most visible symbols of new Jewish entrepreneurship in Shanghai is the Peninsula Hotel on the Bund, which opened in 2009; it is the mainland flagship of the Hong Kong and Shanghai Hotels group, owned by the Kadoorie family. It was the first new building on the Bund in several decades.

Many in Shanghai believe the city chose the Kadoories for this prime site in recognition of their historical friendship with China. Unlike the Sassoons and Silas Hardoon, the family did not trade opium; it also donated its spacious residence, Marble Hall, to the city after 1949. Since then, it has retained good relations with Beijing; its China Light and Power Company was one of the earliest post-1979 investors, in the Daya Bay nuclear power station.

Another important Jewish symbol is the Shanghai Diamond Exchange; as we described in Chapter Seven, setting it up was the last business deal of Shaul Eisenberg three days before he died in March 1997. Three years later, in October 2000, the State Council authorised it as the only channel for the import and export of diamonds in China; it opened on October 27 that year in the Jinmao Tower (金茂大廈) in Pudong.

It was a joint venture between eight mainland Chinese and Hong Kong partners – the only such Sino-foreign jv among the exchanges in China; these include securities, future, metals and grains exchanges. The Diamond Exchange operates according to the practices of the international diamond industry. In October 2009, it moved from the Jinmao Tower into a new China Diamond Exchange Centre building that covers a total floor area of 49,000 square metres. It is an official member of the World Federation of Diamond Bourses.

"In Shanghai, there are many joint ventures between China and Israel," said Wang Jian, deputy director of the city's Jewish Research Centre. "As the city becomes a centre for finance, law and innovation, more Jews will come." (Note 9)

Converting Chinese

Judaism does not seek to convert non-Jews. This suits the PRC government well; it does not allow foreigners to evangelise. Greenberg and his fellow rabbis are careful on this point. "We do not have the right to convert; that has to be done by a Jewish court," he said. "The nearest is in Australia. I can help people prepare for that. Chinese who have married Jews have converted. The government has no problem with that, because the numbers are so small."

In Beijing, Rabbi Freundlich said: "No, it is against the law to convert Chinese. We are too small to offer conversion. I can study with people in the centre here but conversion must be done outside China. If a person is married to a Jew, he or she can take part in our services. The government does not stop them if they wish to convert in another country. We do not proselytise. We obey the laws of the country. We have to pray for the law of the land. We should say 'thank you' to the Chinese government for protecting and tolerating Jews, even though we are not a recognised religion." (Note 10)

One Chinese who did was the wife of Isaac Epstein, an American Jew who came to China in 1998 and to Shanghai in 2004. He married a lady from a farming family in Anhui province. "Few Chinese convert. I made it clear that it was very important to me. She promised to do it. It was a huge life change." (Note 11)

"Normally the process takes one-and-a-half to two years. But we had a baby in the middle, so the process took five years. It was very hard for her. She had to learn Hebrew and the prayers. She had to eat kosher food and follow the Sabbath. That means no use of electricity, money, computer, motor car, mobile phone, an umbrella or a bicycle. You go to synagogue and walk home: you read, play with the children and see friends – but no use of cars. She did not like this at first but likes it now. You turn off the world for a day. My friends know not to call me on a Saturday, because they know my mobile is switched off.

"Then there is the rule of family purity – from the start of the menstrual cycle until five days after, her husband may not touch her, a total of 12 days. We kept all the rules. This meant that she could not eat Chinese food outside the home. When we visited her or my parents, we had to eat out of a separate pot. On the positive side, Judaism creates a wonderful house environment – focussed on the home and education.

"According to Chinese regulations, Rabbi Greenberg is not allowed to convert. So we had to go to a rabbinical court, called Beit Din, in Sydney; it consisted of three rabbis. You do not go to a court until you are prepared and ready. Rabbi Greenberg sent an informal report – did she go to the mikvah, keep the Sabbath and eat kosher food? So, the three rabbis asked her a few simple questions and she passed. Now the community accepts her as one of their own. But she is an introvert and not so social; sometimes she does not know what to talk about to people. That is a matter of culture, not religion.

"Her family had no idea about this. According to Jewish tradition, the religion is passed on through the mother. So, our son, who was born before her conversion, had also to be converted later. This was done when he was 18 months old; it was an ordeal for him to be immersed totally in the *mikvah* three times, with the hold of him released for a second to ensure total immersion. He did not know what was happening; he was not happy and went off baths for a time. My parents are liberal and supported us; there was a period when we did not eat at their house or, if we did, could only eat a salad."

After working in an engineering company for three years, Epstein set up his own business in 2007, doing home textiles and packaging products. He is director of China operations, with a partner in the U.S. He has also done full-time study of Chinese medicine, in Putonghua, the only American in a foreign class largely of Koreans.

"After arrival here, I went to the Jewish centre and felt at home. I made friends there. Since I have come here, I have become more religious. I have learnt a lot more Hebrew. The Jewish centre is Orthodox; men and women worship separately and it serves kosher food. But it accommodates everyone, as is the case in such centres in cities with expats. In Shanghai, Jewish life is very good. The centre says prayers every morning, it provides pre-school up to five years old, organises events at major holidays and has a mikvah, which is very important for the community. Hasidic Jews use it all the time. I use it once a year, on Yom Kippur, the Day of Atonement; you cannot wash away your sins but feel a sense of renewal.

"The centre has a restaurant with kosher food, including imported meat. But there is no Jewish high school in Shanghai and not likely to be one. It costs too much money and there is not enough interest. Many Jews leave when their children reach five, so that they can attend Jewish schools elsewhere; if they stay, they send their children to international schools. I sent my son, four, to the British school, which costs 180,000 yuan a year; I am happy with it."

I asked how long he planned to stay in Shanghai? "If it were just my wife and I, we would stay. But my children and parents are getting older; they only see each other once a year. Family is very important. I would prefer a more Jewish element to my children's schooling. My son studies Hebrew in classes at the Jewish Centre but not to the level I would like. Going to Hong Kong and sending them to the Carmel School there would be one option. It is more like home and much more expensive than Shanghai. But that is still far from my parents." (Note 12)

"There are Jews who are smart and Jews who are stupid"

Joel Epsteinas, a Frenchman, has also become more religious during the 14 years he has lived in Shanghai. "I found the Jewish Centre under Rabbi Greenberg a second home. I have become more religious the longer I stay here and now go for the sabbath service each week. Initially, I only went for the major holidays. I go to the downtown centre, with Rabbi Shlomo Aouizerat.

"Becoming more religious is due to my personal life and also to the presence of the rabbis here. I am not so religious that I cannot eat in a Shanghai restaurant. But I do not eat pork or those foods that are forbidden. Greenberg is a hero. He has recreated a Jewish life here that you can find in Paris, New York or London. He could have stayed in Israel or the United States but chose to come here. He and the other rabbis here aim to attract the non-practitioners; but they do not tell them what to do and not to do. That is up to the members to decide. The rabbis are available all the time if you call on them. A rabbi should love all Jews and share their faith with them."

His parents were born in France; their parents were born in Lithuania and what was then Poland, now Ukraine. "My parents were not so religious; for them, religion was more a matter of identity and culture. My father set up a textile business. With the change in the global economy, the only way for us to remain in this sector was to move the business here. So, in 2003, I came to Shanghai for a week to see if I could live here. I liked it, so I moved to Shanghai.

"I came alone, had no office and no team. I had to start the business from nothing. For 18 months, I lived in a hotel. Thanks to God, I was able to progress. I found factories that made the right quality. It was easy to settle. After 18 months, I found partners; we worked together for six years before parting amicably. For my professional life here, I relied on myself. I found good suppliers quickly.

"The business climate is not easy and not difficult. There is the language barrier. There is a culture of conflict and the balance of power. I stay in Shanghai nine out of 12 months each year. I keep close ties with my family. I would like to spend more time outside China and become more efficient in running my business."

He said that the Chinese had a favourable prejudice toward the Jews. "We are the 'victims' of this good prejudice. In fact, we are like everyone else. There are Jews who are smart and Jews who are stupid. The fact of no prejudice and no anti-Semitism is very good. My grandparents lived in an anti-Semitic climate in Poland before World War Two, but I never suffered from it in France.

"The Chinese do not have a clear idea about the Jews. The Jews played an important role in bringing modernisation and capitalism to Shanghai. Marx was also Jewish – he has had a big impact on China. Shanghai is a good place to be Jewish. The government fears proselytism but we do not proselytise. Look at the problems between China and the Vatican over the appointment of bishops; no such problem exists with Judaism. Here there is total freedom of religion.

"In France, there are some areas where it is hard to wear a *kippa* [skullcap] or symbols of your faith. Not here. We can say a prayer for five minutes outside on the pavement, facing the moon; that could be a problem in

France, which has so many rules about laicity. I will stay in China as long as I have business to do. Without work, you cannot stay.

"We are here for the same reason as those Jews who came in the 1920s and 1930s – a good quality of life and a chance to do business. In those decades, Shanghai was more open than today, when it is very controlled. It was a very free period; if you had money, there were no limits for foreigners. Everything was possible." (Note 13)

The one left behind – "In Israel, everyone wants to be Prime Minister"

The establishment of diplomatic relations between China and Israel made it possible for Chinese Jews to emigrate there. The first was Sara Imas, in 1992. She was born in Shanghai in 1950, the daughter of Leiwi Imas, a Polish Jew, and a lady from Jiangsu province.

A businessman on the German-Polish border, Imas escaped to Shanghai during World War Two; he opened a shop there selling wine and carpets. In 1949, he went to work in the Chinese customs department and, in 1956, received approval to go to Israel; but, aged 71, he suffered from high blood pressure and could not travel. He lived with his daughter in a home for Jewish people in Fuxing Road (復興路) they lived on pensions from the central government and the Jewish Agency, which also sent shipments of kosher food from Hong Kong.

The agency continued to send money to her for 40 years. Imas spoke to his daughter in a mixture of his native Yiddish, English and Hebrew; she learnt Putonghua and the dialects of Shanghai and northern Jiangsu where her mother came from. In 1962, just before he died, Imas told Sara: "Take your chance, have babies and go to Israel."

She was the last Jewish person in the home when the Red Guards took it over in 1967; they stole her possessions, drove her out and confiscated the money she received from the Jewish Agency. In 1971, she took an invitation from the Israeli government to the local Public Security Bureau; they told her that Chairman Mao had banned travel to South Korea, Taiwan and Israel and she could not go.

In 1985, she flew to Tokyo , the nearest Israeli embassy, which gave her a visa and a ticket. But she could not obtain permission to emigrate; she had to wait another seven years until 1992, when diplomatic relations were set up; she finally left for Israel, the first Jewish immigrant from China. She met Prime Minister Yitzhak Rabin.

But things did not work out as she had hoped. At the bank at Ben Gurion Airport, she handed over US$120 and received in shekels the equivalent of US$21. Unable to speak Hebrew or English, Sara lived and worked in Chinese restaurants for a year until her three children came and she was assigned an apartment; they went to school and learnt Hebrew.

"The Russians there have a big community helping new arrivals; so do the Americans, but no-one helped me," Sara said. "I was very disappointed with Israel and do not want to live there. Everyone wants to be Prime Minister."

Her children adapted better and settled there. She returned to China and, in 2002, accepted the post of representative there for a diamond company. (Note 14)

Low-key

The Jews of Shanghai, as in other mainland cities, are low-key and discreet. While they have an intense religious and community life, it is out of the public gaze. As a matter of policy, the mainland media does not report religious news. So, the Shanghai public are only made aware of the Jewish presence when an Israeli or foreign VIP visits the Refugee Museum or other Jewish monument. Most Chinese cannot tell the difference between Jews and other foreigners.

"In our history lessons, we did not learn about the history of the Jews in Shanghai, whether before or after 1992 when relations were set up between Israel and China," said Liu Meixiu (劉美秀) a Shanghai resident who works in the IT industry.

"We regard the Jews like other foreigners and cannot distinguish between them. It was only when I read in the newspaper of a visit to the Refugee Museum by Michael Blumenthal, the former US Treasury Secretary, that I went to the museum myself. Only then did I realise what had happened during World War Two. I believe that Shanghai people were good to the Jews at that time, despite all the privations they were facing themselves. This is not government propaganda. It is one of the features of Chinese – they are kind, perhaps too kind, to foreigners, especially Westerners, but harsh and cruel to each other." (Note 15)

Given what they have experienced in other countries, the Jews of Shanghai treasure this anonymity.

Beijing – "During 16 years, never a word of anti-Semitism"

Before 1949, Beijing did not have a significant Jewish community. Unlike Shanghai, Tianjin or Qingdao, it was neither a treaty port nor a commercial centre for foreign trade. It was a city of administration, education and diplomacy. A small number of Jews worked there as professors, diplomats, doctors and scientists. From 1927 until 1949, the Nationalist government made Nanjing, not Beijing, the national capital.

After the open-door policy, Jews began to arrive in Beijing, as business people, journalists, diplomats and students. In 1979, they established an informal organisation, to organise meetings for Passover and High Holy Days, which were usually celebrated in the homes of members. They held their first *seder* (Passover feast) in 1980. This organisation later became known as Kehillat (from *kehilla*, meaning congregation), which is alive and flourishing today.

In the early 1990s, in addition to people from North America, the city's Jewish community grew with new arrivals from Australia, England, France, Germany, Hungary, Israel, Luxembourg, Poland and Russia. In 1995, Kehillat began to hold regular Friday night services at the Capital Club in northeast Beijing; it has continued to do so until the present.

Later, it added a class for younger children and a discussion group for adults. In 1996, it celebrated its first *bar mitzvah* (coming of age ritual for boys) and in 1997 its first *b'rit milah* (circumcision) – not easy in a city with no rabbi and no *mohel* (person trained in circumcision). It has a Sunday school for children aged four and above; the curriculum covers Hebrew language and Jewish culture, practice and history.

In September 2001, Beijing received the first rabbi in its history – Shimon Freundlich, who is, like Rabbi Greenberg in Shanghai, a member of Chabad Lubavitch. "Its principle is that the first rabbi who goes to a place stays there his whole life, barring emergencies," said Rabbi Freundlich. "Those who follow him may stay for a limited period, depending on circumstances. In 2000, I was in Hong Kong and saw there was no Chabad rabbi in Beijing; the Jewish community then numbered about 400. I came for a visit, gave a class on Judaism and met members of the community. Then I wrote my report. It was decided that I should come. I arrived on September 3, 2001.

"The community here now numbers about 2,000, Many of them are in transit, staying in Beijing for only a few years. The community is very close. We have two places to pray. In other cities, the community is divided into Orthodox, Liberal and Reform; but now here, we pride ourselves on one community. There is no Jewish cemetery in Beijing. If there was, I would be happy to be buried there." (Note 16)

In 2007. Freundlich opened the two-storey Chabad House next to the south gate of Si De Park (四德公園) in the Chaoyang district (朝

陽區) of northeast Beijing. It was built in tribute and memory of the many synagogues that existed in China's history. The Façade and Ark are miniature replicas of the Tianjin synagogue; the Bar in the kosher restaurant is modelled on the Kaifeng synagogue; the wall design in the education room is a copy of the windows of the Jewish school in Harbin.

It has an extensive collection of artefacts, books, letters and mementoes from the many Jewish communities that have existed in China. The second floor contains the house of prayer, where the Torah scrolls are kept. The ground floor contains a café and a kosher restaurant. There is, in addition, the Rohr Family Chabad Community Centre, with 10,000 square feet. The Chabad House and the Community Centre offer: a Jewish day school for children aged between one-and-a-half and 12; adult classes; a Hebrew school; youth activities; holiday services and meals; supplies of kosher food; and a *mikvah*, for ritual bathing. There are two rabbis in addition to Rabbi Freundlich.

On a popular downtown street, the community has also opened Beijing's first kosher restaurant, named after Dini, the wife of Rabbi Freundlich; this is open to the general public. The aim in Beijing, as in Shanghai, is to provide the members of the community with the same elements of a Jewish life as they would enjoy in their home countries.

Beijing is home to about 2,000 Jews, from the United States, Canada, Israel, Europe, Russia, Azerbaijan and Latin America; it is hard to know the exact number. It is also the site of the Israeli embassy, set up by diplomatic relations in January 1992. The embassy is active in organising exchanges between Israel and China in art, culture, academia, science and technology. In addition, about 15,000 Jewish business people and tourists come through Beijing each year.

The rabbi is full of praise for his hosts. "Chinese really respect Jewish people and culture. During my 16 years here, I have never heard a word of anti-Semitism. The overall atmosphere and attitude is one of great admiration and respect.

"I travel all over China. Chinese are fascinated by the fact that we have survived for 2,000 years without a homeland. The second and third generation of Chinese who have emigrated do not identify themselves as Chinese but a citizen of the nation where they are living. But a Jew in France, Australia, South Africa or U.S. sees himself first as a Jew.

"We have a history of 4,000 years and the Chinese of 5,000 years; we are the two oldest civilisations in the world. We are both proud of our history and culture. In January 2017, I took a delegation from the Religious Affairs Bureau of China to Israel for a tour to understand Judaism and Israel. It was the first such visit since 1949, specifically for this purpose. They saw that all religions can operate freely in Israel. They want to create a structure in China in which every religion in the world, whether recognised or not, can operate here. We are very grateful that China respects us and gives us public space; it protects us, even though we are not officially recognised.

"It is wonderful how far China has come in the world in the last 35 years."

said Rabbi Freundlich. "I know Chinese living abroad who have returned to live here because the quality of life is better. During his last visit, (Israeli Prime Minister) Benjamin Netanyahu said that Israel should be the R & D centre of China. More and more Chinese firms are looking to expand in Israel. They admire Israel's knowledge and success.

"In Harbin, there is a Jewish cemetery with 603 graves, including those of two rabbis, who are buried below a large arch that is the entrance. The 603 were moved in 1956 from the old cemetery; the cost was US$36 for each body, but the community had only enough for 603. They have done a wonderful job of maintaining the cemetery. In 2006, I flew there for a visit. I thanked the government officials for looking after the cemetery so well.

"At the entrance, over the graves of the two rabbis, I read words of legal doctrine written by one of them and prayed there. The officials were very respectful and stood with me. The city has spent US$2 million to renovate the main synagogue in Harbin; it has done a magnificent job. It contains a small museum of the history of the Jews and an exhibition of the history."

Harbin – Cherishing the Past

In June 2017, the city of Harbin held a six-day International Conference of Former Foreign Residents. Former Harbiners came from Poland, Israel, Australia, Russia, the USA, Lithuania, Latvia, Canada, and other countries. Among the 200 participants of all colours and faiths, two dozen Jewish people attended the first such international conference.

One was Ester Alon, who lives in Haifa, Israel. She was born in 1939 to a couple who had moved to Harbin from Russia. "I was in Harbin for 22 years, which brought me the most beautiful memories of my whole life," said Ester. "I still remember my friendly Chinese neighbours who taught me their traditional games."

When the family moved to Israel, Ester took all her Chinese clothes and accessories; unfortunately, however, she has forgotten much of her Mandarin, after so many decades. "Harbin cherishes the friendships with all former foreign residents," said Cao Ru (曹儒), deputy director of the Harbin Foreign and Overseas Affairs Office. (Note 17)

Today the city has one Jewish resident – Dan Ben-Canaan, a professor of research and writing methodologies at the School of Postgraduate Studies of Northeast Forestry University, one of China's leading science institutions. Prof. Ben-Canaan is the founder and director of the Sino-Israel Research and Study Centre under the Harbin Jewish Culture Association. He moved to Harbin in 2002, and, being the only Jewish person in the city, he is the gatekeeper of a Jewish legacy and past. "My curiosity and force took me there," he said.

He has written many articles on political and social issues in the Far East, co-written articles for international journals and has authored eight books. Dr Ben-Canaan is a Visiting Professor for Advanced Studies at the Heilongjiang Communist Party School. Besides his university lectures, he serves as editor-in-chief of the Heilongjiang Television English News Services and as an advisor on information and economics management for governmental bodies and enterprises in China.

Since 2003, he has been an honorary Research Fellow at the Heilongjiang Academy of Social Sciences. In 2008, Ben-Canaan received a rank of Honorary Citizen of Harbin, the 15th in the city's history; since 2013, he has been a permanent resident of China.

Since his first encounter with Heilongjiang Province in 1999 and especially over the past 15 years, Professor Ben-Canaan has been instrumental in putting Harbin on the international and national agenda. He has hosted many international conferences, three of them high-level academic events.

In 2009, he organised an international conference and Summer School at Heilongjiang University. He partnered with Heidelberg University in Germany and the German Institute in Washington D.C., and brought to Harbin 40 of the world's leading contemporary historians who contributed studies on the history of Harbin and the cross-cultural dimensions of the Northeast of China, known at the 19th and the beginning of the 20th centuries as Manchuria.

In 2011, he partnered with Bar Ilan University in Israel and hosted a "Meeting of the Minds" international conference which brought to Heilongjiang University's School of Western Studies 75 leading Israeli professors who discussed parallel aspects in Jewish and Chinese thought.

In 2015, he organised an Australian-Chinese conference aiming to form partnership between Australian academic institutions and the Sino-Israel Research and Study Centre under his leadership.

One of his greater contributions was the study of the Huangshan Jewish cemetery. Together with his research students and a German PhD candidate, he supervised the group remapping the place and photographed all the tombstones there, adding a "passport" to each of the names. His study of the history of the Harbin Jewish cemeteries will be published in 2018. His new book *Jewish Footprints in Harbin* will be published soon.

In part because of his influence, the Harbin city government began in 2004 a renovation of the gutted New Synagogue and transformed it into a museum of the Jewish history and culture of Harbin. In 2012, Professor Ben-Canaan was appointed by the mayor of Harbin as the official advisor for the reconstruction of the Main (Old) Synagogue and bringing the structure back into its original state of 1932, after it was destroyed by a fire set off by White Russian fascists; the cost of the project was more than 100 million yuan.

"I welcomed the Harbin government plans and this project with great enthusiasm," said Ben-Canaan. "The reconstruction, restoration, and renovation of the synagogue, the old Jewish gymnasium and the other buildings around, as well as the construction of a large new square between them, will recreate a very large Jewish block here and will reinforce the unique and important Jewish existence in Harbin, its heritage, and its contribution to the development of the city.

"In an absence of a Jewish community here, I suggested that the whole complex – the Jewish High School, a Jewish private house and a small building that served as an apartment quarters for several of the teachers – will become the Harbin Music Centre and that the synagogue will be a concert hall for chamber music. The mayor agreed and, since its opening, the synagogue-concert hall has become very popular among the citizens of Harbin."

During the reconstruction, however, Ben-Canaan encountered several difficulties. One was the refusal of the central government to open the long-shut Jewish archives of Harbin; this, plus the absence of original blueprints, made it very difficult to plan and design the reconstruction. Then, one day, he discovered the workers had painted the exterior of the buildings, including the synagogue, bright yellow – not the colours given to them in earlier meetings. The architect and advisor asked the managers to repaint the exterior with the exact colours given to them in earlier meetings. They refused, saying that they had been ordered to use yellow by Vice Mayor Qu Lei (曲磊); she is known as the 'Iron Lady' of the city.

"We found out later that Qu wanted to paint Harbin in the image of Moscow. She told us Moscow is glowing in yellow. On another occasion, while on an official trip to the Czech Republic, Madam Qu visited a certain church. The grand chandeliers, full of crystal works, made a great impression on her. She sent pictures of the lights through her mobile phone and asked to install such fixtures in the synagogue.

"It became clear that that there was no attempt to understand nor to fully consider the cultural significance of the site. To the contrary, the government made the announcement to name the whole site after a Russian musician named Alexander Konstantinovich Glazunov, who had never set foot in Harbin and had nothing to do with Judaism. The name 'Glazunov' suited the political agenda very well, because in 2013 the Chinese decided to 'warm up' their strategic relations with Russia."

Ben-Canaan said that, in fact, the aim of the project was not to preserve and enrich the historical fragment of the life of Jews in Harbin but to add the structures to the overall Russian-flavour design of historical Harbin. "For them, the buildings represented something Russian, and that could serve the political agenda quite well."

The professor did not agree with the use of the Glazunov name, arguing that the Russian musician was not Jewish and had no connection with Judaism. At a working meeting with a senior official of the government, he suggested that, instead, the area be named Kaufman Square – after Dr. Abraham Kaufman, president of the Jewish community in Harbin from 1919 to 1945 (whose life we described in Chapter Two), and his son Theodor (Teddy) Kaufman who served as the president of the Israel Association of Former Residents in China and the Israel-China Friendship Association for many years.

"The answer given was crystal clear: We may not reconsider ...' All attempts to change the agenda failed." Ben-Canaan suggested then to erect a marble plate in memory of the father and his son. The Vice Mayor agreed, but nothing was done. The name was chosen to improve China's relations with Russia. The project was completed in June 2014.

However, exactly three years later in June 2017, during the proceedings of the International Conference of Former Foreign Residents of Harbin, the city government held a special ceremony; the black memorial marble plaque with the Kaufman names that Ben-Canaan designed was added to an exterior front wall of the synagogue.

In 2016, the Heilongjiang provincial government hosted a Jewish economic conference in Harbin; one of the highlights of the event was an evening of Jewish music at the old synagogue.

The government wants to promote the city as a unique tourist destination. Ben-Canaan has suggested to the city administration that it should promote the unique history of the city, not only her icy winters. "I am glad that my comments and reports fell on open ears and especially on open minds. The city's authorities have come to realise how beneficial it can be when the city promotes her special historical position among all other Chinese cities."

For Professor Dan Ben-Canaan "a present without a past has no future." And thus, the legacy of the Jewish community of Harbin must and will live on and on. This motto has been adopted now by representatives of several countries whose nationals used to live in Harbin. Among those who have studied Ben-Canaan's model are the Lithuanian and Polish governments; with his help, they have started unveiling the past of their communities in Harbin. (Note 18)

Nationwide inspector of kosher food

One key element in the life of an Orthodox Jew is to eat kosher, that is food that has been prepared according to religious regulations. This is very difficult for Jews who live in countries without an established community and regular source of supply. So, one of the first jobs of Chabad rabbis after they arrive in a new country is to arrange the supply of the proper food.

"When we arrived, we could only find Heinz ketchup and lemon juice with the kosher stamp," said Rabbi Freundlich in Beijing. "Now thousands of Chinese factories are producing kosher food for export. Supermarkets that cater to foreigners have many kinds of kosher food. We import beef from Uruguay; and there is a kosher chicken farm outside Beijing."

He has become a nationwide inspector of kosher food. "Each year I make 300-500 visits to Chinese food factories to certify that their products are kosher. I often spend Monday-Thursday of each week doing this. I have done this for 15 years. It is to support my family. The factories pay for my services. The community here is in transit; its members use their donations for their communities at home and have limited capacity to be generous here. Their communities at home are stable, while ours is not.

"The factories want kosher certification because customers ask for it: or because they will get more customers; or because kosher food is seen as cleaner, at a time of many food scandals. I check product records, inspect the storage of raw materials and check the workshops and warehouses. My record was 14 factories in one day, between 0600 and 2100, in Linyi (臨沂) in Shandong; they produce dried fruit and vegetables.

"I spent three days straight at a company in Shanghai that is China's largest producer of vegetable oils. For half a day, I looked at the blueprints and walked around the factory. It is enormous. We found that the margarine was made from tallow and not kosher. All the raw materials and machinery must be kosher; if non-kosher materials are used, it is not kosher. They had to make the margarine factory separate ... The standard of some of the firms is superb. I brought a rabbi from the UK who is a specialist in dairy products and took him to a Beijing plant that makes organic milk. He praised it."

"At the leading edge of healthcare"

The three decades of the open-door era in China have not produced the fortunes of another Sassoon or Hardoon. The Jewish entrepreneurs of today have to work within an economic system that is restricted and regulated – the opposite of the "paradise of capitalists" of pre-1937 Shanghai.

The memory of – and bitterness toward – the wealth earned by the foreign businessmen of that era is imprinted in the minds of those who run the Communist government. They are determined that the Chinese, and especially Chinese state companies, dominate their economy in the 21st century.

Foreigners are excluded from or restricted in many of the most profitable sectors, such as electricity, aviation, telecommunications, petroleum, tobacco, steel, insurance and banking; foreign firms must offer skills, management and technologies that Chinese – for the moment – do not have.

Sir Victor Sassoon and Silas Hardoon had easy access to officials of the two councils who controlled the International and French concessions of Shanghai. The Jewish entrepreneurs of today must work through a large, complex and non-transparent bureaucracy; approval for new projects can take months or even years. Policy can change suddenly and unexpectedly.

Despite these obstacles, some have remarkable achievements. One is Roberta Lipson (李碧菁), a native of Brooklyn, New York, who has lived in Beijing for 38 years and established a nationwide network of hospitals in Beijing, Shanghai, Tianjin, Wuxi, Guangzhou and Ulan Bator, capital of Mongolia. She is chief executive of Chindex International (美中互利) and of its subsidiary United Family Healthcare (UFH, 和睦家醫療).

It employs over 2,000 people, including more than 500 doctors, and has an annual turnover of about US$250 million. In the capital, its flagship Beijing United Family Hospital (BJU, 北京和睦家醫院) is supported by a Rehabilitation Hospital, Cancer Centre and nine satellite clinics and medical centres throughout the capital. No foreigner in China has set up such a network in the post-1949 era.

Lipson earned her MBA from Columbia University in New York; after graduation, she continued to study Mandarin and worked for a few years for an American pharmaceutical company, which allowed her to pursue her secondary interest – health care.

"During my first year in college, I watched Henry Kissinger go to China, which made studying Chinese history all the more exciting," she said. At that time, finding a job in China and obtaining the necessary visa was no simple matter. In 1979, she obtained a job with one of the first American firms to set up an office in Beijing. She started to import medical technology for Chinese hospitals, which desperately needed it. This was spun into a separate company, Chindex which she founded with fellow American Elyse Beth Silverberg, also Jewish; the two spent 10 years building a business that sold medical technology to Chinese hospitals.

One day Lipson accompanied a friend who was heavily pregnant to a Beijing hospital. There was a huge shortage of beds. Thanks to her personal connections, she was able to find a space for her friend. The two arrived during the night in early winter; the nurses told them to walk up three storeys to the delivery area, carrying a wash basin and suitcase. Everyone else – without her connections – was left to wait in a hallway where young men were sitting on the floor smoking cigarettes. No-one was allowed near the delivery room.

That experience – and the pleasure of giving birth to her first baby in the United States – convinced her that residents of Beijing deserved better. She wanted to introduce the philosophy of patient-centred care: a service mentality: systems management and quality control. "The expat community was, at that time, going abroad if they caught a cold, much less to have a baby," she said.

In China, as in all countries, the medical sector is highly regulated, because it affects the life and death of its citizens. In addition, providing private health is lucrative – another reason for a government to control it. Lipson applied to set up a private hospital in Beijing; it was a first in China by a foreigner and involved complex negotiations.

Finally, in 1994, the city government approved it, as a joint venture between Chindex and the Chinese Academy of Medical Sciences (中國醫學科學院) in 1994; it opened in 1997. Very few foreigners – perhaps no-one other than she – would have been able to obtain such approval. She had a track record of 15 years in the health care field in China and knew personally directors of many hospitals which were using equipment her company had imported for them.

That earned for her the necessary level of trust and confidence among government officials. She presented it to them as a project that would "improve the investment environment of Beijing"; a hospital providing international quality of care with foreign and foreign-trained staff would help to persuade expatriates and their families to settle in China.

Initially, 98 per cent of the patients were expats; now almost 70 per cent are local Chinese. The 20 years since it opened have seen a remarkable increase in the wealth of China's upper and upper-middle classes and the development of private health insurance; these have enabled many Chinese to utilise the services of BJU.

"We are proud of being at the leading edge of healthcare," she said. "We are most proud when our innovations can impact the larger health system. Perhaps what has been most impactful is upgrading the position of the patient in the health care process, as it is in family-centred birthing care, to show women actually deserve more respect. As a result, (local) women have started demanding more from the public system."

The next step was to open two satellite clinics in Beijing. In 2004, the company opened the Shanghai United Family Hospital and Clinics; it has since further expanded to Tianjin, Qingdao, Guangzhou and Wuxi. Now it has more than 19 comprehensive premium hospitals and satellite clinic facilities throughout China.

Its hospitals all provide full-service premium inpatient and outpatient medical care, while their satellite clinics can provide personalised outpatient care in convenient locations for the communities they serve.

Among the clinics in Beijing, the United Family New Hope Oncology Center, which opened in 2011, gave China the first of its kind multidisciplinary team approach to treating cancer in a uniquely relaxed setting. In 2005, Beijing United Family Hospital and Clinics was the first integrated health system in Asia to receive accreditation by the Joint Commission International (JCI), the worldwide leader in improving the quality of healthcare.

UFH operations in Shanghai received similar accreditation in 2008, along with its entire system in 2011, placing UFH's multi-city healthcare network as the only one of its kind in China, and within an elite group of the world's best healthcare providers with the JCI "Gold Seal of Approval" for healthcare quality and patient safety.

The Beijing facility is a full-service hospital, offering 24-hour emergency care, family medicine and departments including anaesthesiology, dermatology, eye clinic, internal medicine, neurosurgery, obstetrics and gynaecology, paediatrics, operating rooms and traditional Chinese medicine. It has staff who speak English, Mandarin, Japanese, Korean, Spanish, Russian, Mongolian, German, French and Portuguese. And it has arrangements with over 40 international insurance companies.

In 1994, Chindex, which is registered in Bethesda, Maryland, listed on the Nasdaq. In 2014, Shanghai Fosun Pharmaceutical Group, a maker of modern drugs and traditional Chinese medicine, and TPG Capital began acquiring public shares of the company. In August that year, a group involving the two firms and Lipson, as CEO, acquired the remaining public shares for about US$433 million.

This deal took the company private and it delisted from Nasdaq. Lipson remains Chief Executive Officer of the company. She is proud of the legacy of the development of the United Family Healthcare System in China. The system not only directly impacts the good health of hundreds of thousands of lives per year, saving lives and curing illness; she is also proud of the positive impact it has had in providing new models and concepts of care which the government has referenced in its national healthcare reform. "Creating community institutions is a strong Jewish tradition. Jews have built schools and hospitals wherever in the world they have settled," said Lipson.

Her husband, Ted Plafker, is a veteran journalist. They have three children. "Our children speak Mandarin, regard themselves as Beijing people and see their future careers here," he said. "I visit my friends and relatives in New Jersey, where I grew up, but see no reason to move there." The couple own a house in the Chaoyang district of the capital, which they bought in 1999. They are pillars of Beijing's Jewish community, having seen it grow from modest beginnings in the early 1980s. (Note 19)

They are similar to the Sephardis who went from Bombay to Shanghai in the 1850s and 1860s. They left a known and safe environment to try a new life in a new and unpredictable country. Some prospered, some failed. The Sassoon family left a lasting legacy. So has Roberta Lipson.

Roberta Lipson, chief executive officer of United
Family Healthcare, in Beijing.

Notes

1   Interview with Rabbi Shimon Freundlich, 17/3/2017.

2   Interview with Rabbi Shimon Freundlich, 17/3/2017.

3   Interview with Rabbi Mordechai Avtzon, 27/7/2017.

4   Interview with Rabbi Shalom Greenberg, 13/12/2016.

5   Interview with Professor Wang Jian, 14/12/2016.

6   Interview with Rabbi Shalom Greenberg, 13/12/2016.

7   *Shanghai Daily*, 6/9/2015 and *South China Morning Post*, 7/9/2015.

8   Interview with Maurice Ohana, June 2006.

9   Interview with Professor Wang Jian, 14/12/2016.

10   Interview with Rabbi Shimon Freundlich, 17/3/2017.

11   Interview with Isaac Epstein, 16/12/2016.

12   Interview with Isaac Epstein, 16/12/2016.

13   Interview with Joel Epsteinas, 15/12/2016.

14   Interview with Sara Imas, October 2005.

15   Interview with Liu Meixiu (劉美秀), 14/12/2016.

16   Interview with Rabbi Shimon Freundlich, 17/3/2017.

17   *China Daily*, 30/06/2017.

18   Section on Harbin provided by Professor Dan Ben-Canaan.

19   Interviews with Roberta Lipson and Ted Plafker, April 2017.

In 25 years, economic ties boom – but no peace dividend

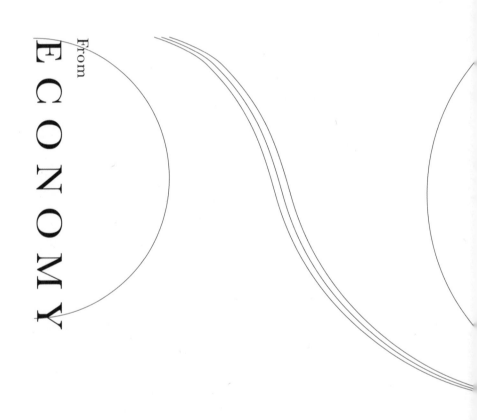

From
ECONOMY

In January 1992, when Israeli diplomats signed the documents that normalised relations with China, they were delighted to finish a job that had taken 42 years to complete. None could have imagined the result 25 years later – China has become one of the biggest foreign investors in Israel, its largest trading partner in Asia and third largest in the world.

In 2016, bilateral trade reached US$11.3 billion, compared to US$50 million in 1992; Chinese investment in Israel was US$16.5 billion in 2016, making China one of Israel's top two foreign investors that year. In the major sea port of Ashdod, China Harbour Engineering (中國港灣建設有限責任公司) is building a new pier at a cost of US$1 billion.

The government has approved a new railway from Ashdod to the port of Eilat on the Red Sea which would supplement the Suez Canal to bring goods from Asia to Europe; in 2012, it signed an agreement with China's Minister of Transport to build the railway line.

Five state-owned Chinese construction firms are building thousands of new homes in Israel; each can import 1,000 workers. Technion, Israel's leading institute of high technology, is opening a campus in Shantou (汕頭), in Guangdong province; the first Israeli university extension in China, Guangdong Technion started to receive students in the autumn of 2017.

In 2016, 70,000 Israelis visited China and 79,000 Chinese went the other way. Since 2017, one Israeli and two Chinese airlines have been providing regular flights between the two countries. When China established the Asian Infrastructure Development Bank in 2015, Israel was one of the 57 founding members – unlike the United States and Japan, which declined to join. China and Israel are discussing a Free Trade Agreement.

This Chinese presence is something completely new. Historically, Israel's economic, social and cultural ties were with Europe and the United States, home to the largest Jewish communities of the diaspora and the birthplace of a large proportion of its citizens. Historically, no Chinese lived in Israel. None of Israel's leaders were born in Asia; most have come from Russia, Eastern Europe or North America. The polyglot Israelis speak Hebrew, Yiddish, Arab, English, Russian, French, German and other European languages; but few learnt Chinese.

The first Department of Chinese and Japanese Studies (later East Asian Studies) was set up at the Hebrew University in 1969; the second only in 1995, at Tel Aviv University. Now the Israeli Ministry of Education includes Mandarin in the school curriculum.

How has this remarkable change come about? It is because each side has much to offer the other. Israel has expertise in agriculture, arms, medicine, science, water treatment, high-technology and counter-terrorism and many investment opportunities for the enormous surplus capital built up by Chinese companies. In exchange, China is one of the fastest-growing economies in the world; because of politics, Israeli firms are excluded from most Arab and Muslim countries and need new markets.

The exchanges are helped by a lack of historical and political baggage. There is no anti-Semitism in China; the Beijing government and public have a very positive view of Israel and the Jewish people, making it easy for them to live and work in China. There is no public debate about the West Bank and occupied territories nor movement to boycott goods produced in them, as in Europe and the United States.

Despite some concerns, the Israeli government welcomes investment by China, in order to diversify its sources of capital and reduce dependence on the U.S. and Europe. But there is an intense public debate about this Chinese capital, given that Beijing is an ally of Iran and other enemies of Israel; some want a stricter approval process and a clearer understanding of China's motives.

Turning the desert green

One of the greatest Israeli contributions to China has been to teach its farmers how to grow crops and plant trees in desert conditions. Israel is a world leader in this technology. In the early 1980s, before diplomatic relations were even established, Beijing had allowed teams of Israeli water engineers to come, in secret, to survey collective farms in the southern region of Guangxi (廣西); they recommended the use of drip irrigation, as well as Israeli seeds better suited to the soil and climate.

The Chinese agreed, but demanded that any markings showing Israeli origin be removed from the equipment and seed packaging. Three years later, again in secret, a team of Israeli hydrologists and geologists was invited to help develop an irrigation plan for the semi-arid Wuwei (武威) district in Gansu (甘肅) province, south of the Gobi desert.

"We have one of the largest areas of desert in the world and our country is one of the worst affected by desertification," wrote Wang Xiumiao (王秀苗) of Zaozhuang College (棗莊學院) in Shandong in a paper in April 2011 called "How Israeli agriculture has inspired the dry lands of northwest China" (以色列農業及其對我國西北乾旱地區的啓示). "China's desert area is 3.33 million square kilometres. The arid areas of the northwest must take inspiration from the success of Israeli agriculture to increase production and farmers' incomes."

Wang said that, in Israel, farmers were well-educated and used the latest technology; but, in northwest China, the best educated young people in rural areas left their homes for lucrative jobs in the cities. As a result, those left behind did not have the intellectual ability to improve techniques and yields. (Note 1)

After normalisation of relations in 1992, this transfer of technology accelerated. There are Israeli irrigation schemes and technologies in operation in many areas of northwest and west China, including Xinjiang (新疆), the largest region in the country which accounts for one sixth of the national territory.

More than a quarter of Xinjiang is desert. One example is Korla (庫爾勒) a city built by demobilised soldiers in the 1950s as a base to explore for oil in the nearby Taklamakan desert; it is the headquarters of Tarim Oilfield Co, a unit of the state giant Petrochina (中國石油). But it is only 70 kilometres from the desert; fierce sandstorms blanket the skies for days on end in spring. Annual rainfall is only 50 millimetres per square metre; the city could plant trees but not irrigate them.

In 2001, an Israeli firm, Eisenberg Agri Company, introduced drip-irrigation technology; it used a pressurised system of main pipes and hundreds of drip lines that can carry water up hills and deliver it to the root of every tree. It can save 75 per cent of the 800-1,000 cubic metres of water needed to irrigate one mu (0.0667 hectare) of land with planted trees. The city says that, as a result, it has planted more than 3,000 hectares with trees. (Note 2)

Israelis agro-companies have skills and technologies suitable for many of its neighbours; but politics prevent them exporting their know-how and equipment to these countries. The large market of China is a good alternative.

Mozart and air conditioning – bovine bliss

Another demonstration of Israeli expertise was provided in 2001 when Mashav, the Foreign Ministry's agency for international co-operation, set up a model dairy farm outside Beijing. The farm, with 800 milking cows and 650 heifers, was rebuilt according to Israel's technological standard and used Afimilk's management system, feeding equipment and training; Afimilk is a world leader in computerized systems for dairy farm and herd management.

Average annual milk production in Israel is 11,770 kilograms per cow per year – compared to 9,500-10,000 kg in other developed countries – and the highest in the world. By the end of 2007, average output at the Beijing model farm exceeded 10,000 kg per cow per year, compared to an average of 6,000 in China; by 2015, it had reached 11,650 kg, the highest in China.

Everything on the farm, from milk production and quality to herd health and fertility, is monitored on a daily basis in the main computer, with software developed and made in Israel. The farm has become a training centre for thousands of Chinese farmers. Its cows are the happiest in the country; kept warm in winter and cool in summer, they listen to classical music; the happier and more comfortable they are, the more milk they produce. Chinese dairy farms have also sent staff to farms and training courses in Israel, to improve their skills and technology.

In March 2015, Bright Food (光明食品), China's second largest food and beverage company, bought a 77 per cent controlling stake in Tnuva, Israel's largest dairy company. It is the country's biggest collective with more than 620 members, specialising in milk and dairy products; it accounts for 70 per cent of the local market. What attracted Bright Food

An Israeli specialist at work in the model Israeli dairy farm outside Beijing.

was Tnuva's advanced technology and production. The kibbutz movement retains a 23 per cent share of Tnuva.

The Dragon in Silicon Wadi

It is in the sector of advanced science and technology that co-operation between the two countries has been most intense. In 2016, Chinese investment in Israel reached a record US$16.5 billion, most of it to buy Internet, cyber-security and medical device start-ups. (Note 3)

What attracts Chinese venture capital to Israel? An article in the *Global People* (環球人物) newsweekly in August 2016 on the Hebrew University of Jerusalem, the second oldest in the Holy Land, gives a good explanation.

The university was built on Mount Scopus in Jerusalem in 1918, 30 years before the establishment of Israel. "Since the state was founded, it has been through four wars but has remained one of the most developed countries in the world and is a leader in many sectors of high technology," the journalist wrote. "How have the Jewish people achieved this despite suffering so many tragedies in their history? One major reason is that they have put science as a core of their life and education as critical to the survival and development of the Jewish race." (Note 4)

It said plans for the university had been made in the early years of the Zionist movement at the end of the 19th century. One of its founders was a distinguished biochemist, Chaim Weizmann, who became the first President of Israel. "The university has produced eight Nobel Prize winners, four national presidents and over 7,000 patents," it said.

It is this relentless innovation, diversity of hi-tech start-ups and rich entrepreneurial talent that have drawn Chinese investors. The value of Israeli technology companies on NASDAQ is over US$100 billion; the country spends 4.1 per cent of GDP on research and development, second in the world after South Korea with 4.3 per cent. (Note 5)

Thanks to this innovation-backed economy, Israel's per capita GDP has reached about US$36,000, making it richer than Italy or Spain. It has a substantial military budget – US$21.7 billion in 2017, more than five per cent of national GDP. This has become an economic asset, since elite intelligence and communications units of the military work with business and academia to serve as key training institutions and an incubator for new firms.

Cyber security exports are worth more than US$4 billion a year. The country is a leader in counter-terrorist systems, such as sensors, data fusion systems and other software, drones and ground systems. There is close co-operation between Israel's government, universities, research institutes and industry to create the best environment for innovation and bringing new ideas and products to market.

The first Chinese to invest heavily in Israel was Hong Kong entrepreneur Li Ka-shing (李嘉誠), one of Asia's richest men. In 1999, Hutchison Telecom, a unit of his Hutchison Whampoa Group (HW, 和記黃埔),

won Israel's third mobile network operating licence, together with two Israeli firms.

In 2008, HW set up a water treatment company in Israel, specialising in desalination, water treatment, wastewater treatment and other water technologies. In 2011, with an Israeli partner, it won a tender to build the world's largest seawater reverse osmosis desalination plant at Sorek in Israel; it provides more than 150 million cubic metres of clean water to 1.5 million Israeli citizens.

Over the last five years, Horizons Ventures (維港投資), the venture capital arm of Li Ka-shing, has invested actively in Israel; it has put money into many of the country's most innovative companies, a total of more than 24 investments.

One of the most successful was Waze, a GPS-based map software company. It was founded in 2006 by three Israelis; it works on smartphones and tablets and provides real-time information and travel times and route details submitted by users. It won the Best Overall App award at the 2013 Mobile World Congress; in 2013, it had 50 million users around the world.

In October 2011, Horizons Ventures and Kleiner Perkins Caufield and Byers invested US$30 million in Waze, its third round of funding. In June 2013, Google paid more than US$1 billion to acquire Waze; with an 11 per cent stake, Li's Horizons Ventures earned an estimated US$143 million from the sale, a spectacular return in less than two years.

In 2013, through the Li Ka-shing Foundation, Li donated US$130 million to the Technion Institute of Technology, Israel's first university founded in 1912. A large part of the money came from the profits made from the sale of Waze; it is being used to develop its campus in Haifa and set up the Guangdong Technion-Israel Institute of Technology (廣東以色列理工學院), a joint venture between the institute and Shantou University (汕頭大學) in Guangdong; the university, in Li's native place, was founded in 1981 with a donation from him of HK$6 billion.

His was the largest donation ever made to Technion and one of the biggest to any Israeli academic institution. Li wants to leave a valuable legacy to his hometown and give Chinese students the opportunity to learn cutting-edge technology in the sectors that will drive the economy of the future.

The cornerstone-laying ceremony for the new institution was held on December 16, 2015; it was attended by 5,000 guests, including Shimon Peres, the ninth president of Israel, who was then 92. It is only Technion's second branch outside Israel. In his address, Technion President Professor Peretz Lavie said: "This partnership, which combines the spirit of Israeli innovation with the power of China, will benefit all parties – the Technion and the University of Shantou, Israel and China – and will give a significant boost to the Chinese education system. The outcomes of this historic project will affect the whole of humanity."

In its first 10 years, from 2017 to 2026, it will have 2,960 students, including 300 post-graduates, in chemical engineering, biotechnology and food engineering and materials engineering programmes. In the long

Israeli and Chinese officials at the ground-breaking ceremony for the Guangdong Technion-Israel Institute of Technology. In the centre is former president Shimon Peres and, second from right, Li Ka-shing, benefactor of Shantou University. (Credit: Guangdong Technion-Israel Institute of Technology)

Israeli president Shimon Peres meets Chinese children on a state visit to Beijing in April 2014.

term, the number will rise to 5,000 graduates, including 1,000 post-graduates. (Note 6)

The success of Li's investments attracted Chinese conglomerates; some decided to follow his example, in venture capital and acquisitions. Up to 2010, foreign venture capital into Israel was largely from the U.S. and Europe; since 2011, that has changed, with a rapid increase in funds from Asia, especially China.

In October 2011, ChemChina (中國化工集團) paid US$2.4 billion for a 60% controlling stake in Makhteshim-Agan Industries, a global crop protection company; in 2014, it changed its name to Adama, which means earth in Hebrew.

Founded in 1945 in Moza near Jerusalem, it is one of the largest companies in the world in its sector, developing products and services to control weeds, insects and disease. Globally, it employs 5,000 people and markets its products in over 100 countries. This was a landmark investment by a major mainland Chinese firm. Adama had the innovation and technology and ChemChina the financial power to enable it to expand in the world market, especially in China.

Other large mainland firms which have invested in Israel are Lenovo (聯想) Fosun (復星), Xiaomi (小米科技), Baidu (百度) and Alibaba (阿里巴巴). Huawei (華為) and Haier (海爾) have established research and development centres there.

At the China-Israel summit in Tel Aviv in September 2016, Chinese IT firm Neusoft (東軟集團) and Infinity Group, a Sino-Israeli private equity fund, set up a US$250 million investment fund and platform for Israeli med-tech companies operating in China.

Amir Gal-Or, founder of the Infinity Fund, said: "Neusoft is considered China's biggest IT corporation, with a 50 per cent share of the health market in China specializing in developing software for the industrial sector." (Note 7)

Ping An Ventures (平安創新投資基金) and China Broadband Capital (中國寬帶產業基金) put venture capital into IronSource, which offers business development and distribution tools for mobile apps. Reuters quoted Tomer Bar-zeev, chief executive of IronSource, as saying strategic Chinese investors were attractive because they offered Israeli firms a way into a Chinese market that is otherwise difficult to crack.

"Once we become a portfolio company of these Chinese investors, they help with opening doors in China … where the business community really relies on connections you build there." (Note 8)

In April 2013, Yingke (盈科律師事務所), one of China's biggest law firms, acquired Eyal Khayat, Zolty, Neiger & Co, a boutique law firm that specialises in high-tech and venture capital. This followed a change in regulations in 2012 that allowed foreign law firms to practise the law of their home jurisdiction in Israel.

Yingke has 20 offices in China and 16 offices and alliances overseas. Its presence in Israel is evidence of the increasing interest of Chinese companies in the market. According to the Chinese media, Chinese entities invested US$500 million in Israeli start-ups in 2015 as well as US$1 billion in Israeli venture capital funds in 2016. (Note 9)

In analysing this flood of Chinese investment, the *First Financial Daily* (第一財經日報)said that 77 per cent of Israel's population had at least 12 years of education, with 20 per cent having attended university. Six per cent of the population was engaged in research and development, the highest percentage in the world.

"Two Chinese have one opinion: one Israeli has two opinions," it said. (Note 10) "In recent years, Chinese investment in Israel has overtaken that from the U.S. In 2015, bilateral trade reached US$11 billion, up from US$5 million in 1992. High-tech companies in Israel have received US$5 billion in Chinese capital, through direct investment, buy out and investment funds."

It quoted an Israeli entrepreneur as saying: "Ten years ago, Israelis had no faith in Chinese and feared they would trick them. Five years ago, they feared Chinese would copy them, but now Israelis believe in the ability of Chinese and are willing to sell their technology to them."

In their book on economic relations between the two countries, *Israel and China, from Silk Road to Innovation Highway*, published in 2015, Lionel Friedfeld and Philippe Metoudi are bullish on the future. "About

66 per cent of the more than 250 multinationals who have established R & D centres are American. In 50 years, given recent trends, we believe it is fair to say that the presence of Chinese conglomerates will at least equal the American presence … Israel is labelled as one of the most dynamic high-tech and start-up ecosystems in the world but has failed to attract global liquidity to its financial market. China, on the other hand, with the world's largest savings ratio, is destined to manage tomorrow's global liquidity and needs a world-renowned high-tech label. The financial markets of Israel and China may be a perfect match." (Note 11)

"At the forefront of global research and development in many fields, Israel invents ideas and technologies that have been revolutionising the world. China, which has no competition in the area of manufacturing, has already identified innovation as its Achilles heel. Even though it has made tremendous progress in increasing the number of scientists and engineers it produces, China knows it needs more than this. Today's 'match in heaven' has been nurtured for centuries, yet was not readily foreseeable until only a few years ago." (Note 12)

Opposition to Chinese investment

But not everything has been plain sailing. Two Chinese bids to buy Israeli insurance companies failed because of regulatory opposition; these firms manage money of the public and require closer official scrutiny than a purchase of a high-tech start-up or manufacturing firm.

There has been an intense public debate in Israel over the strategic risks of selling companies to China. There was a major public protest against the sale of dairy firm Tnuva to Bright Food, because of its position as one of the country's biggest food producers. The Economics Committee of the Knesset (Parliament) called on the company to stop the sale.

"Israel should beware a situation in which a foreign element controls a strategic asset like Tnuva, Israel's largest food company which supplies more than 60 per cent of fresh dairy produce," said former Mossad chief Efraim Halevy.

In a paper in April 2014, Dr Yoram Evron, a research fellow at the Institute for National Security Studies at Tel Aviv University, set out the arguments against Chinese acquisitions. "One major issue concerns China's political and strategic positions, efforts and objectives in the Middle East, which often do not match Israeli interests. China's interest in the Middle East stems first and foremost from its energy dependence, which demands good relations with Iran and Saudi Arabia.

"China even assisted Iran with its nuclear project ... The activity of Chinese companies in Israel can help the Chinese government by gaining control of important Israeli connections and access to information, technological resources and other essential assets."

A second issue, Evron said, is that China did not protect intellectual property rights. A third is the implications of such purchases for relations with U.S., Israel's closest ally. He called for the establishment of a permanent body that would review all foreign investment in Israel: "This body would take into account the gamut of political, strategic, economic and technological aspects involved in Chinese activity in Israel and the region." (Note 13)

No shellfish, please

One evening in the summer of 2000, during a friendship visit, a group of visiting Israeli parliamentarians was sitting down for dinner at an official guest house in Beijing. To their surprise, they found on the walls not the flag of their own country but that of Norway, presumably for the guests of the day before; normally, the Chinese are punctilious in observing protocol. Then the waitresses arrived with the first dish – and the guests were astonished and shocked to see that it contained shellfish, which is not kosher and cannot be eaten by observant Jews. How could their hosts have made such a mistake?

It was, of course, no mistake but a punishment meted out by Beijing for the biggest business setback of the post-1992 period – Israel's cancellation of a contract for a radar system badly wanted by the People's Liberation Army. It had sold an advanced Phalcon Airborne Warning and Control System (AWACs), which was to have been installed on Russian-built Ilyushin-Il-76 aircraft; it would allow military planners to track and target simultaneously large numbers of aircraft and other targets from an airborne command post. The contract was worth US$250 million. The technology had been developed by the Israelis themselves.

"By the mid-1990s, Washington had begun to express its dismay about the

Israeli sale of the system. If satisfied with the sale, Beijing planned to buy three more, at an estimated cost of US$1 billion," according to Professor Yitzhak Shichor in his article "Israel and China: Mutual Demystification in Chinese-Israel Relation". (Note 14)

"Consistently ignoring America's reservations, Israel went on with the sale that seemed to proceed when President Jiang Zemin (江澤民) was paying an exceptionally long visit to Israel in April 2000. Three months later, in July, Washington lost its patience and forced Israel to cancel the deal and improve its arms export supervision through a special parliamentary law and creation of a new department in the Ministry of Defence, whose director had to resign.

"In order to placate the Chinese, Israel paid them US$350 million in compensation but still had to cope with the subsequent cooling in Sino-Israeli relations – less because of the cancellation of the deal but much more because of Jiang Zemin's loss of face and public humiliation. Arriving in Beijing just after the cancellation, the unfortunate new Israeli ambassador Yitzhak Shelef was practically ostracised by high-level Chinese officials throughout his term."

A further punishment came in the autumn of 2000. An exhibition of the life of Albert Einstein was to be held in five Chinese cities. But the Ministry of Culture insisted that three items be deleted – the fact he was Jewish, that he supported a Jewish state in Palestine and was invited to be the nation's second president, an offer he declined. The organisers refused to meet these demands and the exhibition was cancelled.

Officials of the Israeli government said that Washington had made it clear the deal had to be scrapped. U.S. defence officials said the system would alter the strategic balance in the region in the event of a conflict; it could help Chinese forces to threaten U.S. ships if they were defending Taiwan in a war with the mainland. Washington did not compensate Israel for its loss. For Israel, it was a very difficult decision; in the end, it had to put strategic interests with its most important ally above its relationship with a key trading partner.

One motive of the Americans was to damage the reputation of Israel in the Chinese arms market. As we described in Chapter Seven, it was a significant exporter to China in the 1980s. But the world had changed since then. In the 1980s, the main enemy of the U.S. was the Soviet Union; it was in the interests of the Americans for Israel to arm China, also an enemy of the Soviets. But the Soviet Union collapsed in 1991, bringing an end to the Cold War.

Many in Washington had predicted that the Communist regime in China would go the same way. But, in June 1989, it used military force to crush opposition; the Party showed that it was determined not to follow the Soviet example. China had become a rival to the U.S. In the 1990s, Russia became the largest arms supplier to China, which also took great steps to upgrade its own military technology.

It was a historical irony. The arms sales had flourished in a period of great secrecy when the two countries had no diplomatic relations, because Beijing wanted to hide them from its Arab friends. Now, when there were direct flights and normal ties and transfer of money, the arms trade has dried up. It was a financial blow to Israel's defence industry; military sales are a major source of foreign exchange. Yet, shortly afterwards, India, China's rival in Asia, has become Israel's leading arms market in the world.

China has rapidly developed its own arms industry and become a significant exporter, although far behind the United States and Russia. Its customers include countries and organisations in the Middle East hostile to Israel, including Syria, Iran and Yemen.

"Chinese-made or designed weapons, mainly short-range cruise missiles and rockets earlier delivered to Iran, Syria, Yemen and Sudan reached organisations such as Hizbullah in Lebanon and Hamas in the Gaza Strip and were fired against Israel," wrote Professor Shichor. "An Israeli navy corvette was hit. Embarrassed, Beijing asked Israel not to pursue this matter publicly … Visiting China, Israeli leaders have tried to make the Chinese aware of their contribution to Middle East instability, contrary to their own interest, with limited success." (Note 15)

When Hassan Rouhani was re-elected president of Iran on May 21, 2017, President Xi Jinping (習近平) sent him a congratulatory telegram. During a visit to Teheran in January 2016, the first by a Chinese head of state for 14 years, Xi said that the two countries had agreed to form a comprehensive strategic partnership and boost co-operation on all fronts. China is Iran's largest trading partner and biggest buyer of crude oil.

Workers and railways

From the second half of the 19th century, Chinese started to go abroad in large numbers to find work and a new life. They went to North and South America, Australia, South Africa and Russia and, from the early 20th century, to Europe. But they did not go to Palestine. After 1949, the lack of relations between Israel and China meant that Chinese could not go there.

If one of the few former Jewish residents of Harbin or Shanghai who knew Mandarin wanted to practise it, he had to find one of a small number of visiting Taiwan students, professors or businessmen – difficult because Israel never had official relations with Taiwan.

That changed in the early 1990s, when Israel began to import workers from Asia to replace Palestinians; firms no longer wanted to hire them because of the potential security risk. The imported workers came from Turkey, Thailand, the Philippines and China.

The Chinese worked on farms and building sites and numbered 20-30,000; some had work visas and others did not. As they do elsewhere, the illegals paid money to middlemen to smuggle them into the country; many go heavily in debt and are exploited because they have no legal status. The illegals in Israel were especially vulnerable because there was no well-established Chinese community to support them, as there is in the major cities of Western Europe, the U.S. and Australia.

On April 12, 2002, several Chinese workers were standing near the crowded Mahane Yehuda market in Jerusalem, when a terrorist bomb exploded. Six people were killed and 84 injured; among the dead were two Chinese, Cai Xianyang (蔡獻陽) and Lin Chunmei(林春美), both from Putian, Fujian (福建莆田); two other Chinese were seriously injured.

The government investigated the two dead workers and discovered that both were illegals; the Chinese embassy declined to co-operate in the investigation. The Israeli government decided, nonetheless, that the two were entitled to compensation. Officials went to Ben Gurion airport to see off the plane taking home the bodies of the two; an official of the Beijing embassy went to the funeral with the families in Fujian.

To arrange the compensation, the government sent a team to Fujian. According to reports in the Chinese media, it agreed to pay the parents of the two workers US$1,100 a month until their death: US$1,100 a month to the children until they reached the age of 18: and US$1,700 a month to the widows until their death. The two families asked for a single payment and the government agreed; it gave each family US$700,000. It felt a sense of responsibility that, whatever their status, these two foreigners had come to work in their country and died through no fault of their own.

This prompted Chinese on the Net to praise the Israeli government for its generosity and say that it cared for the two men more than their own government.

Initially, Chinese came to work for Israeli firms. Then Chinese state and private companies began to win contracts for important infrastructure projects, like the Akko-Karmiel railway, the Carmel tunnels in Haifa and the Ashdod port.

In March 2015, the international tenders committee of Israel Ports Authority announced that Shanghai International Port Group (SIPG, 上海國際港務集團) would operate a new private harbour being developed in Haifa Bay, under a 25-year contract that is expected to begin in 2021.

Transportation Minister Israel Katz termed the decision a "historic day" for Israel. "The Chinese group that won the tender will bring competition to the sector. Its success is an expression of confidence in the State of Israel by a superpower, which has decided to invest billions of shekels in Israel and turn it into an international cargo centre for all the world," Katz was quoted as saying in *Haaretz* newspaper. (Note 16)

"The new Haifa port – and a second one in Ashdod – are intended to compete with two adjacent harbours owned by the government. The private ports project, which Katz has been championing, is aimed at injecting competition into the sector where powerful unions have imposed rules that make operations costly and inefficient, raising prices for imported products," the newspaper said.

"The new Haifa facility is being built by Shapir Engineering and Ashtrom, two Israeli companies, at a cost of four billion shekels (US$1.16 billion as of January 2018). Sources said SIPG expected to invest another one billion shekels in equipment and upgrading infrastructure before operation can begin. SIPG will pay a license fee for all cargo moving through the port as well as annual usage fees for the facility amounting to 65 shekels a square metre, all of which should generate tens of millions of shekels of income annually for the state." (Note 17)

Chinese firms are also leading suppliers of buses and trucks in Israel; they may provide electric locomotives to Israel Railways and light-rail cars to the mass-transit system of Tel Aviv.

Chinese companies are also important in the construction sector. In April 2017, Israel signed an agreement with China to bring in 6,000 Chinese construction workers; but they will not work in the West Bank because Beijing opposes the building of Jewish settlements in occupied Palestinian territories, including the West Bank.

The men will work for five Chinese companies who have signed contracts with the government to build new homes over five years. Each must show that it has built 250,000 square metres by the fourth year. The government wants to build thousands of new homes in a short time, to ease a serious housing shortage.

From the Red Sea to the Mediterranean

The most ambitious Sino-Israeli project would be a railway running 350 kilometres from Eilat, the country's most southerly point on the Red Sea, to Ashdod on the Mediterranean. In 2012, the Israeli government signed an agreement with China's Minister of Transport to build the railway line; but the project has yet to receive final approval or secure funding. The cost will be at least US$6.5 billion and could reach double that.

The engineering challenges are enormous – the line would cross hundreds of kilometres of rough desert terrain with changes of elevation and subject to flash floods; high-speed trains need a minimum of bends. The project would need 63 bridges and 9.5 kilometres of tunnels. Since the 1950s, successive governments have planned such a train line to Eilat; but the cost and engineering difficulties have always prevented its construction.

The economic benefits would be substantial. Passengers from Tel Aviv would need only two hours to reach Eilat; the line could transport 2.5 million tons of chemicals and 140,000 cars a year. The economic development brought by the line could help Eilat achieve a goal to triple its population to 150,000.

The line would also serve as a land bridge between Asia and Europe; cargo unloaded at Eilat would travel to Ashdod, for onward shipment to ports in Europe. It would complement the Suez Canal. Natural gas could be pumped from Mediterranean fields off Israel through a pipeline to Eilat, for shipment to India, China and other Asian markets.

Israel sees this railway as a link in China's 'One Belt, One Road', the ambitious brainchild of President Xi Jinping; he aims to rebuild the land and sea Silk Roads of ancient China. The railway and the ports of Eilat and Ashdod would enable exporters in Asia, including China, to ship their goods to markets in Europe. But this is many years away – it would require not only the building of the railway but also a massive expansion of the port facilities at Eilat that would cost hundreds of millions of dollars.

Trade

The economic honeymoon between the two countries is reflected in the dramatic increase in trade, which has grown greatly since diplomatic relations were established in 1992. Trade in 2016 was US$11.3 billion, double that of 2010 and up from US$22.8 million in 1991.

Since 1994, China has had a growing trade surplus with Israel. In 2015, it reached US$2.61 billion, with China exporting US$5.86 billion and importing US$3.25 billion. That year China was Israel's second largest export destination, behind the U.S. with US$24 billion and ahead of Hong Kong with US$2.89 billion and Palestine with US$2.86 billion.

China ranked second as the origin of imports to Israel, behind the U.S. with US$8.56 billion and ahead of Switzerland and Germany.

Israel's main exports to China are electronic equipment; medical and technical equipment; fertilisers; machinery; diamonds and other precious metals. For example, Nice Systems, a leading Israeli firm in telephone recording, data security and surveillance, has won contracts to install video security systems in the subway networks of more than two dozen cities in China, including Beijing. Israel's main imports from China are electronic equipment; machinery; clothing; organic chemicals; iron and steel; and furniture, lighting and signs.

The two countries are negotiating a free trade agreement. When he visited Beijing in March 2017, Prime Minister Benjamin Netanyahu agreed with his Chinese counterpart, Li Keqiang (李克強), to accelerate the talks.

President Xi Jinping told Netanyahu: "Israel is a country renowned around the world for its innovation. At the same time, China is pushing forward innovation-driven development, so innovation has become the common focus of our two countries. It is the priority for our co-operation."

The Israeli Prime Minister said that his country should become China's research and development centre. He brought with him more than 100 technology executives. During the visit, the two sides signed agreements for co-operation in economy, science and technology, commerce and aviation valued at US$25 billion. (Note 18)

In 2016, the Israeli embassy in Beijing issued more than 10,000 visas to Chinese business people. In addition to the embassy, there are consulates in Shanghai, Guangzhou, Chengdu and Hong Kong.

Considering that Israel has a population of only 8.7 million and a narrow economic base, it can regard the growth of its exports to China as a success. Its businessmen are competing against well-financed multinationals from Europe, North America and Japan with decades of knowledge, experience and widespread networks in China. It is a market with which most of them are not historically familiar and whose language they do not speak; nor does Israel have the China think tanks and depth of expertise you can find in Europe, the U.S. and Japan.

Tourism from China is a big growth market for Israel. In 2016, a record 79,268 Chinese visited the country, an increase of 60 per cent over 2015; they spent an average of US$267 per day, compared to US$158 by a European.

In November 2016, the two governments introduced a 10-year multiple-entry visa for Chinese and Israeli tourists and businessmen, with a maximum of 90 days; its target is 100,000 Chinese visitors in 2017. The visa allows Chinese to visit Jordan and Egypt and return to Israel.

Three airlines serve Ben Gurion Airport directly from China – El Al and Hainan Airlines from Beijing and Cathay Pacific from Hong Kong. Tourist sites in Israel have started to offer signs and information in Mandarin and hotels to put Chinese food on the menu. Going the other way, about 70,000 Israelis visit China each year. Young people from Israel and China are studying at universities in the other country.

No Peace Dividend

The 25 years of normalisation have seen a remarkable growth in trade, investment, tourism and personal relations, at the official and the individual level. These have brought substantial economic benefits to Israel; China has become an important source of capital, expertise, goods and tourists. Israeli companies have a major new market where they can sell their goods and invest; Israel's citizens can travel there easily, as businessmen, tourists or students. All this is rich reward for those who negotiated the normalisation.

But normalisation has not brought political or diplomatic benefits for Israel – no peace dividend. A permanent member of the United Nations Security Council, China has since the 1950s enjoyed close relations with Israel's Arab neighbours; once it had also established relations with Israel, it could have played the role of peacemaker. But it has chosen not to.

"China's contribution to the resolution of the Arab-Israeli conflict has been so far marginal, at best," wrote Yitzhak Shichor. (Note 19) "Sidestepping the call of international – and Middle Eastern – leaders to become a 'responsible shareholder', Beijing prefers to abstain in crucial votes and avoid taking sides that could alienate allies and friends … many in Israel's diplomatic circles still do not regard Beijing as a real partner in the Middle Eastern peace negotiations, and definitely not as a substitute to Washington or Western Europe."

As we noted above, China is a strong supporter of Iran, Israel's most bitter enemy, and supplies it with arms. In June 2017, the navies of China and Iran held joint exercises near the Strait of Hormuz, through which pass a large proportion of China's oil imports from the Middle East.

Beijing also sells arms to other states that are very hostile to Israel, including Syria, Yemen and Sudan. Beijing supports a two-state solution in the Holy Land but has done little to bring this about.

Its principal interest in the Middle East is economic. It wants access to all the markets for its goods, capital and labour. Involvement in peace-making would mean taking sides and antagonising potential business partners; it does not want to do this. Nor does it have the historic responsibility, like Britain and France, the countries who drew the boundaries of the Middle East after World War One and supported the creation of a Jewish state in Palestine. Beijing's diplomatic priorities are relations with its neighbours and countries in southeast Asia and south Asia. The Middle East is too remote and too complicated.

Professor Shichor said that Beijing would welcome peace in the region as beneficial to its economic expansion and pursuit of raw materials, primarily energy. "Peace may also lessen Israel's dependence on the U.S. and lead to additional opportunities in China in fields that were so far restricted. It may also enable Beijing to become friendlier and more sympathetic to Israel. Still, the prospects of such a settlement – in which China's role would be marginal anyway – are slim." (Note 20)

Going to meet Marx

When leaders of the Communist Party pass away, Chinese say that they have "gone to meet Marx". They cannot say "gone to heaven", "gone to hell" or "on the way to reincarnation", because party members are supposed to be atheist; people suppose that somewhere in the other world is a place for the millions of Communist Party officials from different countries to come together and meet Master Karl, exchange experiences and enjoy an extended break from "building Socialism".

Karl Marx (馬克思) is the Jewish person who has had the greatest impact on China. And he is not the only one. In addition to the many described in this book, others such as Albert Einstein, Sigmund Freud, Henry Kissinger and Shimon Peres have all left a deep mark on this country so far from their own.

Marx is the most remarkable. When I worked in Beijing in the 1980s, a giant portrait of him was the first of four Communist heroes you saw when you entered Tiananmen Square (天安門廣場) on National Day. The others were Friedrich Engels, Josef Stalin and Mao Zedong – Beijing people called it "the history of shaving", because Marx had a luxuriant beard, Engels a smaller one, Stalin a moustache and Mao was clean-shaven.

Since 1949, the study of Marx has been a compulsory subject on the curriculum of mainland schools. Marx was born on May 5, 1818 into a Jewish family; both his grandfathers were rabbis and his mother came from a prosperous Dutch Jewish family who later founded Philips Electronics.

When he wrote *Das Kapital* and *The Communist Manifesto*, he was describing the industrial economies of France, Germany and U.K. and forecast the death of capitalism in those countries. As he did research for *Das Kapital* in the spacious, well-lit reading room of the British Museum in London, he could not have imagined that one day it would inspire a revolution in the world's most populous country on the other side of the globe.

After World War One and the overthrow of the Qing dynasty, there were two competing political movements in China. One was the Nationalists who were inspired by European and American republics; the other was the Communists who wanted to follow the model of the Soviet Union.

Most people, Chinese and foreign, believed that the former would win out, because they controlled the government and were supported by the Western powers. But, thanks to a 14-year war with Japan, help from the Soviet Union, the mistakes of the Nationalists and the military genius of Mao, the Communists won – and Marxism became the state ideology. Ever since, Chinese have been studying the writings of the man with the luxuriant beard and making pilgrimages to his family home in Trier in the Lower Rhine and his burial place and statue in Highgate Cemetery in London.

Another Jew who has left a deep mark on China is Henry Kissinger. He was the pioneer in restoring diplomatic relations between the United States and China after 20 years of deep hostility. From July 9-11 1971, as President Richard Nixon's National Security Advisor, he made a secret visit to Beijing to meet Premier Zhou Enlai (周恩來); he flew there after an official trip to Pakistan.

Since the two countries had no relations, the visit had to be arranged

A Chinese propaganda poster with the face of Karl Marx that reads: "Long Live the Dictatorship of the Proletariat".

Chairman Mao Zedong meets U.S. Secretary of State Henry Kissinger in Beijing in July 1971. This landmark meeting paved the way for Sino-U.S. normalisation of diplomatic relations.

through the leaders of Romania and Pakistan. Thanks to Kissinger's diplomacy, President Nixon went to China in February 1972, paving the way for diplomatic relations in 1979, after a 30-year hiatus. While Nixon took the final decision, it was Kissinger who convinced him that relations with China were in the best interests of the U.S.

Many Chinese believe that only someone of Kissinger's experience, intelligence and cunning could have made such a breakthrough; a Jewish refugee from Germany, he arrived with his family in New York in 1938 at the age of 15.

During World War Two, he served in the intelligence division of the U.S. army in Germany and, for a period, was put in charge of the administration of the city of Krefeld.

The Republican party of Richard Nixon was fiercely anti-Communist and anti-China as a little brother of the "evil" Soviet Union; but Kissinger was able to persuade Nixon and other Republican leaders to take the dramatic step of recognising the PRC. He changed the world.

Ever since then, Kissinger has remained a confidant of successive Chinese leaders who recognise his contribution to their country's new place in the world. They find time to meet him in Beijing and in the U.S.; they have accorded few foreigners this privilege.

The contribution of Sigmund Freud, the father of psychoanalysis, is not so dramatic; but he has left a deep mark on the treatment of mental illness in China. "Freudian theory had a significant impact on Chinese thought," said Gao Xi (高晞), then associate professor of history at Fudan University in Shanghai. "All his works have been translated. Since I was at university in the 1980s, Freudianism has been a hot topic, in books and magazines. Freud and sexualism are very popular, if hard to understand. His theories of the unconscious are completely different to Chinese thinking." (Note 21)

Freudianism arrived in China in May 1914, when a magazine in Shanghai introduced his *Interpretation of Dreams*. It then carried many articles about his life and work. His ideas were widely used in novels and stories of the pre-war period, as writers saw them as illuminating many parts of the human psyche.

Among the more than 20,000 European Jews that escaped to Shanghai in the late 1930s and early 1940s were distinguished Freudians, including Fanny Gisela Halpern, a psychologist from Vienna who taught at universities and worked at hospitals in the city. She remained in Shanghai for more than ten years and was a pioneer in the treatment of mental illness in China. When the Communists took power, she emigrated to Canada.

For the first 35 years after 1949, Freudianism was dismissed as "corrupt" and "immoral"; but it was rehabilitated in the mid-1980s and the first psychiatric clinic of the post-1949 period opened at a Shanghai hospital in 1986. Such clinics now operate in many of China's major hospitals. "Chinese find it difficult to talk about sex, even to a doctor," said Gao. "They prefer anonymous channels, such as radio talk shows." (Note 22)

Among the leaders of Israel, the one who engaged most with China and drove relations forward was Shimon Peres, president from 2007 to 2014. He was a friend of Li Ka-shing; he visited China more than any other Israeli leader. After he died on September 28, 2016, China's official media gave him extensive and positive coverage, calling him an "old friend of China".

Just six days before his passing, Zhang Dejiang (張德江), head of China's Parliament, visited him in hospital in Tel Aviv, during an official visit to Israel. Peres first visited China as Foreign Minister in May 1993, 16 months after diplomatic relations were established.

A polyglot who spoke at least six languages, Peres impressed his hosts by quoting a poem of Li Bai (李白) of the Tang dynasty. In 2008, he attended the opening ceremony of the Beijing Olympics and wrote a poem in English for the event. In April 2014, he set up an account on the Sina Weibo social media platform, to communicate with the Chinese public; within minutes of the launch, 50 million users had viewed the page – a record for a launch, said Weibo.

As we mentioned above, in December 2015, at the age of 92, he flew to Shantou to take part in the cornerstone-laying ceremony for the new Technion institution. He wanted to support what he saw as a project of great historical significance. "China is one of Israel's major partners in hi-tech and more than 1,000 Israeli companies are active in China. Both countries have much to share with, and learn from, each other," he said at the ceremony.

At the Beijing Olympics, he told Chinese reporters: "The Chinese and the Jewish people are nations ancient and young and full of wisdom. Both are constantly creating new knowledge and miracles." (Note 23) In his poem for the event, he seemed to be writing for both his own country and for China:

"Forget your borders, ignore your cages and fly free.
Reject your different nightmares and have one dream.
The same dream, of glory, of harmony, of peace.
An equal dream for poor and rich, black and white.
An equal right to compete and champion.
Run and throw, shoot and swim and pin, row and hit.
You can be the best on our globe.
Win, don't kill, lose, don't hate, Hope, don't regret.
Go home with an olive branch in your lips: together in harmony.
Breathing fresh air and singing for the newly born in the cradles and the nests."

Notes

1 "How Israeli agriculture has inspired the dry lands of northwest China" (以色列農業及其對我國西北乾旱地區的啓示), Paper by Wang Xiumiao (王秀苗), of Zaozhuang College (山東棗莊學院) in Shandong, April 2011.

2 Article by Antoaneta Bevlova in *Asia Times*, 10/11/2006.

3 "China's tech money heads for Israel as US welcome wanes", Article in Reuters, 11/5/2017.

4 Article in *Global Times* (環球人物) on Hebrew University, 26/8/2016.

5 World Bank figures, 2014.

6 Technion website (https://www.technion.ac.il/en/), 20/12/2016.

7 *Jewish Times Asia*, November 2016.

8 "China's tech money heads for Israel as U.S. welcome wanes", Article in Reuters, 11/5/2017.

9 *China Daily*, 22/3/2017.

10 *First Finance Daily* (第一財經日報), 22/2/2017.

11 *Israel and China, From Silk Road to Innovation Highway*, by Lionel Friedfeld and Philippe Metoudi, Partridge, 2015, page 162.

12 Same, page 149.

13 Article in *INSS Insight*, by Dr Yoram Evron, Institute for National Security Studies, Tel Aviv University, No.538, 8/4/2014.

14 *Israel and China: Mutual Demystification in Chinese-Israeli Relations*, by Yitzhak Shichor, April 2013, page 117.

15 Same, page 121.

16 Article in *Haaretz* newspaper, 24/3/3015.

17 Same.

18 *China Daily*, 22/3/2017.

19   Yitzhak Shichor, page 120.

20   Yitzhak Shichor, page 122.

21   Gao Xi (高晞), associate professor of history at Fudan University in Shanghai interview with author, 10/6/2006.

22   Same.

23   *Global Times* (環球時報), 29/9/2016.

Haven of stability

From

WORKPLACE

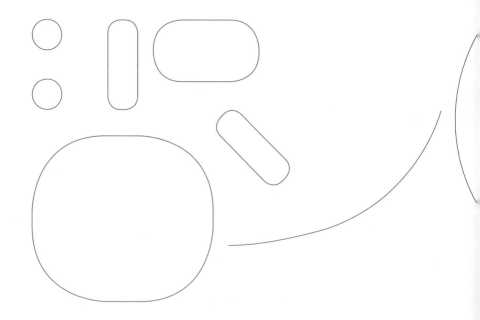

Of all the cities of China, Hong Kong is the only one to have offered Jews a safe environment for life, work and worship for the last 170 years, except for nearly four years of Japanese occupation from 1941 to 1945. It is the site of the only free-standing synagogue in China, Ohel Leah, in continuous use for more than a century, and a Jewish cemetery that has been used ever since it opened in 1855.

The Jews enjoyed this stability first under British colonial rule, which ended in 1997, and under the "one country, two systems" introduced by China since then. The booming economy of Hong Kong over the last 20 years has caused the community to double; it now numbers 5,000-6,000, in seven congregations, including Chabad Lubavitch, Orthodox, Reform and Liberal.

They are mainly expatriates from the U.K., U.S., France, Australia, South Africa, Israel and Canada; there are also a few families from India. They share the Jewish Community Centre (JCC), next to the synagogue in the upmarket Mid-levels district, and the Carmel School, which celebrated its 25th anniversary in 2016; it is the only Jewish school in Asia that offers education from kindergarten to secondary school.

Hong Kong is also home to a Holocaust & Tolerance

To

HOME

Centre and the Jewish Historical Society set up in 1985; it has hosted an annual Jewish Film Festival every year since 1999. It is a prosperous community; its members work as judges, lawyers, bankers, architects, engineers, professors, civil servants, business people, journalists and in foreign trade and the diamond industry. About half are long-term residents; the other half stay for short-term contracts before going to another assignment or returning to their home country.

As in other cities in China, there has never been anti-Semitism in Hong Kong; relations with the city's 300,000 Muslims are good. Nonetheless, visitors to the JCC and the synagogue must present identity documents and have their bags checked by professional security staff. There are few cities in the world that have offered such peace and economic opportunity to Jews over the last 170 years as Hong Kong.

Early arrivals

The Sassoon family had offices in Guangzhou even before Hong Kong became a British colony in 1842. The establishment of British rule and law persuaded the family to move to the new location. The first Jews to set up home were Iraqis who arrived in the 1840s. They were descendants of Jews expelled from Spain and Portugal who had settled in Baghdad.

As we described in Chapter Three, some moved from there to Bombay and Calcutta; as foreign trade became possible in China, they set up offices in Guangzhou, Macau and Hong Kong. One of the first was the Sassoon family; its patriarch, David, sent one of his sons to establish the office in

Hong Kong. He purchased from the British Crown a 10,750-square foot plot of farmland, with a 999-year lease. It was for use only as a Jewish burial ground and was officially opened in 1855 by his son Reuben David Sassoon. This was a landmark, a sign that the Jewish community expected to stay in Hong Kong for the long term.

The first burial, of a man named Leon Bin Baruel, was in 1857. Most of those buried there in the early years were single men; it was not the custom to bring wives and families, because Hong Kong was considered too dangerous for health.

It is one of the few Jewish cemeteries in the Far East that remains in its original 19th century location and is still in use. There are now about 360 graves in the cemetery; the gravestones are mostly in Hebrew and English, as well as Russian, French and German and Dutch. They reflect the diversity of the countries from where the members came.

The Sassoon family and their staff, also Baghdadi Jews sent from Bombay, formed the core of the early community. "They were deeply religious people," said Judy Green, chairwoman of the Jewish History Society of Hong Kong; her ancestors moved to the city from South Africa. "They always made sure they had somewhere to worship – until they built a synagogue, it was usually just a room in one of their offices." (Note 1)

Arthur, one of the sons of David Sassoon, was on the provisional committee that founded the Hongkong and Shanghai Banking Corporation in 1864. Another son, Frederick, served on the Legislative

Council in 1884. For business, Shanghai was a larger and more attractive city than Hong Kong; so, the community there grew faster. In 1882, there were 60 Jews in Hong Kong, all Sephardic. By the end of the 19th century, they wished to have their own synagogue. Three grandsons of David Sassoon purchased land on Robinson Road, on the northern slope of Mount Victoria, 500 feet above the harbour, and donated the synagogue to the community. They asked that it be named in memory of their mother Leah Gubbay.

It was built by Hong Kong architects Leigh & Orange in Edwardian free-baroque style, popular at that time. The exterior was red brick with white detailing; the interior followed Sephardic style. The foundation stone was laid in May 1901 and the opening ceremony held on April 8, 1902. (Note 2)

This was, like the cemetery, a milestone, a symbol that the community had put down roots in the city. During their occupation from December 1941 to August 1945, the Japanese military took over the building; the Torah (holy scripture) scrolls were smuggled out and safely hidden for the duration of the war. Some date from the 1830s. Unlike their Nazi allies, however, the Japanese did not damage or destroy the synagogue. So, for 115 years, it has been the centre of Jewish spiritual life in the city.

First and only Jewish governor

On July 29, 1904, a new governor, the 13th, took office in Hong Kong – Matthew Nathan; he was the first and only Jewish governor. He was just 42 and the second youngest governor until that time. His appointment was a symbol of the respected place Jews occupied in the British Empire. It was a time of pogroms and persecution of Jews in Tsarist Russia. Between 1894 and 1906, France was involved in a scandal involving the false conviction of Captain Alfred Dreyfus, a Jewish artillery officer, for allegedly giving military secrets to Germany; he was not finally exonerated until 1906.

Covering Dreyfus' trial was an Austro-Hungarian journalist named Theodor Herzl; so shocked by the anti-Semitism he saw, he abandoned the idea of Jews assimilating into European society and proposed instead that they build their own state in Palestine. He organised the first Zionist Congress in Basel in August 1897.

Unlike Dreyfus, Nathan enjoyed a smooth and successful career. His father, a Jewish businessman in London, had three sons – one became an officer in the Royal Artillery, another a colonial judge in Trinidad and Tobago and Matthew a Major in the Royal Engineers. After military expeditions in Sudan and India, Matthew was appointed acting governor of Sierra Leone in 1899 and Governor of the Gold Coast (Ghana) from 1900 to 1903. In April 1907, he left Hong Kong to become Governor of Natal; later he served as Governor of Queensland, where he promoted British migration. On retirement, he retired to the comfort of rural Somerset in the west of England, where he died in 1939 at the age of 77.

He is best remembered in Hong Kong for Nathan Road, the main north-south road in Kowloon; home to major hotels and department stores, it has become a mecca for shoppers from round the world.

"He wanted to develop Kowloon, which was a muddy backwater in those days," said Judy Green. "My husband's grandfather remembers walking around in gumboots because it was a swamp. Nathan decided that, for it to flourish, it needed an access road, to link it to the hinterland of the New Territories. Many thought he was making a mistake but he was determined to push the project through." (Note 3)

He also played a leading role in the construction of a railway line from Hong Kong to Guangzhou; an engineer, he oversaw the building of the line from Kowloon to the border with China. The whole line was completed in 1910.

Nathan also proposed a landfill project on the southern tip of the Kowloon peninsula, to accommodate the train, bus and cross-harbour ferry terminals. This was done and the area has been a major transport hub ever since.

On the morning of September 18, 1906, the city was hit by a devastating typhoon that caused heavy loss of life and great damage to property, Nathan established a signal station next to the Hong Kong Observatory; ever since, it has given advance warning of approaching storms to the city's residents and the ships in the harbour. (Note 4)

During Nathan's tenure, the government granted a 75-year lease on a piece of land adjoining the Jewish cemetery; on this land was built a chapel, *Tahara* (ritual purity) room and other small buildings.

In 1979, the lease was renewed for a further 75 years. Green said that, a bachelor, Nathan had no wife to act as hostess at functions at Government House. "I think he found that aspect of colonial life very difficult. A lot of expat socialising was centred on the Hong Kong Club, which did not admit Jews in those days, and there were Sunday gatherings at church, which he could not attend."

These social exclusions aside, the fact that London appointed a Jew to the highest post in Hong Kong was a sign of equality. Many Jews in Hong Kong, Shanghai and other cities of the empire took British nationality and enjoyed the same rights as their fellow countrymen and women.

Kadoories – betting on Hong Kong

In the 1880s, there arrived from India two brothers from a family who have since World War Two been the city's most important and wealthiest Jewish family – the Kadoories. Its current head is Sir Michael Kadoorie; he is chairman of China Light & Power (CLP) and the Hongkong and Shanghai Hotels (HSH). Forbes magazine estimated the wealth of his family in March 2017 at US$6.7 billion, making him one of the 10 richest men in Hong Kong.

In a talk to the Jewish Historical Society on December 16, 2008, Sir Michael described the arrival of his ancestors. "My family comes from Baghdad. In 1880, the family sent two brothers from India to Hong Kong and two remained in India. The two in HK were Sir Elly [Eleazar Silas], my grandfather who was sent to Shanghai, and Sir Ellis, who remained in

Hong Kong.

"The map of the world was pink – the British empire. You did not need a passport, but a laissez-passer. Sir Elly worked for Sassoon and was sent to a warehouse in Ningpo (寧波), where he was the number-three person. Bubonic plague struck the city. His two superiors were away; he opened the warehouse to the patients and gave a disinfectant to those who needed it; some could pay and some could not. No problem. Then his two superiors returned and objected. So, Elly resigned and went to Hong Kong; his brother gave him HK$500, a substantial sum in those days, and told him not to come back for more.

"With two partners, he set up a brokerage and did well. He went to the U.K. and married a member of the Mocatta family, who had been expelled from Spain and gone to the U.K.; they had been bullion dealers for 200 years before the Bank of England became the Bank of England. At that time, the people in the colonies were more British than the British.

"My grandmother was educated. They had two sons, Horace and Lawrence, my father. At 28, Elly retired to the U.K., bought homes in London and in the country and sent the two boys to Ascot St Vincent preparatory school.

"But one of his partners in Hong Kong was alcoholic and the other did not work hard. So, Elly had to return to Hong Kong where he found his wealth diminished to 10 per cent of what it had been.

"He had to sell the house in the country and start again. His wife moved to Hong Kong, while the sons remained in boarding school. He set up a brokerage and specialised in rubber. When rubber prices crashed, Chartered Bank called in the loans he had made from it. He was sitting forlorn in Statue Square, when Sir Thomas Jackson, the head of HSBC (滙豐銀行), told him there was another bank. So, he got a new loan, paid off his loans and started again.

"The bank closed 300 rubber companies and reduced the number to three, aided by Elly's knowledge in this field. After an 18-month lean period, prices picked up and he made a fortune. He diversified." (Note 5)

The Hongkong and Shanghai Hotels (HSH), established in 1866, and China Light and Power (CLP), in 1901, have long been and remain today the jewels of the Kadoorie business empire. The Peninsula Hotel (半島酒店) in Hong Kong, HSH's flagship, opened in 1928; the company branded it as "the finest hotel east of Suez". It was, and is, in Tsim Sha Tsui, opposite the three terminals created by Governor Nathan.

In 1903, CLP opened its first power station in the Hung Hom district of Hong Kong. By 1921, the size of the Jewish community in the city had reached 100, mainly Sephardim.

During World War Two, the Kadoories were detained by the Japanese, first in Hong Kong and then in Shanghai. Elly died a prisoner of the Japanese in Shanghai in 1944. Only after August 1945 were the rest of the family able to return to Hong Kong. The war had devastated the city,

Sir Elly Kadoorie with his two sons
Lawrence and Horace. (Credit: The
Hong Kong Heritage Project)

Sir Michael Kadoorie (Credit: The Hong
Kong Heritage Project)

including CLP's plants that generated power for Kowloon and the New Territories; the city's population had fallen to 600,000 from 1.4 million before the conflict. With a civil war in China, nobody knew the outcome nor if the city would recover.

"It took great courage to see a future for such a desolate place," said Sir Michael. His father, Lawrence, returned from Shanghai in 1945 on an RAF Halifax.

Lawrence and his brother Horace made a major decision – they would not emigrate but would stay in Hong Kong and rebuild the plant. "When he arrived, everyone was working hard to get the power back on. It needed a Royal Navy submarine," said Sir Michael.

This decision and the subsequent expansion of CLP's generating capacity to meet soaring demand was one of the most important factors in the city's economic recovery after the war.

The two brothers made another big gamble, after the Communists won the civil war and tens of thousands fled the mainland to Hong Kong and Taiwan. Would the victors occupy the city and nationalise businesses as they did in the mainland? In the event, the People's Liberation Army stopped at the border and allowed the British colony to continue.

Among Jewish families, the Kadoories were unusual in having major businesses in both Shanghai and Hong Kong. While they lost those in Shanghai, the two they had in Hong Kong were in strategic sectors.

"YC Wang, chairman of the Cotton Spinners Association, was looking at Mauritius as well as Hong Kong. My father said to him: 'I will give you electricity. He got a turbine. It was a turning point for Hong Kong. That brought manufacturing and prosperity. The Korean War had a huge impact. By the 1950s, the population had reached 2.5 million." (Note 6)

By contrast, Sir Victor Sassoon chose to sell all his China assets and move to Nassau; the Kadoories bet on Hong Kong.

Luxury hotel becomes refugee centre

During the war, The Peninsula served as the temporary headquarters of the Japanese and re-opened for business as the Toa (East Asia, 東亞) Hotel in 1942. Afterwards, it served another important purpose – a transit place for Jewish refugees leaving Shanghai for new lives abroad. As we described in Chapter Four, there were about 20,000 of them.

"They had no money, no nothing," said Judy Green. "The Jewish community in Shanghai had galvanised and looked after them and Horace Kadoorie was particularly active in that."

It was a huge undertaking because the community was small and the refugees so numerous; most had to come to Hong Kong to collect visas for their new homes – in the U.S., Australia or Europe.

"Horace gathered information about each batch of refugees in Shanghai and sent it to his brother Lawrence in Hong Kong. He visited the

Immigration Department almost daily, with lists of names, final destinations and petitions for permission to transit."

Since they had nowhere to stay in Hong Kong, Lawrence threw open the doors of The Peninsula. The floors of the luxury hotel became full of beds and cabinets for the refugees; one group of nearly 200 bound for Australia stayed for several months because the ship assigned to them was diverted to carry troops. The refugees held religious services in the hotel. Other members of the Jewish community helped with clothing and medical aid, handling baggage and helping their brothers and sisters with their journey.

In 1947, the Jewish Women's Association was set up to help the refugees; it celebrated its 70th anniversary in 2017. "The Jewish people were very important to Lawrence and he was unstinting in his efforts to help them," said Green. (Note 7)

Community grows with Hong Kong

After 1949, against all expectations, Hong Kong prospered and became a major industrial and trading centre. A flood of refugees more than tripled the population from 600,000 in 1945 to 2.1 million in 1950. Among them were entrepreneurs who re-established their factories and businesses in the city; immigrants from Shanghai created a cotton spinning industry. Others were people with nothing who were more than willing to work in the new factories and businesses.

Hong Kong became a global centre for production of clothing, electronics,

Peninsula Hotel in Kowloon, Hong Kong before World War Two. (Credit: The Peninsula Hong Kong)

Entrance to Peninsula Hotel. (Credit: The Peninsula Hong Kong)

Jewish refugees in transit stay in the main hall of the Peninsula Hotel after World War Two. (Credit: The Hong Kong Heritage Project)

plastics and other labour-intensive goods, mainly for export, and for goods shipped in and out of China. Exports accounted for 54 per cent of GDP in the 1960s, rising to 64 per cent in the 1970s.

The Jewish community remained small – 250 in 1954, 230 in 1959 and 200 in 1968. Some were long-term residents, others had moved from Harbin, Tianjin, Shanghai and other mainland cities where they had made their homes. Others arrived from overseas, eager to take advantage of the new commercial opportunities; their strong point was links to overseas markets for a city that had suddenly become an important export centre. (Note 8)

In 1978, the Chinese government announced a new policy of reform and open door. Hong Kong developed a new role as a trade and finance centre to serve the booming economy of the mainland.

It attracted thousands of new foreigners, including Jews from the U.S., Israel, the UK, Australia and Canada. By 1997, their number had reached 2,500, two thirds of them Americans and Israelis; they included professionals in the financial sector, some of whom had relocated from Tokyo, and Israelis working in trade, technology and the diamond industry. By 2017, it had doubled again to 5,000. This influx revitalised the community.

"Our community is similar to that of the expat community as a whole," said Erica Lyons, editor of *Asian Jewish Life* and Hong Kong delegate to the World Jewish Congress. "It is disproportionately young and wealthy. If you have no economic opportunity, you leave. There are few old people – they retire elsewhere. We are more valued than in other places. The Hong Kong government is very serious in providing security to us. When the flights arrive from Israel, there are armed police at the gate in the airport. You do not find this in airports in Europe. The government sees the community as productive and making a contribution." (Note 9)

Doctor, archaeologist and conductor

One man who left a great mark on Hong Kong was Dr Solomon Matthew Bard. Born in 1916 to Russian Jewish parents, he spent his first eight years in Chita, Siberia before moving with his family to Harbin. By the age of 13, he could play the flute and the violin. He was educated in Harbin for seven years before moving to Shanghai in 1932 to attend an English-language school. His parents emigrated to Argentina: he earned his school fees from playing the violin in Shanghai nightclubs.

In 1934, he was admitted into the faculty of medicine at the University of Hong Kong (HKU); he graduated in 1939 and met his future wife there. During World War Two, he was interned in a prisoner-of-war camp in Sham Shui Po (深水埗). After two years as a medical doctor in Britain, he returned in September 1947 to Hong Kong where he spent the rest of his working life. This included eight years as a general practitioner, 20 years in the University Health Service of HKU, including nine as director.

He had many interests, notably serving as a founder and later chairman of the Hong Kong Archaeological Society and the first Executive Secretary of the Antiquities and Monuments Office. From 1976 to 2014, he was a Museum Expert Advisor to the Leisure and Cultural Services Department (LCSD).

Bard learnt to play the Chinese flute and served as chairman of the Hong Kong Philharmonic Orchestra for many years, as well as assistant music director of the Hong Kong Chinese Orchestra from 1983 to 1987. In 1993, he and his family emigrated to Sydney. But, into his 90s, he still regularly appeared as a guest conductor in Hong Kong, dressed in a long cheongsam. Fluent in four languages, he wrote four books and many academic papers.

Bard passed away in Sydney, Australia in November 2014, aged 98. "His passing is a great loss for his family and friends and also to the Leisure and Culture Services Department," the department said in its obituary. "We always miss him who was a friend and teacher to us." (Note 10)

From Harbin, Tianjin and Tokyo to Hong Kong

Another descendant of the Russian Jewish diaspora and long-term resident of Hong Kong is Robert Dorfman. His great-grandparents travelled the trans-Siberian railway from Russia to Harbin, where three of his grandparents were born. Both his parents were born in China and attended the Tianjin Jewish School. They lived under Japanese occupation in China during World War Two.

After 1949, they moved to Tokyo, where Robert was born in October

1954. In early 1956, the family moved to Hong Kong. In 1969, his step-father George Bloch set up Herald Metal & Plastic Works Ltd with two partners. Robert attended primary and secondary school in Hong Kong.

"Life was peaceful," he said in an interview. (Note 11) "I never felt anti-Semitic prejudice here, not at the Glenealy Junior School, nor were any clubs closed to us. At my school, there were people of all backgrounds, including British children of officials in the big hongs as well as Hong Kong Chinese. As it is today, Hong Kong was very open and welcoming. There were Jews in the Department of Justice. I experienced anti-Semitism for the first time in the summer of 1967 in New York, when I saw *Fiddler on the Roof*, about the persecution of Jews in Russia."

After obtaining a BA in Government and International Relations from the University of Washington in Seattle, Dorfman returned to Hong Kong to work in the family business.

"During my studies, I had always thought to return. I had spent the summers as an intern in the firm. In addition, I was a British and not a U.S. citizen, so staying there would have meant changing my visa."

In 1992, he became Executive Director and Vice-chairman of Herald Holdings and chairman in April 2014. Today it is a publicly listed company quoted on the Hong Kong Stock Exchange, with four business units engaged in the manufacture and global distribution of toys, timepieces, houseware and computer components.

After his return to Hong Kong, Dorfman became involved in Jewish community life. "My family was secular; they did not eat kosher and were not observant but did celebrate the High Holidays. In 1983, I became involved in the Hong Kong branch of the United Israel Appeal (UIA). Its chairman was Eric Beare, who had moved to Hong Kong in 1963 from South Africa to set up his own trading company. He was interested in Jewish religion and culture. He was a mentor to me.

"UIA is a worldwide organisation that raises money for social services in Israel. Because of its situation, Israel has to spend a high proportion of its budget on defence and does not have enough money for social services. It is a tradition to ask Jews in the Diaspora to help.

"For the last 30 years, this UIA money has been used to help children at risk and to absorb new immigrants. For example, migrants from East Europe are skilled, like doctors and lawyers; how to convert their skills into jobs that can be used in Israel. Or migrants from Ethiopia; they have arrived from the Stone Age, unable to read or write, and have never taken a lift or an escalator. There are a lot of costs.

"In June 2015, I was invited to Jerusalem to attend a ceremony at which I received the Yakir Keren Hayesod award for my UIA work in Hong Kong. I had been involved for 34 years and was chairman for 10 years until 2015. Four of us received awards – the others were from Geneva, Sao Paulo and Cape Town. I was delighted to be recognised. The ceremony was held at the residence of President Reuven Rivlin; we had a private meeting with him, as well as one with Prime Minister Benjamin Netanyahu.

"I have been to Israel many times but have not considered living there. I live happily in Hong Kong. It is important that Jewish people live in the Diaspora, as part of international communities. I have no calling to go to settle in Israel. I am very proud of what it has achieved. It is like a good house in a bad neighbourhood, surrounded by countries that do not want it to exist.

"It has the new technology to defend itself fully, such as the Iron Dome anti-missile system. During the 2014 war in Gaza, this system shot down missiles landing in populated areas and left those that would land in the sea or unpopulated areas. Israel is very realistic and prepared in every way. It has two big challenges – to ensure that the U.S. is always on its side. It must persuade China to be on its side. All will change dramatically in the next 20 years. There will be new energy sources that will reduce China's dependence on Middle East oil. Israel will become more valuable to China in technology, so that China will find it in its interest to keep Israel safe."
(Note 12)

Rebuilding the synagogue

The centre of the community's social life was the Jewish Recreation Club (JRC), built in 1905 next to the synagogue and renovated in 1909 with funding from the Kadoorie family. The JRC was a two-storey building, with a large hall, restaurant, bar, library and billiards room, a tennis court and spacious lawn with a spectacular view of Victoria Harbour.

In 1937, J.E. Joseph donated a property below to the club to preserve the view of the harbour; it was used to house the rabbi, with a *mikvah* (ritual bath) on the ground floor. During World War Two, the club was totally destroyed; in 1949, the Kadoorie family again financed construction of a new club on the same site.

With the boom in Hong Kong's economy, the area surrounding the synagogue became prime residential land, with towering residential blocks built one next to the other on the side of the mountain above the harbour.

The large granite retaining wall between the synagogue and Robinson Road next to it became dangerously unstable. In the late 1980s, the government ordered the trustees of the Jewish community to stabilise the whole length of the wall, at their own expense.

After much deliberation, the trustees of the Ohel Leah Synagogue Charity decided to redevelop the site and signed an agreement with Swire Properties to build two residential towers; one would contain a Jewish Community Centre (JCC), a kosher supermarket, kosher meat and dairy restaurants, an indoor swimming pool, functions rooms and offices and a new *mikvah*.

The JCC would own one and Swire Properties the other; thanks to rents from the apartments, the financial future of the JCC would be secure. Lost would be the JRC, its tennis court and pretty lawn overlooking the harbour.

Some proposed demolishing the synagogue and replacing it with a new building. It was in poor condition, with water dripping down the walls and the floors sometimes covered in water. A new structure would be safer, more comfortable and allow new facilities, such as classrooms.

The issue sharply divided the community. Opponents of demolition argued that it was a precious piece of history and a historical symbol of Jewish life in Hong Kong. Religious Jews had bought or rented properties nearby so that they could walk there on the Sabbath; an observant Jew may not use a motor vehicle on Saturdays.

In the two-three years needed for rebuilding, how would they perform their religious duties? It would have been very difficult to find alternative facilities nearby. In the end, the community found a compromise. In 1997, work began with painstaking care to restore the fabric of the building, its furniture and fittings to its original feeling.

New tiered seating, better lighting and air conditioning were added to the women's section upstairs, so that they could see better; the acoustics were improved. They found old photos in Israel and brought in experts in stained glass and rattan who were not available in Hong Kong.

On October 18, 1998, a re-dedication ceremony was held. In 2000, the UNESCO Asia-Pacific Heritage Awards recognised the "Conservation and Restoration of the Ohel Leah Synagogue, Hong Kong" as a winning entry for the Outstanding Project Award for Cultural Heritage Conservation.

Because it is an Orthodox synagogue, the women worship on the second floor, separate from the men on the ground floor. Today its membership comprises more than 200 families from over 17 different countries. Some of its *Torahs* date from the 1830s; they are stored in steel containers, with designs of the Baghdad style, behind a curtain at one end of the synagogue.

The rabbis say the prayers in Hebrew and give sermons in English, the native language of most of the congregation. (Note 13)

Ohel Leah historical heart of Judaism in Hong Kong

Since October 2010, the rabbi of the synagogue has been Asher Oser, an Australian. In January that year, the Ohel Leah Rabbi Search Committee began a global search and received 80 applicants. It narrowed the field to a final three; each was invited to Hong Kong to meet the community. The community chose Oser. He holds a B.A. from the University of Sydney and an M.A. from McGill University; after studying at yeshivas in Israel, he was ordained at the Rabbi Isaac Elchanan Theological Seminary of Yeshiva University in New York. Before moving to Hong Kong, he served as a rabbi in Connecticut and Rhode Island.

"You find diversity everywhere. But the diversity here was above and beyond anything I had experienced before," he said. (Note 14) "There was a colonial and Anglo-Jewry aftertaste, in which Orthodoxy was prestigious and had social cachet; you did not find that in the U.S.

"There are different schools (of Judaism) in Hong Kong, but the Ohel Leal

Interior of Ohel Leah synagogue, Hong Kong.

Torah scrolls in the Ohel Leah synagogue.

synagogue remains the centre. It holds more *bar-mitzvahs* than anywhere else. It is the only purpose-built synagogue in Hong Kong and is the historical heart of Judaism. The Ultra-Orthodox separated from us and set up their own place – but this year (2017) they came to our synagogue centre for all the festivals. You feel the gravity of the place. When you sit inside, you feel something in the air.

"On a regular Sabbath, there are 150 people. On the Jewish High Holidays, it is packed, standing room only. We are here for everyone. I serve others in addition to the regular members. Jews cannot have here the same Jewish life available in New York or Israel. But it cuts both ways. If you come from elsewhere, you can feel a little lost. When people arrive, they feel they are floating in anonymity. This is a community for them."

I asked how his members could keep dietary laws in a city with the most enticing cuisine in the world and in a Chinese society in which eating is the most important social ritual. "People respect integrity. They see that you believe in something and respect it. It is a shock at first. I have had this conversation on cuisine. Not all the community have a high level of observance. People ask why they should follow that standard. I answer that this is what God wants from us."

For an Orthodox Jew, the Sabbath begins at sunset on Friday and lasts 24 hours. During that time, he or she is prohibited from many activities – such as writing, doing business, using motor vehicles or telephones, shopping and turning on or off anything that uses electricity. It is a day set aside for the family and friends, for reading, for reflection and for sleep. Many of the Jews in Hong Kong work in high-pressure jobs, such as in finance, the law or business where people are on call 24/7. How do they keep the Sabbath?

"It runs from Friday afternoon until Saturday night. People can check their e-mails on Saturday evenings. In New York, people know that you are out of contact for that period. Here, once people know, they accept it. A human being needs one day of rest."

The rabbi's congregation includes Chinese. "I have facilitated conversions for Chinese children adopted by Jewish families. The number of Chinese in our synagogue is not negligible. Some are spouses of Jewish men and women.

"There are Chinese converts who have divorced their spouses and remained members. We have two single Chinese ladies who attend services regularly; one of them works in an international law firm. Judaism is a religion, not a culture. Jews speak French, Chinese, English – many languages."

He said that he facilitated conversion. "We are warm and welcoming to everyone who comes. The synagogue is not competing with other places of worship but with the street, with the rest of the world. The procedure for conversion is that you study and we help you meet with the *Beth Din* [a rabbinical court with the authority to convert]. The procedure takes one-to-two years. There is not an exam, more a conversation about what level they have come to. I become a sponsoring rabbi and send people to *Beth*

Din in Chicago, New York and Israel."

Like other Jews in the city, he cherishes the good public order and absence of anti-Semitism in Hong Kong. "In France, they have good laws that aim to protect Jews but Jews live in fear. In China, they do not have such laws but Jews do not live in fear. Which is better?"

In May 2016, he attended a public seminar at Hong Kong University on "Radical Peace – Theologies and Practices of Reconciliation" with Anglican Canon Andrew White, the Bishop of Baghdad, and Mufti Muhammad Arshad, the chief Imam of Hong Kong. The three men had a warm and friendly discussion and embraced warmly at the end. It was a powerful symbol of friendship in a world where thousands are killed every year in the name of religion (https://youtu.be/wQa7sstgtxs).

Building Chabad Lubavitch in Asia

Having arrived in the city in 1985, Mordechai Avtzon is the senior rabbi of Hong Kong. He belongs to the Chabad Lubavitch movement, like Rabbi Greenberg in Shanghai and Rabbi Freundlich in Beijing; he is its head in Asia. His office and religious centre is in an apartment building in the Mid-levels, a wealthy residential district of the city. He was the first emissary (*shluchim*) of the Chabad movement to Asia in the post-war era.

He has opened a total of 30 Chabad houses across the continent, including three in Hong Kong: 11 in eight cities in the mainland and Taiwan: and 16 in Cambodia, Laos, Thailand, Singapore, Vietnam, Nepal,

Rabbi Asher Oser stands at the lectern of the Ohel Leah synagogue.

India, Japan and South Korea.

"Chabad is the infrastructure of Jewish life in Asia. Our unique philosophy is that no Jew is judged on his level of observance. Every Jew is welcome. We cater to the highest level of commitment."

This expansion into 10 countries is a remarkable achievement of the Rabbi's three decades in Asia, one of which the CEO of a multinational would be proud. It is also testimony to the willingness of his movement to send rabbis to these cities and provide funding where necessary to build the infrastructure of each Jewish community.

After 32 years, he has no plans to leave. "Chabad appointments are generally for life, unless there are other circumstances or health issues," he said. (Note 15)

"I was born in the U.S. to parents who survived World War Two and Stalin's campaigns against humanity and Jews in particular. They were grateful to be alive. There were many miracles. In 1946, they left Russia on Polish papers, lived as refugees in France and came to the U.S. in the early 1950s. I am the 10th of 15 children.

"I was raised with the feeling that we were in this world to restore the love of the Jewish people and not to apologise for who we were. Since I was a child, I had the dream to further the mission of the Rebbe of blessed memory to reach every Jew in the world."

The Rebbe

The Rebbe was Rabbi Menachem Mendel Schneerson, who led the movement until his passing on June 12, 1994, at the age of 92. Chabad Lubavitch was founded in 1775 in a village in what is now Belarus; the Rebbe transformed it into the largest Hasidic Orthodox Jewish movement in the world.

One of the most influential Jewish scholars of the 20th century, Schneerson was born in April 1902 in what was then Nikolaev in Russia and is now Mykolaiv in Ukraine. He studied at the University of Berlin but left for Paris in 1933, when the Nazi party took power.

On June 11, 1940, three days before Paris fell to the Wehrmacht, he and his wife fled the city for Vichy and later Nice. In 1941, they escaped from Europe via Portugal and arrived in New York on June 23 that year. According to the movement's website: "The Rebbe and Rebbetzin (his wife) arrived in the United States, having been miraculously rescued, by the grace of Almighty G-d, from the European holocaust."

In January 1951, he became the leader of the Chabad Lubavitch movement. In his opening speech, he said: "One must go to a place where nothing is known of godliness, nothing is known of Judaism, nothing is even known of the Hebrew alphabet, and while there to put oneself aside and ensure that the other calls out to God."

One of his most important missions was to send rabbis to cities around the world with Jewish communities and reawaken their faith; Chabad is especially active in places where a community is newly established and has no rabbi. It has 4,500 such full-time *shluchim* (emissaries) around the world, including Rabbis Avtzon, Greenberg and Freundlich.

The Rebbe also established kindergartens, drug rehabilitation centres and care-homes for the disabled as well as synagogues. He spoke English, Yiddish, Hebrew, French, Russian, German and Italian. His published teachings fill more than 300 volumes and greatly enrich *Torah* scholarship. He worked 18 hours a day and never took a holiday; he was opposed to retirement, regarding it as a waste of precious time. His charisma, his words and his work inspired thousands to follow in his footsteps.

Chosen for Asia

Rabbi Avtzon had been working for 18 months with Chabad of Argentina, preparing a prayer book in spoken Spanish, when the Rebbe asked him to be his first emissary to Asia. After several visits to Hong Kong, he was invited by the community of Ohel Leah to be its rabbi in 1985. "I accepted the offer. I went back to New York and married my wife, from Philadelphia, and concluded a one-year contract with Ohel Leah," said Rabbi Avtzon.

"I found a small community with no Jewish school except a Sunday school, no proper infrastructure for Jewish education and no kosher food in an organised way – only prepared by individuals. The JCC was not kosher. The *mikvah* had fallen into disuse.

"There was no daily service. Even on Sabbat, services were a struggle. Once I announced a service on a Jewish Holiday and found the door of the synagogue locked. When I came with my wife, there were no grants. We struggled with very minimal funding. Hong Kong was and is an expensive city."

He was one of the founders of the Carmel school, which we describe in the next section.

There were conflicts within the community over the kind of rabbi they wanted; some members desired a very high level of observance and others did not. "I made it clear from the start that I was personally committed to be as observant as possible." So, he decided to set up Chabad in Hong Kong as an independent organisation; the synagogue chose another rabbi. Now Chabad has three houses in Hong Kong.

His presence attracted the interest of Jewish communities in other cities in Asia. He went several times to meet the members in Shanghai, then a small number. They asked Chabad to send a rabbi; he told them that they would be responsible for his salary and upkeep.

"I went to Atlanta to see the owner of the Portman Centre in Shanghai, who was a member of Chabad in Atlanta. He agreed to give the rabbi and his wife an apartment in a residential tower next to the hotel free for two years. There were other grants from the U.S.

"China is a very friendly government. Our experience has been regarded favourably. They are clearly aware of what we are doing; there are police cameras at our centre in Shanghai. While Judaism is not a recognised religion, it is clear that we do not do anything divisive to Chinese people. The government is satisfied as long as there are no conversions. We are as wary of proselytising as they are."

In Shanghai, the rabbi established regular religious services and the provision of Jewish education and kosher food. This became the model for other Chabad centres in China and in Asia; the headquarters in Crown Heights, New York sent a rabbi who gradually provided these services. There are now centres in Beijing (北京), Chengdu (成都), Guangzhou (廣州), Ningbo (寧波), Shenzhen (深圳) and Yiwu (義烏), in addition to Shanghai.

The Rabbi has also spread the movement to 10 countries in Asia. This involved flying to meet the members of the community in different cities, finding out their needs and, at their request, sending a rabbi from Chabad's headquarters.

"Our experience here inspired me. As soon as we opened in a city, we started, even if the numbers were small. We would be the infrastructure of the community. Each place is autonomously managed. I was very involved in Vietnam, where we have opened houses in Ho Chi Minh City and Hanoi."

Sometimes, he needed to raise money from private donors to rent or buy premises and pay the living costs of the rabbi and his family.

"We are not God's judge or policeman, we are His salesman," he said. "Our job is to make Judaism so enjoyable. We make every event enjoyable and meaningful. A person realises that Judaism is like a mother's milk, without which he cannot live. It is his lifeline."

Asked how easy it was for people to observe Jewish dietary rules among the rich diversity and temptation of Asian cuisines, he said: "We should not do things that are against how a Jew should live. Is it more difficult than surviving during World War Two? Chinese respect Jews who respect themselves. They are perplexed when a Jew does not want kosher food."

Asked if he felt a sense of pride at what he had achieved, he read a passage from a speech by the Rebbe who said that a person should devote every moment to fulfilling his mission and have no feeling of self-satisfaction. "There is no time to think of accomplishment."

Carmel School

Together with the Ohel Leah synagogue, the Carmel School is one of the centres of Jewish life in Hong Kong. In December 2016, the school celebrated its 25th anniversary, with the SAR Secretary for Education in attendance. It has 400 children of 20 nationalities, from elementary to high school, of whom over 80 per cent are Jewish, across all grades. It offers courses to the level of the International Baccalaureate Diploma; its students go on to attend Oxford, Cambridge and other famous universities in the U.S., Canada and Israel.

"Amid the expat life, Jewish continuity is very important," said Dr Mark Konyn, who was on the school's board for 11 years from 1999 and chairman for seven years. (Note 16) "At its most fundamental level, Jewish Identity is about a sense of shared destiny. The school is a centre that brings together people of all levels of observance, including Orthodox and Progressive; from the observant to the less observant.

"From the outset, Carmel School was careful not to disaffect any of our various congregations in Hong Kong, being inclusive rather than judgmental. The central role of education in Jewish life is common to all congregations and those that are not affiliated at all. Carmel brings people together and plays an important role in Hong Kong Jewish life."

The school is on three campuses. The elementary school is located in a colonial-era building in Borrett Road (波老道), with ancient trees, high ceilings and broad corridors. The school has two other sites –two floors in the building of the JCC and one in Shau Kei Wan (筲箕灣). All three sites are on Hong Kong Island, where a majority of the Jewish community lives.

The JCC owns the two floors in its building; the school has enjoyed good support from the Hong Kong Government over the years and benefits from education institutional rental terms and has invested heavily in the refurbishment of the high school in Shau Kei Wan.

The school was established in 1991 by a handful of passionate parents who believed that every Jewish child has a right to a Jewish education. Previously, parents had sent their children to one of Hong Kong's many international schools or boarding schools abroad. From the late 1980s, the community increased sharply, with an influx of professionals in the financial sector and Israelis working in trade, technology and the diamond industry.

The school began with 12 children at pre-school level in a room above the synagogue. It expanded gradually to elementary, then middle and, finally, high school. "We have always had very warm relations with the government, before and after the transition of sovereignty" said Konyn, referring to the 1997 handover of Hong Kong from Britain to China.

"We feel valued and have been included in several general tenders for potential premises – a critical constraint when establishing a school. The lease fees are commensurate with those of an international school in Hong Kong and we rely heavily on donations to sustain our operating costs and for key capital projects."

The students have a full and stimulating curriculum, including both academic and life skills aspects. Central to the approach are the Jewish and Hebrew studies. Over the years, Carmel has developed a strong Mandarin department in response to parents wanting to take advantage of being in China and learning both language and culture. The school recruits the teachers for the teaching of Hebrew and Jewish studies primarily through specialised agencies in Israel; it sources the others from the pool of international teachers.

"They need not be Jewish," said Konyn. "We have teachers from the U.S., South Africa, Australia, the U.K, Hong Kong and Canada amongst others. Our parents have high expectations, in terms of both Judaism and academic outcomes."

He said that the school is very community-based: "It has a human touch, very caring and nurturing. It is a wonderful experience for our students and the Parent Teachers Association is very active."

The students visit historical and cultural sites in Asia, Israel and Europe, and have in the past visited the Warsaw ghetto and the Auschwitz concentration camp. They also conduct projects in Hong Kong, the Mainland and Thailand. Since Hong Kong is on the international speaking circuit, eminent Jewish people who visit the city often speak at the school, including Nobel Prize winners, educationalists, notable Israelis and Holocaust survivors.

It is the only school in Asia that offers a Jewish education to pre-university level. So, the school board has in the past considered a boarding option for students in the region; but this has not materialised.

In June 2001, it achieved full accreditation by the Western Association of Schools and Colleges, an American accreditation body. In December 2016, at the auditorium of its Elsa High School campus, it hosted an evening to celebrate its 25 years. In attendance were Eddie Ng (吳克儉), Secretary of Education of the Hong Kong government, and Regina Ip (葉劉淑儀), a Legislative Councillor and chairperson of the New People's Party. Their attendance showed the school's good relations with the government.

The evening included a performance by the choir of the elementary school, an act by a Jewish comedian and speeches looking back at the last quarter century. One of the speakers was Shay Razon, chairman of the board; his eldest son Rom graduated from the school with a perfect score of 45 points in the International Baccalaureate Programme, one of only 160 of the 15,000 candidates worldwide to do. Now he is studying at the Technion Institute in Haifa, of which we spoke in Chapter Nine.

The winning bet on Hong Kong

The most important Jew in the city in the post-war period was Lord Lawrence Kadoorie; he was the first man born in Hong Kong to be named to the British House of Lords, in 1981. He served in the policy-making Executive Council from 1951 to 1954. His China Light and Power (CLP) company ensured sufficient electricity to power the thousands of new factories, hotels, offices and apartments Hong Kong built from the 1950s. Today the company provides electricity to 75 per cent of the city and has equity interests in power plants in China, Southeast Asia, Australia and India.

Like many of the people profiled in this book, he had a story worthy of a Hollywood film. Born in Hong Kong in 1899, he was educated at Clifton College, an elite private school in Britain; he studied law at Lincoln's Inn but did not finish his degree. In the 1920s, he and his brother Horace went to work at Sir Elly Kadoorie & Sons, then headquartered in Shanghai, before returning to Hong Kong to head the family businesses there. During World War Two, with his family, he was imprisoned first in Stanley (赤柱) in Hong Kong and then in Chabei (閘北) Camp in Shanghai.

After the war, with Horace, he rebuilt the Peninsula Hotel and CLP. He also set up cotton and carpet mills, was a majority shareholder in the Peak Tram, which would later become part of HSH, and held a major stake in the Star Ferry, which carries people from Hong Kong to Kowloon.

The next trial came when Mao Zedong launched the Cultural Revolution in August 1966; China was thrown into chaos as millions of urban residents were sent to the countryside "to learn from the farmers" and economic growth slumped. In 1967, leftists in Hong Kong copied their comrades in the mainland, held demonstrations and attacked the police as "yellow dogs of imperialism".

Believing that the Communist army would take over the colony, many people sold their homes; property prices slumped and many of the business class emigrated. But Kadoorie kept his nerve. He started night-shifts for construction crews working on his projects, particularly St George's Building in Central District, under floodlights to show his faith in the city's future and in defiance of the threats from the mainland.

As in 1945 and 1949, his judgement proved correct. The leftists on the streets of Hong Kong represented local interests but not those of the central government; it wanted to leave Hong Kong in British hands as a well-run economy that brought many benefits to the mainland.

The long experience of the Kadoorie family in China and their low profile enabled Lord Lawrence Kadoorie to maintain good relations with the leadership in Beijing as well as with the British colonial administration that governed Hong Kong. In 1985, CLP took a 25-per-cent stake in China's first large-scale nuclear power stations in Daya Bay (大亞灣核電廠), 50 km from Hong Kong; the rest was owned by a Chinese state company. It involved a total investment of more than US$5 billion.

While Beijing had launched a policy of welcoming foreign capital seven years before, few foreign firms were willing to make large investments; they did not know how long the policy would last nor if written agreements would be honoured. Fearful of radiation and not confident of mainland technology, one million people in Hong Kong signed a petition opposing the plant.

But Lord Kadoorie went ahead; the plant began commercial operations in 1994, with CLP buying about 70 per cent of output to supply the needs of Hong Kong. In more than 20 years of operations, there has been no major safety problem. Lord Kadoorie earned enormous gratitude from Beijing from his major vote of confidence in their new policy.

He was repaid soon after when CLP was building the Black Point Power Station (龍鼓灘發電廠) in the Tuen Mun district close to the border with the mainland; it was only a few years before the handover to China in 1997. Fearful that Britain would plunder the wealth of Hong Kong before it left, Beijing had made it agree to restrict land sales to 50 hectares a year in the Joint Declaration the two countries signed in 1984.

"We were building Black Point but did not have the land," recalled Sir Michael. "We sent someone to Beijing. It signed an agreement with us on trust, giving us the land, so that we could go ahead. The Hong Kong government was not happy that we had approached Beijing on our own." (Note 17)

The government in Beijing would have made such an agreement with very few non-Chinese companies. The plant started operating in 1996; it is one of the world's largest gas-fired combined-cycle power stations with ultra low-sulphur diesel as backup fuel source. It is owned by a joint venture between CLP Power Hong Kong Limited (70%) and China Southern Power Grid International (HK) Co., Limited (30%), and is operated by CLP.

Lawrence and Horace were very active in philanthropy. In 1951, they founded the Kadoorie Agricultural Aid Association, which set up an experimental farm in the New Territories and provided training in sustainable agriculture, livestock and interest-free loans. From 1968, it offered training to thousands of Gurkhas – Nepalese serving in the British Army – stationed in Hong Kong, so they could work as farmers when they left the army and returned home. Now it is run as the Kadoorie Farm and Botanic Garden.

High-quality carpets

In 1956, with six associates, Lawrence set up an enterprise to give employment to boat women; Tai Ping Carpets started life in a house in

Experimental farm in the New Territories of Hong Kong set up by the Kadoories. (Credit: The Hong Kong Heritage Project)

Tuen Mun (屯門).

With the widespread use of air conditioning that could protect carpets from humidity, sales increased sharply. In 1959, Tai Ping moved its headquarters and factory to Tai Po (大埔), where it remained for 32 years before it moved production to Nanhai (南海) in Guangdong province; it also has a factory in Thailand. It was listed on the Hong Kong stock market in 1973; the Kadoorie family retains a majority stake. Tai Ping Carpets International is a global firm, the largest hand-tufted carpet company in the world, with factories, design studios and showrooms in 100 countries in four continents.

In 2016, its sales turnover was HK$1.33 billion, triple the HK$400 million in 2000. Its clients include Tom Hanks, Brad Pitt, the British Royal family, Hong Kong International Airport and luxury hotels like Sands, Parisian and Venetian in Macau and the Mandarin Oriental. It is one of the few Hong Kong home-grown luxury brands with a global footprint. (Note 18)

In 1974, Lawrence was knighted and, in September 1981, made Baron Kadoorie of Kowloon and of the City of Westminster. In 1962, he and Horace both received the Ramon Magsaysay Award for public service; this is an honour named after a former Filipino president for achievements in Asia. He also received honours from the French and Belgian governments. Lord Kadoorie died on August 25, 1993 and is buried in the Jewish cemetery in Hong Kong.

Lord Kadoorie (Lawrence) (Credit: The Hong Kong Heritage Project)

Sir Horace Kadoorie (Credit: The Hong Kong Heritage Project)

Entertainment king who became a Chinese

The most famous Jewish person in Hong Kong today is Allan Zeman; he moved to the city in 1975 from Canada. After making his first fortune from exporting Chinese clothing to Canada, in the 1980s he created Lan Kwai Fong (蘭桂坊) in the Central (中環) district and transformed it into one of the important bar and nightlife districts in the city; he has since expanded the LKF brand to Chengdu (成都), Haikou (海口), Shanghai (上海) and Wuxi (無錫).

From 2003 to 2014, he was chairman of Ocean Park (海洋公園), which defeated the nearby Disneyland to become Hong Kong's most popular tourist destination. He has also produced films, developed a five-star resort complex in Phuket, Thailand, and is a partner in the Shanghai Dream Centre project, which has a ground floor area of over 400,000 square metres. He is a director of several major companies listed on the Hong Kong Stock Exchange and has a net worth of US$1 billion.

Having lived in Hong Kong for over 40 years, Zeman is very active in government and community service, holding numerous positions on government committees. In 2001, he was appointed a Justice of the Peace; in 2004, the government awarded him the Gold Bauhinia Star and, in 2011, the Grand Bauhinia Medal.

In September 2008, he renounced his Canadian nationality and became a naturalised citizen of the People's Republic of China; he carries a Hong Kong SAR passport.

"I have lived and worked in Hong Kong for 38 years and always considered it to be my home," he said at the time. He is one of a handful of westerners to have taken such a drastic step – a decision warmly welcomed by the central government in Beijing.

He speaks conversational Cantonese, as well as English and French. Immigration officers in China and abroad have been unable to keep pace with this dramatic change. "Whenever I go abroad, I write 'Chinese National' on the immigration card. The immigration officer says 'You are not Chinese' and I say 'It's a genetic problem.' Then they look at me and let me go. Whenever I go to China, I line up in the queue for Chinese Nationals. The immigration officer always says to me: 'No, you should queue in the Foreigners line'. I say 'No, no, no, I am a Chinese national'. They check my Home Return Permit for a long time to see if it is a fake. Sometimes they even call their supervisor. It is really quite funny. I always say that I am an 'egg' – white on the outside and yellow on the inside." (Note 19)

His story is one of rigorous self-discipline, hard work and no alcohol. He was raised in Montreal; his father died when he was seven. "Seeing my mother play the role of victim taught me what not to do. The important thing is that you pick yourself up and move on from those problems."

At 10, he was delivering newspapers; at 12, he was clearing tables three days a week at a steakhouse. He dropped out of college and, at 19, started a business importing ladies' sweaters from Hong Kong, which made him US$1 million in profit in the first year. It was that which gave him the idea to move to Hong Kong.

"The most important thing in life is health," he said. Each morning for 38 years, he has done 100 sit-ups with his feet in the air, 100 forward crunches, 40 dumbbell curls with each arm and an hour on the elliptical. "Be positive, be confident in yourself and don't be afraid to make mistakes. Money is important, but it should not be the most important thing in your life."

He is not a very practising Jew. He does not eat pork but eats shellfish; he goes to synagogue on major Holy Days. "I think that a Jewish upbringing gives you self-discipline and an ethic of hard work, which are very important qualities. I think every religion should be tolerant of the others and we would have a better world. Religion in general is something that you are born into and not something you choose. The key is to be a good person."

With associates, he is in the process of setting up an Israeli-China Tech Fund, as many Chinese companies are seeking to do business with Israeli companies. "My business model is 'I look at things not for what they are; I look at things for what they could be'."

Notes

1   Judy Green interview with *South China Morning Post*, 14/12/2014.

2   Booklet of Jewish Historical Society (JHS) of Hong Kong.

3   Judy Green interview with *South China Morning Post*, 14/12/2014.

4   Jewish Times Asia, issue of December 2009/January 2010.

5   Sir Michael Kadoorie, Fireside Chat 16/12/2008 from the library of the Jewish Community Centre, Hong Kong.

6   Same.

7   Judy Green interview with *South China Morning Post*, 14/12/2014.

8   "Jewish Community of Hong Kong", by Erica Lyons on website of Beit Hatfutsot, August 2011.

9   Interview with author, 10/8/2017.

10   Obituary of Dr Solomon Matthew Bard on website of Leisure and Cultural Services Department, Hong Kong government (www.lcsd.gov.hk); articles on him in *South China Morning Post*, 29/11/2014 and *Sydney Morning* Herald, 2/4/2015.

11   Author interview with Robert Dorfman, 22/6/2017.

12   Same.

13   Booklet of Jewish Historical Society (JHS) of Hong Kong.

14   Author interview with Rabbi Asher Oser, 19/6/2017.

15   Author interview with Rabbi Mordechai Avtzon, 27/7/2017.

16   Author interview with Mark Konyn, 26/7/2017.

17   Sir Michael Kadoorie, Fireside Chat 16/12/2008 from the library of the Jewish Community Centre, Hong Kong.

18   Article on Tai Ping Carpets, *South China Morning Post*, 29/7/2017.

19   Author e-mail interview with Allan Zeman, 24/7/2017.

Thanks and Acknowledgements

In September 2016, I presented an outline of this book to Anne Lee, Deputy Editor in Chief of Joint Publishing in Hong Kong. She graciously accepted it; I was delighted to take on such a fascinating story. However, as an ignorant gentile, I was nervous to take on this complicated subject.

So I must say a big thank you to many Jewish friends who have done their best to save me from ignorance. Yitzhak Shichor, Professor of Political Science at the Hebrew University of Jerusalem, most graciously reviewed and corrected Chapters Seven and Nine; he also provided many of his excellent articles, from which I have quoted extensively.

Professor Dan Ben-Canaan, the sole Jewish resident of Harbin since 2002, most graciously reviewed and corrected Chapters Two, Three, Four and Six, and contributed to Chapter Eight a section about his remarkable work in Harbin. He also provided 59 historical photographs from his precious collection; readers can see the results of his generosity.

Erica Lyons, founder and editor-in-chief of *Asian Jewish Life*, reviewed

Chapter Ten. She also showed me the Ohel Leah synagogue in Hong Kong, including its precious *Torah* scrolls.

I thank the three for their precious time and corrections and providing much material and guidance through complicated and difficult subjects. I also thank Rabbi Marvin Tokayer, a great scholar of the Jews in Asia.

I thank very much those who spared their precious time for an interview. These included Rabbi Mordechai Avtzon and Rabbi Asher Oser in Hong Kong, Rabbi Shalom Greenberg in Shanghai and Rabbi Shimon Freundlich in Beijing.

Also Ted Plafker and his wife Roberta Lipson in Beijing: members of Rabbi Greenberg's congregation in Shanghai: and many members of the community in Hong Kong, including Robert Dorfman, Mark Konyn, Roy Delbyck, Allan Zeman, Judy Green, Stephen Vines, Michael Hartmann and Jeanette Lewis.

Susan Raymond, librarian of the Jewish Community Centre in Hong Kong, provided excellent books and documents. The Jewish Historical Society of Hong Kong arranged talks that were interesting and instructive. Alan Goldstein helped with introductions, accompanied me to interviews and provided guidance and many funny stories.

We thank the Hong Kong Heritage Project for providing precious historical photos and reviewing and correcting four of the ten chapters.

We thank Ho Manli (何曼禮) for sending photographs of her father Ho Feng-shan (何鳳山) and reviewing the section about him. Similarly, Nobuki Sugihara (杉原伸生) reviewed the text on his father Chiune Sugihara (杉原千畝) and provided pictures.

For material in Chinese, we must particularly thank Pan Guang (潘光) and Wang Jian (王健). Their *The Jews and China* (猶太人與中國) was the most important single source for this book. Professor Wang also graciously gave me a long interview in Shanghai in December 2016. He gave me a copy of his latest book *Escape and Rescue, Jewish Refugees and Shanghai in World War Two* (逃亡與拯救：二戰中的猶太難民與上海), which was very helpful. Also useful were *Harbin Jews in Early 1900s: their Political and Religious Lives* (20世紀上半期哈爾濱猶太人的宗教生活與政治生活) by Wang Zhijun (王志軍) and Li Wei (李薇) and the biography of Wang Ti-fu (王替夫), *The Life Story of the Diplomat of Manchukuo* (一位偽滿外交官的人生告白) by Chen Ming (陳明).

For pictures, we thank our friend Kevin Lee (李安民) for going to the office of Roy Delbyck and taking images of some of his remarkable collection of Republican China. Rabbi Greenberg in Shanghai kindly sent images of his centre and the *mikvah* (ritual bath). Our good friend in Shanghai, Helen Wu (吳蔚然), took many pictures of buildings and places connected to the Jews in the city.

We also deeply thank Norman Ching (程翰), who patiently translated this long book, full of historical detail and names of people and places. It required a great deal of time and hard work. He did this quickly and efficiently.

We also thank members of the Israeli Foreign Ministry. One was Sagi Karni, consul-general in Hong Kong until July 2017, who provided excellent advice and contacts in Israel.

Also members of the consulate in Shanghai from 2003 to 2006 – Uri Gutman, Ilan Maor and Eliav Benjamin. They graciously invited me to many events at the consulate, which was an opportunity to meet many Israelis working or active in projects in China.

Those three years were an opportunity to learn the rich Jewish history of Shanghai and meet the new Jewish citizens who had arrived after China's open-door and reform policies.

Also we must thank Anne Lee and many colleagues at Joint Publishing, including Betty Chiu, who edited the book and Donal Scully, who proof-read the English version. And my beloved wife Louise, who listened patiently to endless stories and jokes about Jewish history and people.

Bibliography

Books

China and Israel, 1948-1998, A Fifty Year Retrospective, edited by Jonathan Goldstein, Praeger Publishers, 1999.

Escape and Rescue, Jewish Refugees and Shanghai in World War II (逃亡與拯救：二戰中的猶太難民與上海), by Wang Jian (王健), Shanghai Jiaotong University Press (上海交通大學出版社), 2016.

Harbin Jews in Early 1900s: Their Political and Religious Lives (20 世紀上半期哈爾濱猶太人的宗教生活與政治生活), by Wang Zhijun (王志軍) and Li Wei (李薇), People's Publishing House (人民出版社), April 2013.

Refuge in Shanghai, by Ernest Heppner, University of Nebraska Press, 1993.

Secrets and Spies: the Harbin Files, by Mara Moustafine, published by Random House Australia, 2002.

Shanghai's Baghdadi Jews, by Maisie Meyer, Blacksmith Books, 2015.

The Chronology of the Jews of Shanghai from 1832 to the Present Day, by the Jewish Communities of China.

The Fugu Plan, the Untold Story of the Japanese and the Jews During World War Two, by Marvin Tokayer and Mary Swartz, Gefen Publishing House.

The Jews and China (猶太人與中國) by Professors Pan Guang (潘光) and Wang Jian (王健), Shishi Publishing Company (時事出版社), 2010.

The Jews in Kaifeng, Reflections on Sino-Judaic History, by Chan Sui-jeung, The Jewish Historical Society of Hong Kong, 1986.

The Jews of Harbin, China, by Dr Irena Vladimirsky, of the Department of History, Achva College of Education, Israel.

The Personal Statement of a Manchukuo Diplomat (一個偽滿外交官的人生告白), by Chen Ming (陳明), Chun Feng Wenyi Publishing Company (春風文藝出版社), October 2001.

The Sassoon Group in Old China, by Zhang Zhongli (張仲禮) and Chen Zengnian (陳曾年), People's Publishing Company (人民出版社), 1985.

Treaty Ports in Modern China: Law, Land and Power, by Chiara Betta, edited by Robert Bickers, Isabella Jackson.

Warum Japan Keine Juden verfolgte, Die Judenpolitik des Kaiserreches Japan wahrend der Zeit des National-sozialismus, 1933-1945, by Heinz Eberhard Maul, Iudicium Verlag GmbH, 2007.

Newspapers and magazines

"Ernest David Bergman and Israel's Role in Taiwan's Defense", by Professor Yitzhak Shichor, the *Asia Papers*, Number 2, 2016, published by the Center for International and Regional Studies, Georgetown University School of Foreign Service, Qatar.

Eye on History magazine (看歷史), by Chen Zhongdan (陳仲丹：上海開埠：從江南小鎮到十里洋場), December 2016.

Eye on History magazine (看歷史), by Mao Jianjie (毛劍傑：十里洋場的猶太印記), April 2012.

Eye on History magazine, by Liu Dong (劉棟：新沙遜洋行：舊上海的地產生意), April 2017.

"Jewish Immigration after the Second World War", by Suzanne Rutland, University of Sydney, in the *Journal of the History Teachers' Association*, New South Wales, 2006.

"Maple Hardoon Doron", by Maisie Meyer, Essay in *Shanghai's Baghdadi Jews*, published by Blacksmith Books, 2015.

"Moscow of the Orient" (東方莫斯科) by *National Humanity History* (*NHH*) magazine (國家人文歷史), July 2016.

"My family and its city: 50 years in Harbin", Paper by Mara Moustafine, given at an international seminar on the History and Culture of Harbin Jews at the Shangri-La Hotel, Harbin on August 3-September 2, 2004.

"Shanghai: a Haven for Holocaust Victims" (上海：大屠殺倖存者的天堂), by Professors Pan Guang (潘光), in "The Holocaust and United Nations Outreach Programme".

"*The Descendants of the Jews of Kaifeng*" (開封猶太人後裔，身份之謎被揭開) in *Overseas Chinese* magazine (僑園), June 2016.

"The Extraordinary Adventures of Two-Gun Cohen", by Sara Jo Ben Zvi, *Asian Jewish Life*, issue 12.

"The Fate of Harbin Jewish Community under Japanese Occupation, 1931-1945", paper by Dr Zvia Bowman, King's College, University of London.

"The Harbin Kidnapping of 1933 that shook the world" (1933 年震驚中外的哈爾濱綁架案) in *Eye on History* (看歷史), January 2017.

"The Japanese Convert", by D. Sofer, in www.aish.com, 20/11/2004.

"The Rising Strategic Value of Global Technology Assets and its Impact on Sino-Israeli Relations", magazine article by Ariella Berger, senior fellow of SIGNAL and founder of UnBounded Research.

"The Tragic Destiny of the founder of the Modern Hotel" (馬迭爾創始人的悲劇命運), *Global People* magazine (環球人物), 2011, Number 27.

"The Westerners who became Chinese" (那些加入中國籍的洋人們), *National Humanities History magazine* (國家人文歷史), April 2017.

Article in *Changchun Evening News* (長春晚報), 14/6/2014.

Article on Major-General Kiichiro Higuchi from *Asahi Shimbun* (朝日新聞), 4/5/2010.

Article in *Manitoba History,* by Michael R. Angel, Elizabeth Dafoe Library, University of Manitoba, Number 7, Spring 1984.

Article in *The Jerusalem Post*, 10/4/2014.

Article in *The New York Times*, 26/9/2016.

Israel Epstein: obituaries in *The New York Times* 2/6/2005 and in the *Daily Telegraph* (14/6/2005).

Sidney Rittenberg: article by *Financial Times,* 12/1/2013.

Sidney Shapiro: article by *Financial Times,* 24/10/2014.

Sanlian Shenghuo magazine (三聯生活週刊), 2011, number 49.

Scribe Magazine

Others

Sir Michael Kadoorie, Fireside Chat 16/12/2008 from the library of the Jewish Community Centre, Hong Kong.

Website of Israel Ministry of Foreign Affairs (www.mfa.gov.il/).

Website of Japanese Foreign Ministry (http://www.mofa.go.jp/mofaj/).

Website of Shavei Israel (https://shavei.org/).

ISRAEL AND CHINA:
FROM THE TANG DYNASTY TO SILICON WADI

Author	Mark O'Neill
Editor	Donal Scully
Designer	Vincent Yiu

Published by Joint Publishing (H.K.) Co., Ltd.
20/F., North Point Industrial Building, 499 King's Road, North Point,
Hong Kong

Printed by Elegance Printing & Book Binding Co., Ltd.
Block A, 4/F., 6 Wing Yip Street, Kwun Tong, Kowloon, Hong Kong

Distributed by SUP Publishing Logistics (HK) Ltd.
3/F., 36 Ting Lai Road, Tai Po, N.T., Hong Kong

First published in January 2018
Second impression in January 2019
ISBN 978-962-04-4297-1

三聯書店
http://jointpublishing.com

JPBooks.Plus
http://jpbooks.plus